NO
SELL
OUT!

Ten Years in the life
of a Black Man

BY

FRANK JAMES IV

ISBN: 1-4140-2353-7 (e-book)
ISBN: 1-4140-2352-9 (Paperback)

Library of Congress Control Number: 2003097855

This book is printed on acid free paper.

Printed in the United States of America
Bloomington, IN

1stBooks – rev. 11/06/03

...ask him his dream,
what does it mean
he wouldn't know.

Can't be like the rest
is the most he'll confess,
but the times running out
and there's no happiness...

Curtis Mayfield, *Superfly*

CHAPTER I

1987

My boys' Herbert and Sherbert and I are tripping on the yard. We are trying to get chose for this brotherhood on the yard Beep. I was a second semester freshman at good old Willyfarce, the first black university in America. The whole thing about Willyfarce being the first black university was a joke. Hell it had to be a black school because whites wouldn't have the decrepit institution. The place was a damn disgrace, it consisted of two dilapidated boys' dorms, and two girls dorms that were not too much better.

Well anyway the twin brothers, Herbert and Sherbert, were wondering if we would be picked up by this brotherhood, the twins really wanted to be picked up. I, on the other hand, was just doing it to see how pledging was. I really didn't give a damn about being down with the dudes because in my brain I was the shit, and everybody else was the smell, so that group stuff didn't faze me. We let a few of the brothers know about us being interested in their clique. We also walked around the yard spotting the ones we knew and acting courteous to them, sucking up.

About three days later one of the brothers came around and let us know about an interest meeting for those who want to be down. The twins were happy, me I was kind of skeptical cause I wasn't for that physical pain stuff and I had heard that pledging can get kind of rough on you. Also, in truth I just wasn't really into that group thing. I was not really impressed with the dudes I had met and I felt why not start our own organization. I had run this idea around with some other freshman the previous semester but none of them wanted to upset the status quo of the yard. They just wanted to follow the normal pattern and get their heads cracked to be down with some other fools. I almost made the same stupid mistake.

On the night of the meeting we met in a little dude's room I had seen around the yard named Mouse. There were a few of the other brothers there, Ace, Ken and Tim. They gave us a brief intro to what the deal was and how to be down. They seemed like some cool brothers so we agreed to meet in Mouse's room the next night. Blue jeans and a white T-shirt was the attire for the evening. We were required to have a fifth of *Wild Irish Rose*, one for each person that was going on line. We had to also have beer and other items for the brothers. There were six people on line including myself.

The brothers had us line up in a line and explained that these dudes were going to be our best friends for the next few weeks. They explained that our line should never be broken. To offset this ever happening they showed us how to lock up. For those of you who never wasted time pledging, this is when you line up and wrap your arms around the man in front of you. Once they felt we understood the principle the drinking started.

They cracked those fifths and started passing them down the line. The logic was supposed to be each person on line drank a fifth. The bottle started at the front man and was supposed to be empty when the last man put it down. We were lined up shortest to the tallest. Tico was the front man followed by Deion then the twins, and then me, the tail dog. Tico started drinking and it was on. Every man was supposed to drink as much as he could and then pass it over his shoulder to the next man. All while this was going on the brothers were screaming and yelling in our ears.

I want to get one thing straight. The Beep's didn't pressure anyone to drink. You didn't have to if you didn't want to. I was not forced to do anything. When the bottle came to me, I had already made up my mind to drink. I guess I had made the decision a long time ago. I was just waiting for the right opportunity. Now, as I was saying, when those bottles came to me they had better be dry when I put them down. That sounds easy if everybody was drinking their share, yeah right.

The first fifth was split equal, but after that Tico started feeling drunk and the Deion twins were next. The only ones holding up were the twins. The bottles started coming with more and more wine in them. Sherbert was like "Spit what you can't drink down my back." Hell I was into it by the time the fourth one came to me. Why waste good wine? I was drinking hard. The last one had to have been at least 3/4 full, I downed it. Most people start off drinking a little brew or wine coolers and maybe some gin. I started drinking the right way. I started off with Wild Irish Rose Red. A star was born.

Well I dropped Beep, no loss. The pledge process started to get old quickly. The thing about getting dudes food and catering to other cats' needs, was for ho-cakes not the dog. The Beeps couldn't even step at parties! Well one night this big rock-headed trick named Lil' Petey and his ho-ass-boy, Wide Mouth from Center State came to the yard to join in on the pledging process.

The brothers on the yard were cool, up to a point. They seemed to at least give a damn about the pledges. In comes this little five-foot pussy with a small man's complex! Shit hit the fan. First off he had a problem with the fact that I had a curl. Funny how things work out. I have a problem with silly fools wearing curls today. But anyway this was 1987, over a decade ago. Lil' Petey starts tripping about my hair, we are all lined up when this silly fool started playing with cigarettes around my hair! Now any fool knows what happened to Michael Jackson when those sparks hit his hair. I snapped! I got out of line and looked to the other brothers who were from Willyfarce, to check this fool. But the brothers were just laughing. This punk was yelling "He dropped, he dropped!" I looked around and just walked out.

I felt, how the hell was I going to be down with some fools who didn't look out for my well being. Ace hollered out "Wait" and we went outside in the hall. We rapped but the ordeal was over for me. I liked the brothers who were down like Ken, Mouse, Ace and Tim, but their agenda wasn't mine so we parted ways.

Two things came out of my experience with Beep outside of drinking. One was getting used to going to the library to study and read. The other was how to run lines and what to do to break a pledge down when he's on line. The latter came in handy when I launched PFA.

After all the stuff I went through that semester, guess what? I made the Dean's List. Yep, a dude who barely had a two-point grade average in high school was carrying a 3.2 in college. Up until that point I wasn't sure that college was for me, but after that I was. It was the perfect excuse to keep from getting a real job. One major point that needs to be brought out is that I had started drinking. The drinking did not stop when I dropped Beep. It kept going. A little brew here, a little wine there, you know drinking every Friday, things like that.

I remember going to the Que ball that semester high as a kite. In addition, add in the fact that there really wasn't a damn thing to do at Willyfarce outside of drinking or sex. The school was in the middle of some worn out cornfields. At that time, I had a girl at home who I was still crazy about, so I wanted to stay true to her. Ahh how innocent I was in my deluded thinking. This ruled me out from chasing females on the yard.

Another factor in dealing with the girls down there was everything seemed to be ruled by what clique you fit into. To tell the truth I really did not fit into any clique there, and didn't really want to. My one foolish attempt at "being down" had only solidified my resolve that I was better off rolling solo, or creating my own clique. I watched some of the ugliest fools on campus hook-up with some of the finest females on the yard simply because they were either in a fraternity or in some brotherhood. The situation just didn't make sense to me. If you are ugly then how are three Greek letters going to make you look better?

So drink it was. I played basketball as much as I could but not nearly as much as I could back in Racine so that option was out. I started lifting weights and got a little bit big and played a lot of cards. Up until I went to Willyfarce I never had even heard of Spades, by the time I left for the summer I was a master at the game. Around the time close to summer break I was sitting at the desk in our room writing a letter to Tina, my girl. I was telling my roommate Dontae that I had not heard from her and I was really ready to break up with her. Dontae asked why? I said, "Man this relationship was getting old. When I go home I want to be free, not carrying any dead weight." Dontae agreed, so I started writing the letter trying to be nice saying something to the effect that we should not see one another anymore, the "nice guy" escape clause type of letter. Then it happened, I cannot explain to this day what happened, but it was like a veil was lifted from my eyes and I saw how our relationship truly was.

I had been writing Tina at least twice a week since I got to school. I used to put all of my little change into the phones trying to call Tina until I discovered calling card numbers, somebody else's. That was how I kept my end of the relationship going. What did I get in return? I might get a letter once every two weeks, if that. I don't remember Tina ever calling me until later.

This, plus the things that went on in the past like making me wait three months for a kiss started flashing through my head. The times the chick would just get quiet for nothing and I'd beg what was wrong. Hell, I would apologize for things I didn't do or didn't even know what I was apologizing for. The mind games Tina ran on me finally came to light.

I balled up that nice letter. It was time for a new letter, a real letter. I can't remember the exact contents of the letter but I know it started like this: "Yeah I know you been having a good laugh with your sister about the hoops you put me through, but the game is over!" Then it went on to say "When I come home do not say a damn thing to me, we ain't friends or nothing! Stay away from me!" I signed it Perfect Frankie that was my nickname at the time and I knew Tina hated that. After I wrote and mailed it I felt like a burden was lifted off of my shoulders. I could settle down and get to work on my finals.

4

Three days later I was sitting in the room chilling listening to *DMC* when a brother knocked on the door and told me I had a call on the fourth floor. The phone on the third floor had been torn off the wall. I'm wondering, "Who in hell can this be?" They must want to talk to me awfully bad to try to call me on a different floor.

I picked up the phone, "Hello?" The voice on the other end says, "Monte I don't want to break up." Tina had finally called me. I said, "Man it is over. You should have thought about that when you were playing games." I heard a few garbled words then a long wail and the phone dropped. Now by this time I'm shaking my head cause the situation is ironic. Tina's mother got on the phone, "What's going on with you and Tina?" I said, "Nothing Mrs. Bias, it's just over." Tina's mother said, "Just like that." I said, "Yeah." I heard more loud sobs in the background and Tina's mother said, "Girl, shut up! What brought this on?" I said, "I was tired of the relationship and it was time to move on." Tina's mother said, "Huh, one of them girls down there done got you." Something to that effect, well I knew that was wrong cause I had been "faithful" to her daughter and I told her so. Tina's mother conceded that I was through with her daughter and I said goodnight and hung up. The phone call was crazy, I laughed with Dontae about it.

Two days later I went to check my mailbox and oh baby! I had letters up the ass in it. I swear it was around two weeks left in the semester and every day I got two letters. The first day I tripped cause a card was in there. All of this correspondence was from Tina. I really lost respect for the girl. The situation was like, before I couldn't get a letter, now when I didn't want her I was getting one daily. I didn't even open them. Some I wrote return to sender on, and placed them back into the mail. Sherbert wanted to read those babies bad but, I just took them and threw them into the garbage. I remember thinking I'm glad I got out of that pitfall. I aced my finals and as I said I made the Dean's List that semester, the year was over and it was time to go home.

CHAPTER II

The first thing I did when I got home was to get my Jerri-curl cut off. I was back home and I wanted to have a fresh look when I hit my old stomping grounds. Plus, my experience at college had let me know that the curl thing was played out. The day I got there I talked to May, the lady who did my hair, and arranged to get my hair cut into a *Cameo* cut, like *Larry Blackmon*. She hooked me up the very next day. When I was finally saw by my boys I had a new look. It was on.

First off I had to acquire a job. Willyfarce was high as hell so I had to get a job to buy clothes and books. Well my old man got me in touch with this cat who worked for the city and he got me a gig working for the highway department. This shows how screwed up my career path was going. My field was communications but my summer job was picking up dead animals off the damn road and shoveling black top.

The first day on the job I was training with this stupid dude named Paul. I later found out his nickname was, "Moto." They called him this because he talked so much. Our job was to patrol the highway for dead animals and to make sure the street signs were up. We also had to pick up paper on the side of the road. Paul was showing me the roads I would have to patrol, and he pulled over for me to pick up every shred of paper on the side of the road. I later found out that the fool was only doing that because he had help. This went on all morning, me jumping in and out of the truck and Paul talking, until about 10:00. Keep in mind that this dump truck is big as hell and getting in and out was a chore. Listening to Paul talk about his son was an even bigger chore. We're going up the side of the highway he's blabbing, and I'm wondering how I can quit and still stay at home with Mama when the shit hit the fan. We had passed up a piece of paper that looked like it

6

was no bigger than half of a piece of notebook paper, when Paul decided to back up and have me pick it up. I was tripping on this fool.

As we were backing up, I was looking in the side mirror, and I could tell Paul was about to run into a ditch. I was about to warn the idiot but, as usual Paul was talking it up about his son, so I thought "Skip it let the fool get stuck." Then we can stop working for a while. Thirty seconds later I was crawling out of the truck on Paul's side. The fool had tipped this big dump truck over on its side! I guess I should have been scared because earlier that morning, I know this sounds corny, the door on my side was having trouble closing, and that same door saved me. I should have sued the county but I was young and stupid to the ways of the world. I stayed at work and finished the day working like a good peon. All I wanted to do was get off work so I could go kick it that was why I came home anyway.

You have to understand that I'm from a little town called Racine, in rural Wisconsin. I knew a lot of people in this little country town. See, everybody basically knew or heard of everybody, or if not they knew someone who did know the person. So I came home like a star, in my mind. I had left and went to school and made the Deans list, I was somebody. That summer was quite literally the beginning of the end.

I was drinking now so I did not hang with my high school ace PJ, cause he did not drink. PJ and I considered ourselves the two livest dudes in Park High School when we went there. He was my ace boon coon, PJ and FJ, things change.

One Friday right after I got back in town, I was out drinking with some of my church friends kicking it. I was getting lit because it was a party at the South Side center and I intended on kicking it. I was drinking *Red Bull* malt liquor and I wasn't short stopping either. By the time I got up to the center the party was in full swing. There were plenty of women around and it felt good to be home kicking it. Well needless to say I had drunk a little too much brew for my system. I was drunk and acting like it.

I was riding with my guy Dee and he was buzzing but not as much as I was. The following scenario is a collection of stories that were told to me the next day. The reason being, I don't remember the night clearly. Dee told me that when we got to the center I was tripping, hollering and stumbling into people. I ran into my other partner Del, and me and him made a scene because he was drunk also. I pushed some fool down and almost came to blows with dude. Del said the one thing that really sent me off tripping was the fact I ran into Tina, my ex-girlfriend. Del said that when I seen her I just started tripping saying things like, "Get that fool away from me!" I guess that is when Dee and Del decided to take me out of the party.

Outside we ran into PJ. Dee and other people said that when I seen my old buddy I was glad to see him but he wasn't glad to see me. I guess I must have embarrassed him because he told them to get me away from him, in short terms he dissed me. To many of you out there, this may not seem like anything bad but to real ones out there they know this is the one thing you should never do, flake out on a partner when he is in a bad way. You should always look out for your homeboys or home girls no questions asked.

The funny thing about that night is I remember being at an after-party later on that night and having my mother come and get me. How embarrassing this was. It later came out that my cousin had called my mother and told her I was drunk so she came and got me, how foul can things get? Mama didn't really say anything but just the fact that she came and got me was messed up.

Of course the next day everybody knew what had happened. I got lectures from everyone from my Aunt to my father. Daddy just said to make sure that when I was out drinking that I did not overdo it. Everyone agreed on one thing though, that PJ was not a true friend. Everybody I knew had a basic theme about dude and it stated that the way he acted was weak as hell. I never held it against dude that he didn't help me out. He was still PJ to me and this was just another facet of his mental make-up. I looked at it as a learning experience.

I had vowed I would never drink in my life because of how it messed up my father. Vows are like laws made to be broken, and I had shattered that particular one.

The funny thing is that most of my drinking partners were my church buddies, I guess they got carried away with the wine thing from church. That summer I hung with my church partners Dee and Del or the Twins. Next on the agenda was using my college student status to acquire some women. Even back then I knew that women look for promising young men to hook up with, men who have something going for them. If only I had of known the deeper implications of what this rule really meant.

I hit Case High School one day with PJ. We were up there just tripping. PJ was messing with some young females he knew, when I seen this cutie named Kia. Kia was a junior or a senior. I didn't give a damn I was only 18, so I got her digits. I was loving this. See, I had missed almost my whole senior year and three fourths of my freshman year in college thinking I was in love with Tina, so I had ground to cover.

Also by me being with one girl for so long I decided I wanted four, one for each Frank James, I am the fourth of a prestigious line. Kia was my first prospect. Next up was a chick I should have had back in high school cause her cousin had brought her up to Park to meet me when I was a senior there.

Oh well, it was never too late in my book. Nia was her name, she was prospect number two. Man as I look back on those days game was easy, I think my best line was, "What's up?"

Let me clear something up, all this did not happen in a day. This took about two or three weeks for the process to even begin to click. Also Kia never came into my fold like I wanted her to. One day while cruising in Dee's mama's car drinking brews I seen number three, Sandra. If I had any sense I would have stayed in the car and made Dee speed up and not stop. But, if I had any sense I wouldn't be writing this book. Sandra was pushing a baby carriage up the street. Sandra was light skinned and built. Sandra was tight.

Sandra was so tight the fact that she was pushing a baby carriage didn't even register in my head. I don't think that fact registered in no one's head in that car that day. I had Dee pull over cause I could see Sandra's future had Frank written on it. Now I know the art of game is all washed up now cause dudes don't have it anymore. All they do is cater to females now but at that time you had to have either game or looks I had a little of both.

As I get out of the car, I do a quick assertion of my standing. I was wearing some ripped up pants I cut up in college. Keep in mind this was three to four years before *Damage* or *Used* jeans got hip to the concept. Plus I had fever blisters on my mouth from working in the sun with no Vaseline. On the other hand Sandra's looking like a cool million, Sandra had on some stone washed gear that had her looking wonderful. To me I was coming from a position of weakness because of my attire but mainly because of those fever blisters. Who wants to talk to a dude with sores on his mouth? Well Sandra did.

I still look back on that scene and wonder why in hell would this woman want to be bothered with a dude with some ripped pants on and messed up lips? I used to think it was my weak game but as I grow older I know it had to be that garbage about women wanting men with promise. I think Sandra saw FJ as her ticket out of the hood. Why? Because remember what I said earlier, everybody in Racine knows everybody, and Sandra knew me from school. That was my third prospect.

The fourth one really isn't worth mentioning but I will her name was Val. Val really was a loss. One reason is I think Val and Nia was cousins, no loss. These were my four prospects the next stage was to wrap them up.

You couldn't tell me anything. I was like a man out of prison. My day consisted of: work till four, get home, shower, hoop till 7:30, then try to make it over all of their houses. Kia was the first one I had to chalk up as a loss, she was cool but a tad bit square. It was relatively easy to make the rounds cause I balled on the south side and all of the rest lived in that area.

When I got home from work, I would have my secretary, my sister Chasity, call and make sure they knew when I was coming, to confirm our appointment. I was full of myself. Chasity would call and check to see if they would be home at the appointed time, I wouldn't even get on the phone. I swore I was doing something and the funny thing is I wasn't boning any of them. Well Sandra was the exception to this.

I would go hoop then stop by Nia's house mess with her, then before Val quit my flock stop by her house. The last stop would be Sandra's house on my way to the pad. Once Val hit the wind it became real easy. I'd hoop go by Nia's then hit Sandra's. The only drawback was this might last until 12:30 at night. I had to be up and gone by 5:30. I learned a lesson that would help me throughout my working life, just make it to the job. By the time you wake up or sober up it will be time to go home.

My routine was getting old quick with my mother. I needed my own car. Mama had grown tired of me using her little Accord, the main reason was, my hours had changed. I went from being home at 10:30-11:00 to 2:30-3:00 in the morning. That wasn't going down too well with my old "G." I had to start catching a ride around with Dee or Del to the places I needed to go. This scenario also helped me get away from one girl's house to another. All I had to say was, "My ride's here" and I'm gone. As I look back on this that was my last fun summer before my life really went awry.

The relationship Nia and I started was a crazy ass love hate type of thing. I would go over Nia's house and dog her out. Nia thought she was the shit. Everybody knew that was my title, so I went over Nia's house to let her know this. Nia called herself Gucci and her crew used to pump her head full of bullshit to keep the hype going. Nia's main girl was Cathy. Her nickname was "Louie" after Louis Vuitton. Nia's other partner was Rikki nicknamed Fendi. Rikki wasn't around much but Cathy was there almost every day. We would kick it around in front of Nia's house tripping.

I was a straight up fool. Instead of trying to get this girl's pants off I would be trying to dog Nia. It was all because of the way Nia's girls related to her. They were always like, "Nia this, "and "Don't nobody talk to Nia like that" that type of propaganda. So I just went over there and did what came natural to me, dog her. For example: instead of having Nia kiss me I'd make Nia kiss the tree in front of her house, or I'd give Cathy horse back rides and not her, stupid stuff. Throughout all of this I was still seeing Sandra so I was having cake and ice cream! Alas all things must come to an end.

Before we go on, I know some of you out there are wondering what happened to my ex-girl Tina. You're figuring I'd go back to hit the cat for old time sake. Well I never repeat myself, once I leave 'em I'm gone. But I did have an interesting encounter with Tina. This is how it went.

Nia and I were sitting on her porch chilling. This was when I was first really trying to hook up with Nia. Now the first question out of her mouth is what about Tina. Hell that was easy for me to answer. I had left Tina before I came home. Nia was skeptical because of this trend most people go through, break up then make up. Well that was most people. I've never been one of them. So as I was explaining this to Nia we noticed this car inching up the block. I know you have heard of drive by shootings, this was a family by.

Inside the car was Tina and her whole family except her father! At first I figured they was just going someplace and came down Nia's block. As they passed, before Nia could say something I told her this. So we kept talking when low and behold here come these fools again. As they went past, I see them motioning toward the porch. I can't believe this. Nia now asked me, "What's up with that Frank?" Well I don't know so I saw them turn like they were going around the block for another pass so I told Nia, "Come on, lets go."

I was driving the Accord so we jumped in and as I was pulling off I saw their headlights coming up the block. Keep in mind the car they was driving was a *Seville*, clean as hell. I guess the family seen me leaving so they zoomed up till they were in back of us. I drove a few blocks the car stayed on my tail.

Nia was looking at me like this was my fault so I sped up. They stayed right on my tail. I turned a few corners they followed. The scene was so sad it was funny. Nia was like, "What's up with them?" "Ain't that they mama driving?" If it wasn't it damn sure was her twin. I sped up and faked like I was turning left then swung right, the Accord could maneuver like that. The caddy couldn't.

I sped down a few blocks and went back by Nia's house. As we sat outside in the car she said, "You ought to go back with her." I could tell Nia was saying that to see where my head was. I replied, "I'm where I want to be." She grinned. While we were grinning I seen some lights coming up the street, "Hell naw!" I thought. Oh yes, it was them. They cruised by I guess to let me know I could run but not hide. Nia looked at me and said, "They crazy." At that point I was in full agreement.

That may sound crazy but that was not the only close encounter I had with Tina. Later on in the summer I was driving Dee's mama's car and he was driving my mama's ride. Dee had this system that you could hear a block away so I was leaning with the music blasting headed up to the gym to meet up with Dee and get my mother's car back. I passed a car at an intersection waiting to turn right, it was the Cadillac from hell.

After the scene over Nia's house I was a little paranoid of those people. I mean those people too because they used to ride around with the whole family inside the car, except the father. I knew they had seen me and I wasn't taking any chances, I hit it. I sped up to put some space between us, they sped up too. I got to a stop sign and darted out in front of a car so they couldn't follow exactly behind me. I then sped up and turned into the gym parking lot. I seen Dee and Toya sitting on the back of my mother's car, I made a beeline for them. By this time the Cadillac had turned into the lot I saw it as I was pulling up next to Dee. Dee leaned into the car and I jumped onto the floor and said, "Man they following me! Don't tell them I'm in here, please!" He looked up and backed away from the window. For the next few tension filled minutes I crouched on the floor of that old Ford. I expected at any minute for Tina to come into the window and drag me out of the car. I heard Dee say, "They gone man." I remember asking him if he was sure and Toya came to the other window and confirmed that they had left. I got out of the car and Dee told me that they had pulled right up on the car pointing and saying, "He in that car." Dee claimed they said some other things then drove off. Toya wanted to know what I had done I said nothing and went and sat at the front of the gym and thought, "These people are crazy!"

CHAPTER III

As the summer went on I was learning a lot of stuff. One thing I learned was white people on the job play games on black people. What I mean is that if there are two of you at a job they play you off against one another. Or if you happen to be the first black on the job you have to excel way above their performance. The way I got tricked up that first year was they played "The last black was lazy" game on me. There were other black men who worked at the county but they were full-time older men. I was the only black summer help. This actually was a good job because you had it every summer you came home and it kept me in money because it paid well.

The trick bag was though, the summer before I came on board there were two brothers before me who worked there. The whites played me against them. The cats were some dudes I knew from school, big time hoop stars, and they got the jobs and didn't do any work. The whites were constantly telling me stories about how lazy they were and how they got fired. So dumb me I damn near fried myself in the sun trying to prove I wasn't like them. This is a game I learned that was played on all black people on all levels of this society. I've always been a quick learner though before it was over I was the one getting over.

The party was soon to be over with Nia and I. I'll admit though that Nia was the coolest chick I had met at the time. Nia was fun as hell it was a big difference from stiff Tina. The only drawback was I never got the draws. Nia also has this one distinction; she is the only female I have ever argued with in public.

The situation jumped off like this. I was out with Del, drinking brews chilling in his old man's van when we stopped by the Action club. This was the place everybody hung out at. The joint was packed but most of the people hung outside drinking and smoking weed or whatever. So I was brewed up feeling good, at that time I still had a tolerance level, just kicking back listening to the tunes in my man's pop's van. When I spotted Nia, right then Devastator got hard.

I was thinking that maybe tonight I could hit this female's guts. All those thoughts quickly vanished when I seen Nia go mosey up and start jocking on another dude. I was shocked Devastator went limp. My boy Del followed my eyes and peeped the scene and said "Man don't let that shit bother you." I just nodded, Nia was jumping in and out of a car playing with some trick and he was grabbing all on her.

Man to tell you the truth I started feeling sick cause I liked the girl. I started walking down the street to make sure I'm seeing this picture clear. I was in a state of denial, when I bumped into one of Nia's girls. When she seen me she got a funny look on her face. I played the role I said, "Where is Nia?" She knew I had to have saw Nia already so she just pointed her finger where Nia was at. By this time Nia was all up in the car on the fool's lap. So I remarked, "Oh that's how Nia cut." Her girl was like, "Uhn-uhn." and she walked over to the car and leaned in and started talking to Nia. I walked off and went by the corner to holler at some cats I knew. I then turned and started walking back toward the van. Nia came over there by me I could tell by the way the girl's face was twitching she was scheming and fixing to lie. I just sat back to hear the tale. Nia said, "What's up Frank?" I was furious Nia was trying to play the situation off like wasn't anything happening.

Later on in life I knew how I should have played Nia. I should have said, "You." Then took Nia back to dude's van and tried to bone her. I should not have even mentioned dude. But I was still young and stupid. My cool was already slipping. I blurted out, "What's up with dude?" Nia replied, "He is just my friend." I waved her off. Nia said, "Fuck you Frank!" I just walked off. My cool was totally blown cause I walked the wrong way. I was headed back up to the corner instead of back towards the van. I played it off hollered at my boys then turned around and headed to the van. I glimpsed the ride Nia was at before, now Nia was all in the back seat with dude giggling! I was very perturbed at this stage in the game.

This is where the situation gets kind of hairy in my mind. I can't remember if Nia said something to me. I may have said something to Nia but, the fan once again got covered with shit. The next thing I know Nia had jumped out the car and was in my face yelling putting me on Front Street! At first I was shocked, the fool was really putting on a show! Nia was rushing at me yelling! Her girls were holding her back, yelling and cursing. I was just standing there like, what the hell? Then all of my cool points went down the toilet. I started yelling, "Let her go!" Dudes started pulling on me saying she ain't worth it, trying to calm me down. The scene was a joke! The sad part was I lost my watch.

That may not seem like much to most people but I had a *Seiko* that was a big deal at the time every other fool had *Swatch* watches. I had a 200-dollar *Seiko*. My watch was on display at the jewelry store in the mall. The watch was tight for a sixteen-year-old boy that was when I got it. Anyway in the melee I lost my watch, Del drug me to the van. I was pissed. I slammed some more brews. Del pulled off. While I rode around Del was talking trying to calm me down but I was highly agitated. I couldn't believe it. A female tried to play me, me! I kept drinking then after I was drunk as a skunk I told him to ride by Sandra's pad. We picked her up and I kicked it with her. I guess that was my way at getting back at Nia.

The next day I was hung over that is when it dawned on me I had lost my watch. I searched everywhere for it but it never came up. I made two vows that day: one to never argue with a female no matter what. Two, I would not buy another watch until I could spend five times what my old watch cost on a new one. To this day I have not broken either one of those vows. One reason after I seen *The Mack*, I realized why I shouldn't argue with females. As far as the watch I always say I'm on my time. Plus my bankroll never got big enough for me to blow a grand on a timepiece.

Well after I couldn't find my watch I figured the next thing to do was to see what was up with Nia. I can't remember if Nia called me or if I called her, but we put the situation behind us. Once again I was back over there tripping with Nia and her friends. This was destined to end and end it did.

One day I was over Sandra's house, sitting on the porch when Nia's cousin rode by. He spoke. I didn't think anything about it, he was supposed to be a player too. I don't know if he told her or not but a few days later I was up at the store with Sandra when Nia's cousin, who put me up on Nia, drove through the lot. To this day I think Nia was in the car scrunched down on the rider's side and seen me. I just knew I was done. For one, she had already seen me with old girl at the carnival once before. But I explained that off. I stopped by her house the next day and she didn't mention it so I didn't either. As I look back, she probably was doing her thing too. You can't point the finger when your are all the way wrong. The situation officially crashed on a Friday night.

My boy Steve, who was boning Sandra's cousin Lisa, decided we should take the girls up to Sonnies on Broadway in Milwaukee one Friday. I was cool with it. I knew his girl Lisa from high school and she was cool. We were picking them up from Sandra's house. Steve swooped me up and we went to pick the females up. When we got to Sandra's house I hopped out to go up to the door. I was feeling good it was going to be a good night.

Sandra's house was on a busy street and not ten feet from the street. I was waiting for someone to come open the door when I heard a familiar voice say, "What's up Frank?" If it had of been a drive by I would have been sprayed. In a sense it was one though. I turned around and Nia was sitting right there in the passenger seat of her cousin's car. Man I started sobering up fast and just as it dawned on me how screwed I was I heard Sandra's voice say, "Who is that?" Oh baby!

I was on the nexus of two worlds, caught in a crossfire. I was at the crossroads of my destiny. On one side I had Sandra my china doll and petite beauty. On the other was my thoroughbred, Nia. My mind was clicking fast. I realized Sandra did not know about Nia so I could play it off with her. Plus she was quiet so there would be no yelling or violence. Hell Nia was rough she might want to fight. Also Nia was probably just confirming what she already knew so I was through already. The final factor was Sandra was giving up cat, case closed.

I pushed Sandra back into the house and followed her and shut the door. I took the easy way out. As I look back on that, I wonder what would have happened if I went the other way. If I had of went and jumped into the car with Nia. Just drove off and said, "Fuck it!" Left with the female I had fun with instead of the one that was setting it out. That's one I will not know in this incarnation.

Well anyway I was inside of Sandra's house grinning like a damn chess cat. Sandra was looking up into my face all inquisitive like. I immediately jumped to damage control. I didn't want to give Sandra a chance to put two and two together so I immediately went to flattery, "Damn you looking fine tonight." I pointed at Lisa and said, "You looking good but my baby got you beat by a mile." She just waved me off. I glanced at Sandra, she was grinning so I knew it was cool. As the girls was putting on their finishing touches I cracked the door to make sure Nia was gone, she was so I was cool. I gathered up the women and went out to the car. Steve just looked at me and shook his head. I just reached for the joint he was smoking. I wanted to get high as hell, cause in my head I was already trying to figure some way to get back in good with Nia.

That night was a total bust. I got high as hell but when we got up to Milwaukee Steve drove the wrong way up a one way street and got a ticket. I wanted to bust out laughing but Steve was mad so I chilled. We wound up back in Racine. I got Steve to drop me off at home. I was high as hell and horny but I really didn't want to do Sandra. My mind was on Nia. I hopped into the Nova and rode around Racine trying to clear my head, trying to come up with a plan to cover up this mess I had let happen. My best option was to play like I didn't know if Nia cared for me or not. Play like I was kicking it with Sandra just to protect myself. The story was weak as hell but mostly true. I felt refreshed so I went to the pad to rest.

I got tied up that weekend drinking so I didn't call Nia until Monday. She went off on me so I let it ride. I chalked it up as a loss. I figured it was getting close to me going back to school so I'll just stay with Sandra and not try to get another broad in my flock. Plus I had to start facing the fact that I hadn't saved a dime for school. I had to save my last few checks to buy books and some gear.

One day I was riding with the twin's cousin Ronnie when he cut into Nia's cousin Kiesha. Kiesha must have pumped his head full of bullshit. Later Ronnie got hot in the nuts and wanted to go by Nia's house to see Kiesha. I told him, "Man I don't want to go by that house, drop me off at the gym." Ronnie was like, "Man just chill, Nia won't even know you in the car." I don't know why I listened to that asshole. Ronnie pulled up right in front of Nia's house. Right then I should have had an alarm bell going off in my head, but I wasn't paying attention. Ronnie went into the house and left the radio playing.

I was in the car vibing and nodding my head to the beat spacing out on the tunes. The next thing I heard was, "Hell naw!" I turned and looked up Nia was right at the window! Nia was not happy. If Nia had of had a gun she could have blew my fool head off and I would not have known what hit me. That broad went off! Nia was calling me everything but a child of god, Keisha and her friends was trying to pull her back into the house away from the car. All I could do was lean over away from the window with a stupid ass grin on my face.

Nia's friends pulled her into the house. I looked over at Ronnie he was standing on the curb grinning like a chess cat! I was like, "Dude let's go!" Ronnie was still bullshitting, talking about, "Let me see if old girl is coming." Then he ran up the walkway. I couldn't believe my ears! Keisha met Ronnie at the door. I guess she wasn't coming.

Ronnie turned to come to the car when the door exploded open! It was Nia. She hollered, "Don't even come on my block!" Hell that was fine by me I didn't want to come here in the first place. Dude got his ass back into the car and we pulled off. I said, "I told you I did not want to come over here!" Ronnie just laughed and drove on. I always thought that trick set me up for that confrontation. Keisha probably conned Ronnie into doing it for some sex he never got. Well that was the end of Nia for about three weeks, we never really quit playing with one another but that is another story.

Around this time I had hooked up with my boy Wally. We were kicking it off and on, drinking and hooping stuff like that. I used to wear this shirt that said, "Snow what snow" it was a summer T-shirt. I used to say to him you know what snow this shirt is talking about. Wally would laugh and wave me off. One day we was kicking it on a Friday and I told him I want some snow. Wally looked at me and started to laugh. But I guess he seen I was serious Wally said, "You bullshitting." I said, "Boy, don't you know I'm city slick and hip to all thangs?" I was lying through my teeth.

To this day I don't know why I went to Wally to find some cocaine but he did not disappoint me. We tooted cocaine that whole night. I remember feeling a tad bit disappointed because it didn't make me feel like a superman, but it was cool no big deal. Well I had done cocaine so I would have something to talk about back on the yard. I was going fast for a dude who only six months before hadn't even drank a beer.

Well it was time to go back to school. By this time I had grown tired of Sandra. I was too lazy though to go grab more females, plus Sandra was fine so I kept her around. I was hanging out off and on around some of Sandra's cousins towards the end of the summer. Sandra's cousin Lisa had started making remarks about pregnancies. Me, I wasn't paying attention. As I look back I think Lisa was trying to pull my coat that old girl was framing me like a Picasso. So a few nights before I was leaving Racine me and Sandra's cousin Jim was out drinking and riding around town. I stopped and grabbed us two fifths of Orange Jubilee. We parked the car and got out and started walking, drinking wine.

We finished that and stopped at another store I grabbed two fifths of rose and kept stepping. We started in Midtown and ended up on the south side. Since we were over there, I conned Jim into going up to Nia's house to knock on the door. I was drunk as hell so I was feeling bold, but not bold enough to go up to the door.

I stood a couple of house away behind one of the trees I used to make her kiss. This was my protection, if Nia came out mad I wanted to be able to run. It was all for naught. Nia came out and we rapped and joked so everything went cool. I felt good cause I knew when I came back for break I could look up my buddy. So Jim and I left. We had one problem though, I had forgotten where I had parked the car. Jim was drunker than me so he wasn't any help. I finally found it over on 13th street about two miles from Nia's house. I dropped Jim off at home and made it back to the pad. It had been a good night.

A few days before I left for college I was talking to Lisa and she all but told me Sandra was pregnant. My dumb ass had finally gotten the picture. I went over Sandra's pad to rap with her. I asked Sandra and she claimed that she was taking the test, now this situation couldn't have happened at a worse time. For one I was leaving in the next day or two, plus I was mentally through with Sandra. I had long since decided when I leave for college I was never going to speak to Sandra again. I was sick of her. Right before I left she let me know the results: I had crapped out. The female was pregnant.

CHAPTER IV

I went to school as planned. I did good seeing as my nuts were in a sling. I got my classes and even partied for a week. I then started scheming. I got in contact with the broad over Lisa's house and told Sandra I was going to come home. Sandra could then get an abortion. The dog mentality had not totally taken over my psyche yet. I was still a little soft around the edges. I was trying to play nice with Sandra like I still gave a damn about her, as if I cared if she lived or died. Realistically if she died that would solve my problem. I told Sandra she shouldn't have the baby because she would get fat and lose her figure. I was playing a ho-ass role cause I hadn't yet developed the nerve to just "raw-dog" a female yet.

I got a ride home one weekend to get the abortion taken care of. I didn't know zero about abortions so I was behind the white ball from the beginning. Sandra had saved some scratch to get the procedure done. So I called up to Milwaukee and they said Sandra had to have an appointment to get it done. I was pissed I wanted to be there and know the procedure was done. I got hard and told Sandra to get the abortion done cause I did not give a damn about her. This was the truth. I left Sandra sitting on the stoop in front of her house.

For some ass-hole reason I went around the block and came back. Sandra was sitting on the stoop crying. I went soft. I tried to be nice about the abortion and show her the benefits from getting it. This was a horrible mistake. I should have never gone back and attempted to rationalize with her. You need a hammer to drive a nail and I had just thrown mine away for a sponge. I was about to pay dearly for my mistake.

Sandra needed more scratch so I went and hollered at my boy PJ, he lent me some scratch. My Aunt Darla was next, then my cousin Rita. I went back and gave Sandra all the money I could scrape up about sixty dollars.

20

With that money and the scratch Sandra had saved she had enough to get the abortion done. I had to go back to school. I felt guilty but only for a day.

Before I left, I had made sure Sandra had a ride up to the clinic. My boy Del said all Sandra had to do was call him and he would take her. I had everything taken care of, wrong! The situation started getting flaky as a piecrust right after I left. The abortion was supposed to be done the week after I left. I called my boy Del Sandra hadn't called him. I couldn't be mad at Del cause he was waiting on Sandra to call him. So catching up with this woman was hard because Sandra didn't have a phone. I had to catch Sandra at Lisa's house. When I finally could catch Sandra, the fool always had a weak excuse like, "I over slept," or something.

All the while the clock is ticking. After a time you cannot get the abortion done for the cheap price. I damn sure did not have any more scratch to give up. I called Del and told him it was this Saturday coming up. Del was cool with it. I let Sandra know he was coming and it was O.K. with her. Finally I can sleep. Wrong. That Saturday came and I had partied the day before so I slept late. I was in the shower so someone hollered to me, "Frank you have a phone call." I came out wet I wanted to hear the good news from Del saying it was taken care of. The conversation went like this: Me, "What's up?" Del, "She didn't get it done." Me, "What!" Del, "She was too far gone." Me, "How far?" Del, "Thirteen weeks, it would have taken another hundred dollars to get it done." Me, "Where is she now?" Del, "Shopping for some coats." I think I mumbled bye and hung up.

Then it hit me Sandra had put off the abortion until she knew it was too late. It was only too obvious. Sandra knew how many weeks she was pregnant. So she knew she had to hold out for twelve and then the abortion rates would go up. She knew I could not give her any more money hence here comes the child. Sandra spent the scratch so there could be no more chances. To further insult, Sandra spent the little money I gave her as if I owed her something! The female dog didn't even send what was mine to me!

I still didn't realize how screwed I was until a few weeks later. My birthday was coming up and I needed some loot to enjoy it. Now I knew Sandra had scratch coming in from her first kid so I cracked on her to send me a few bones. Add in the fact that she still owed me sixty dollars and I figured I was due some loot. I did not hear from the Sandra until the day after my birthday. Sandra sent a card with a dollar in it with "Ha-Ha" written in it.

A few days later I received a letter from Sandra saying that when I get home we have to have a talk about: me, her, the baby and her son. I did not even finish reading it. It hit me. I had been played. I thought I was the one fucking her but in the end I had been fucked.

I guess it wouldn't have been so bitter if Sandra had of just been real from the beginning. Sandra had known she was not going to have an abortion from the start. If an abortion was going to be her escape from childbirth then Sandra knew she was pregnant two or three weeks before I left Racine. I could have taken her myself. Sandra had her con down.

Sandra knew that once I left Racine it would be hard for me to come back from Ohio to take her to the clinic. The con Sandra ran about wanting an abortion was unnecessary. If she had of came clean from the jump, we would have had a whole different type of relationship in the years to follow. All the Sandra had to say was, "Frank, I'm pregnant. I'm having the baby." I still would not have married Sandra or touched her again but, I would not have felt as played as I did. By Sandra playing like she was going to get an abortion and not, froze any feeling I may have had for her.

The person that was really at fault was myself, only at the time I could not see it. I did not listen to my parents when they literally said Sandra was not shit. They did not use those words but they knew once they seen her that she was flaky. My mother even stated more than once she was going to jam me with a child. I did not listen so I paid the price.

From that day on the smile left my face. Fuck grinning in females faces they were all trick bitches to me. Out of the whole ordeal the fact that galled me the most was I was being forced to be a father. Add in the fact that, this was supposed to be quiet nice girl had ran one of the oldest scams on me. This female probably had never even been to Chicago before! It was all that nice garbage, Sandra probably had never even been talked to before when she was getting boned. Just, "Ho take 'em off!" Oh well you learn the hard way sometimes. Well the usual thing would be to keep up some type of relationship with your baby's mama. Well I was far from usual. I got hard as hell.

I was determined to not let this stop me from finishing up school. I damn sure was not going to let this peon, Sandra, hinder me from living my life. So I hit the books even harder, I hit the malt liquor harder too. If I had a woman at that time then her name was *Private Stock* and I cheated on her with *Old English 800*. I went home for Thanksgiving. I had to start laying down the future of our "relationship" to Sandra.

Soon as I hit Racine I touched base with Nia so we started hanging. One evening I was up at Total 24 with Nia and her girls when I seen Sandra's sister. I spoke to her we laughed and she went her way I went mine. I was in Racine from Tuesday through Sunday. I had a good time kicking it with my partners and family. Sandra never crossed my mind until Saturday night.

I was riding with the Twins and they rode up 6th street. I told them to pull over by Sandra's grandmother's house. Sandra was inside. The kids out front told me so. I told them to go tell her to come outside. Sandra was upset and acted like she did not want to come out, but she did.

This was the last conversation I had with Sandra for at least the next six years. It went like this: me, "So you're having my baby, don't be drinking and also make sure you read at night I don't want no dumb kids." I turned and got into the car with my boys and drove off. I didn't look back. I could not make Sandra not have the child but I damn sure wasn't going to let her live in a fantasy like I was going to be with her or even, heaven forbid, marry her. I didn't give a damn about Sandra or her kids and it was important that she knew this. Also secretly I was hoping Sandra dropped dead or something. Hey I had a right to dream.

Back at school I had to finish out the semester. I did well on my finals I think I made the Dean's List that semester. I came home for the holidays, kicked it with family and friends. The word Sandra never came out of my mouth, she was forgotten. New Year's came I was high as hell partying in the *Club New Yorker*. 1987 was a blast 1988 was going to be an explosion.

CHAPTER V
1988

I went back to school for the second semester of my sophomore year and I was partying and drinking all the time. Once again though I was on the dean's list. Through it all I was hearing about the *United Negro College Fund* and financial aid that was all bullshit. I constantly heard that my mother made too much money for me to qualify for grants. I couldn't figure it out. I was a Negro, I thought. Later I realized I was not a Negro but a Nigger. That came later in life after I read, *The Nigger Bible*. So by my mother having to come up with so much scratch to send me to school the situation felt like a burden. I knew my mother wasn't rich so I felt obligated to do my best. Even then I was trying to find ways to find scratch so Mama wouldn't have to pay. So I started looking at some state schools to go to that would be cheaper. Also around this time PFA was starting to gain some people who were interested in joining. PFA was the brotherhood I created my freshman year after I dropped Beep. I patterned it after the MFA, the Midnight Funk Association. It was a brotherhood like Beep except it was mine. The history states the number one person is FJ, now this was more like it. My first pledge was my boy Len. I don't know what I had him do to get in but he was in. Then later we got my ace CJ to join, there were others but they are not worth mentioning at this time. The one I remember, who stayed true, was my roommate Dontae and his buddy Mickey. These fools caught Len and I drunk and conned us into letting them in for some *Burger King.* You can do that when you run the show.

Well at the time in the winter of 1988 we had a few brothers. But outside Len and CJ and I they were not cool. They didn't get sauced up enough for me. Plus these squares didn't hang with the real dogs enough for me. I look back on that scenario and realize that I would have had it made if

I could have just gotten my head together. I could have been running things. How many dudes do you know have people pledging their name? I was just too consumed with hatred to think straight. The fact that Sandra was having that baby just ate me up on the inside. I was a bitter man who didn't give a damn about nothing. I was changing fast. The nice carefree FJ was being transformed into an empty hate-filled vessel with no love for no one. I also hadn't bothered to tell my mother about the baby. Mama found out off the streets. I got a phone call about the situation. My mother, I love her, but I wonder if she really gave a damn about Sandra? Or was she just pissed that someone laughed at her when they told her about it. Mama called me with this song and dance about how could I be so cruel. I laughed on the inside I was just getting started. If I had my way I was going to take cruelty to a whole new level, as far as Sandra was concerned. Another thing that was adding to my degeneration was the environment I was in.

My environment was screwed up. There wasn't a damn thing to do at Willyfarce except drink and have sex. I had stopped playing ball cause the gym was half open. The bitterness that I felt was quickly coming out of me I could not hide it. So I constantly drove women away. That led to more fun times with the malt liquor.

I was headed down a shitty road fast. Len and this chick Deja and I would kick it. Deja had a child and I would ask her all types of ways to get rid of the baby. Deja was telling me about shots that could be administered so the baby would be born dead, all types of stuff. Man I'm glad I was 500 miles away from that female, Sandra, or I would have tried some of those procedures. I also figured if worse came to worse Sandra would have miscarried the hard way. I had came to this conclusion: if I pushed the girl down some stairs I would only get five years at the most, but by her having a baby I was hit for eighteen years. It was a no-brainer to me, which was the better deal. At this time I was real messed up in the head.

It was time for me to leave this raggedy place. The whole concept of Willyfarce was a joke. This was the first black university in America and it was a total sham. At the time I remember some students saying that a white man controlled the money. I don't know if it was true but looking at the state of the school I could believe it. The dorms were a mess and the food was a joke.

I remember one time sitting down on the toilet to take a dump and just as I was getting started a big roach comes crawling up the toilet. This roach is crawling right up like it was about to hop on my Johnson! You had to keep boric acid on the floor under your bed and in your closet to keep the roaches under control. They never left. Sometimes you could strike up a peace treaty with them.

On the other side of the coin, administration knew there was drinking and screwing going on. This went on at a school that was supposed to be a church school! Oh how rare was that? Let me give you a quick insight. At any time I could go into a room on any floor and find some alcoholic beverage to drink. Whether it was beer or liquor there was some alcohol somewhere around. You have to keep in mind this was supposed to be a dry campus, no alcoholic beverages allowed. Security knew that people were smuggling brew and liquor into the dorms they didn't give a damn. A few of the security guards were too busy getting their jimmies jacked by the students. Hell I don't blame them I would have been freaking those young females too. They were eighteen.

There were not too many days where you could not walk onto a floor and not smell weed. That type of endeavor was right up my alley too as long as I did not have to pay for it. I guess the administration figured as long as the tuition was paid, oh well. I came through this garbage with a 3.2 or something. It was time for me to exit stage left. I wasn't coming back. My grades were good enough for me to go to any school I damn near wanted to.

I got home in late April of that year. The first thing I did was contact my old job to get it back. I got the Nova running and once again it was on. The previous year at the county I was a good worker this year was different. All I wanted to do now was sleep on the job. I was driving these big dump trucks asleep at the wheel. Once I remember nodding off and waking up on the wrong side of the road heading towards the ditch. Another time I was asleep driving in traffic. The reason I would be so tired was because of my lifestyle. I just kicked it too much.

In early May I got a call from Sandra, she had a girl. Sandra had given her my last name. I hung up. I couldn't figure out why the fool was calling me. I could really care less. Two days later I was drinking with my boy Brian. Brian and his girl conned me into going up to the hospital to see the baby. Sandra had been released, oh well no loss.

A few days later PJ and I was riding down Memorial Drive when I said, "Let's go check out the kid." We went in and Sandra's mother was holding the baby. PJ sat down. I went by Sandra's mother she asked would I like to hold the baby grinning. I remember looking into that woman's face and seeing everything I despised about her daughter and would see in the child and calmly said "No." I looked at the child turned and walked out.

It was all I could do to keep from just snapping and doing some severe damage to everyone in the house. I looked at the dilapidated furniture and the gooney grin on Sandra's mother's face and realized this kid tied me to this trash! I thought about how raggedy the furniture was inside the joint and wanted to throw up when I realized my child was going to have to live in such squalor. I know what you are thinking. Why didn't I gain custody of the child? Because I was a realist, I could never care for a child. I could barely care for myself. Any other type of thinking would be foolish. I couldn't help the baby without finishing school and paying support. I knew even back then that no matter how much I paid, my child would always be lacking because I had betrayed my own genes by mixing with scum.

PJ was tripping on the scene that had just went down inside the house, he said I was sick. I had stopped listening to dude. I was already thinking of a way for me to get rid of him and go get me some brew and do some personal introspection.

One day I was at mama's house bullshitting around when the postman came and said he had a registered letter for me. I was excited! I was always filling out for sweepstakes, so maybe I had finally won one. I could see that prize patrol van pulling into my driveway giving me a check for a couple million. I opened the letter anxiously. I had won! But it wasn't *Publishers Clearing House,* it was the state of Wisconsin telling me I was named in a paternity suit. Sandra had turned me over to the state. That vision of the prize patrol quickly vanished. It turned into a vision of flat out hell. The one with the flames and people being burned.

Well the letter stated I had three options: claim the child, deny the child, or request a blood test. I took the third option. I was sure the child was probably mine but, as Jessie Jackson says, "Keep hope alive!" I was definitely hoping. I took my blood test praying to anyone that would listen to let them come back negative.

I had to go to court to get the results of my blood test. It was a formal session to establish paternity. I went down there with hopes that I could be exonerated. When I got into the court room guess who was sitting there as pert as could be, Sandra. I felt the walls closing in on my ass. The court commissioner read the results: 99.987 that the child was mine. See what hope gets you. The commissioner continued on that in light of the results there was no doubt that I was the father. I glanced over at Sandra. She was loving this. I guess Sandra was feeling good that the system would force me to do what I refused to do up until that point, claim my child.

As I sat there, I wanted to scream that I had been duped! I had been tricked and lied to. The state only wanted to get my name on those papers so I could start paying support. The reason being Sandra was on welfare. The funny thing though they were not sweating her about her other child's father. At the time Sandra had never told the state who the father of her other child was. The state didn't want to pay if I was around. I could not blame them I didn't want to pay. Sandra was smiling like she had beaten me. I couldn't have this. If I was going out, I was going out in a blaze of glory. The female dog had me but I'll be damned if I was going to let Sandra know it.

As I sat there listening to the commissioner talk. He said something that I knew could help me snatch victory out of the jaws of defeat. He said, "You can sign now, deny the child and go to court or seek legal help." I paused and let out a sigh. Sandra was sitting there just bubbling over with happiness, I guess she thought I was broken, wrong. I straightened up and said, "I want to wait to sign until I have sought out legal representation." Wham! Score two for the home team. As I said it I looked at Sandra with a sneer on my face that said, "Not today cow, you won't get the satisfaction today."

When I said those words the grin dropped off of the peon's face. Sandra got red as hell. Sandra couldn't even sit still until the man gave me six more months to get a lawyer. As soon as the court dismissed us, Sandra jumped up and sped out of the courtroom. I took my time and sauntered into the hall. Sandra was out there waiting for the elevator. When it came Sandra seen me heading for it and walked towards the stairwell. I guess she preferred the stairs. I pushed the down button laughing. She was fat and needed the exercise anyway. I really had a good laugh when I seen Sandra walking fast down the block.

I went and talked to a lawyer and she was sympathetic to my cause but she told me I was screwed. She agreed that Sandra was scum and was playing on me with the hope one day I would get rich. But there was no law against it. It is hypocritical isn't it. If someone runs a con game on someone and beats him or her out of two or three hundred dollars the law will step in and deal with the con person.

On the other hand if some no good female gets pregnant by some guy, not out of love, but because he may have some money. Or maybe he has potential he gets dragged into court and sentenced to eighteen years of paying child support. I know what your thinking the guy should have kept his Johnson in his pants, true. But then the victim of the con man should have kept his money in his pocket and not let greed take over. I eventually signed the papers but Sandra was not present when I signed them.

One quick side note. Before all of you females and males out there throw the book down think about this: my baby's mother has three children by three different fathers. At the time I was the only one whose name she had ever turned over to the state. You figure it out.

I put in an application for Pickeville University in Wisconsin. As I stated before, Willyfarce was costing too much and I wanted to change my scenery anyway. Also, Pickeville was supposed to be one of the top broadcasting schools in the Midwest. Whoo-hoo, they accepted me, once that was taken care of I just kicked it hard as hell with my boys. Wally, Keith and I just partied all the damn time.

CHAPTER VI

Keith had a bullshit job working at *Great America* in one of the game booths. The boy was peeling them like oranges. Keith had to be taking at least two to three hundred a day from them fools. I was getting paid every other week so on the Fridays I got paid, I'd have a couple hundred in my pocket, skip saving for school it was party time. To the Christians Good Friday comes once a year, to me it came every other Friday.

This is how the evening would go, Keith would get off the bus from his job at around 11:30 at night. I would swing over and swoop Keith up as he was getting off the bus. We would then rush to the store to get some forties and then hit the New Yorker. One weekend we took partying to a new level.

I swung through *Total 24* where Keith got off the bus. The bus had not made it in yet and it was close to 12:00 so I went and grabbed two six packs of our brand *Old English 800*. I rode up Sixth street looking for Wally to see if he was hanging with us that night. I caught up with Wally but he was chilling with Liza, his girl. So I hopped back into the Ultimate Homeboy Car, my Nova, and went back up by Total to see if Keith was up there. Sure enough he was walking down the street looking around for the ride. Keith knew the protocol about Fridays. I rolled by Keith, he jumped in and I pointed to the brew he said, "Hell yeah!" As I pulled off Keith reached into his pocket and the fool pulled out a wad of bills. Keith had peeled *Great America* for about seven to eight hundred that day, I just shook my head. It was Good Friday. I did not want to be out done so I reached in my pocket and pulled out my bankroll. Keith looked and we slapped five. It was going to be a good night.

We sat outside the New Yorker drinking the brews and scheming on how we could get in. We had gone in before, but, I was nineteen and Keith was seventeen or eighteen. Our age was an issue. After we finished the six

30

packs we was buzzed and agreed to just look hard and keep walking when we got to the door. When we got to the door Keith and I both frowned up. The dude at the door just asked for the money and let us in. Party time!

We grabbed a table and started ordering our favorite, *Jack Daniel*'s. I asked Keith, "Man are we going to do it?" Drink like a fish was my intent, Keith responded, "Yeah." I said, "Cool." The waitress asked what we wanted I said, "Bring two double shots of *Jack Daniel's* I'm buying." The waitress came back with the drinks and we toasted to ourselves and downed it. Keith caught the waitress and ordered two more. We toasted this one to Wally. I flagged her down and ordered two more. This time we toasted our mothers and Keith's girl. By now we were fairly high, add the brew and the double shots together, and we had put some shit away. Keith wanted to order more, I said, "Man just get me a *Corona*, I'll be straight." The waitress was taking too long so Keith went to the bar. I was high as hell. I was just sitting there nodding to the music checking out which female I was going to try to bone. When I looked toward the bar and saw Ron, the owner. He was pulling glasses down and filling them with *Jack Daniel's*. I thought man somebody is getting messed up. So I looked the other way and the table shifted so I turned around. It was Keith putting these glasses on the table damn near full of *Jack Daniel's*. This nut had come back with four double shots of *Jack Daniel's*, he was grinning like a chess cat. My mouth was gaping, he explained, "They was out of *Corona*, so I got these. Dude hooked us up!" I just shook my head and asked, "Who are we toasting?"

After we finished those two drinks I was blitzed. I got up and said, "Man I have to dance or I'm going to fall out." *Guy* was the group back then and the deejay was playing one of their songs. I danced and rubbed on females' butts like a maniac trying to get a genie out of a lamp! Keith and I partied all night doing the Donkey Back, a dance I had concocted. Keith was yelling, and I was acting a fool. We both were hollering, "I wish Wally was here!" Since he wasn't we were obligated to leave the dance floor and order another round to toast our buddy. There were plenty of women in the club too. I was trying to talk to all of them.

By the time the club closed we had drank the New Yorker out of *Jack Daniel's*. Keith and I staggered back to the ultimate homeboy car and rolled out. When we got by his house Wally was out front in the car with a dude we knew named Tip. Keith was out. I was shaking him and slapping him, trying to wake him up when we rolled into Tip's car. Keith woke up laughing and got out. I was on the verge of passing out myself so I hollered at Wally and rolled. I was driving drunk as hell trying to stay focused cause I did not want to get pulled over. I made it safely and blacked out on my bed with my clothes on.

To this day Keith and I reflect back upon that night as one of the best parties we ever had. The coolest thing to come out of the night was we had established a relationship with Ron, the owner of the New Yorker, so we never had a problem with getting carded. To Ron we were cool, we spent so much money in there that summer, that he would buy me drinks when I would come back from school. That summer I kicked it tough.

Even though I was having fun if someone came up to me and mentioned Sandra and the kid, my mood would swiftly change. For example, one Saturday Wally Keith and I were up by Tip's house chilling and drinking brews. Some females Wally knew, Brittney and Clairese, stopped by and brought a female I knew from high school, named Halle.

Halle used to dig me back in the day, but I really wasn't feeling her too tough at the time. So we were all laughing and having a good time when Halle started tripping. Halle must have been upset about the attention I was giving her, or the lack of it, so she started saying, "That's why you got a baby." Halle kept saying this over and over. I told her to shut up but she refused. Nobody else was paying attention to what she was saying, it seemed she meant it for my ears only.

Finally I snapped. Halle was sitting in the back seat of my Nova and I guess she saw the look on my face, so she quickly rolled the window up and locked the door. Well the Nova was a four door and Wally was in the front seat talking to Brittney with the door open. I was in a rage by then because Halle had pointed at me through the window and laughed. I elbowed Wally out of the way and reached in the back and unlocked the door and snatched it open. Halle fell back into the car, kind of laughing like this was a game. Boy, was she wrong.

I dragged her out of the back seat by her legs until she fell out onto the pavement. When she came out she hit her butt on the ground with a thud by this time I was standing over her ready to blow her mouth out for such insolence. When she recovered from the shock of being drug and dumped onto the ground she looked up with a puzzled look on her face that froze me. That look of utter disbelief and embarrassment made me forget how mad I was and made me want to bust out laughing.

By this time everybody was quiet because they realized I was not playing anymore. I had to bite the insides of my jaws to keep from laughing in her face, but I had to let her know not to play with me again. I mumbled something about do not mention this to me again or I will kick your ass. I then spun around and walked away.

Wally caught up with me and asked if I was all right. I was walking fast because I knew I was going to bust out laughing and I didn't want Halle to see me because she would think I was playing with her and I really did not want to hear that baby talk again. When Wally saw my face as we rounded the corner he busted out laughing right with me. I laughed until I cried about how stupid Halle looked. I told him what she was saying and he agreed that she got what she deserved. Deep down I knew I wasn't going to hit Halle because I had never hit a woman before and didn't intend on starting. This was not my last encounter with Halle, in the end she got the last laugh. This was just an example of how much the baby situation was starting to wear on my mental make up.

In my book there hasn't ever been three downer brothers than Keith, Wally and me. We would see a female and instead of us easing over one at a time possibly stepping on each other's toes, we would go over to her all at once. All three of us would start firing game at her. This eliminated us from back stabbing each other. We would usually wrap up with the fact that she would have to choose one of us, who was it going to be? Our motto was we had what you needed. Tall light bald, Keith, brown with brush waves, me, and dark with a perm, Wally. We never had any beef. If the girl picked one of us the other two just faded out. It was cool to us. We looked at it like the cat was kept in the family. We partied until I had to go back to school. It felt funny cause I was not headed to the bus station in Chicago to go to Willyfarce I was headed to Pickeville. That was a story in itself.

Pickeville

I should have known I was headed into trouble because on the way up there we did not pass any black people on the highway. I'll never forget when we got to Pickeville and found my room and the feeling I had. I was sick. When mama, Chuck and Chasity drove away I had a bad feeling. The situation was so bad Chuck later remarked, "I felt bad leaving you there." Welcome to hell Frank James.

The school was at least 10,000 students and when I went there it was only ten or eleven black students. Four were black females, and only two looked good. One was engaged to be married, the other, my boy Mel wrapped up. My first room assignment was with three white boys. That lasted a few days then I moved into my room.

My roommate then was a white kid named Biff. Biff was from Illinois. It's funny, if I saw the man now I wouldn't even know his face. He probably wouldn't know mine either. The only whites I was used to seeing at Willyfarce in the dorms was the cracker security guard Yakov, the others were on television. Now the only blacks I saw were on the tube. Keep in mind that I was literally PE crazy. Public Enemy was my group and earlier that summer they had released, *It takes a Nation of Millions to hold us Back.* I listened to the tape every day. *No Sellout* was to become my life standard.

The one thing that made it bearable was there were a few cats I knew from Racine in Pickeville, Lyle and Sam. Lyle became my running buddy. Sam played hoop. Sam had been at Pickeville for four years. Sam was used to the atmosphere. Lyle was a freshman so the situation was new to him like it was to me. My man Mel had just graduated from Pickeville and now worked for the university. This was to be the most unproductive semester of my college career.

I used to blast the hell out of my roommate's system. One day Lyle came in saying he could hear the music down the road. There were also a few brothers from Chi-town (*Chicago*), who played basketball and they were cool. Other than that the situation was foul. Some of the classes were interesting though. I liked the television/radio class but it was at 8:00 in the morning, so scratch that one.

One thing I had to give the Caucasians though, was that they had more stuff for their students. We had a phone in our room! That was a long way from Willyfarce when there was only one phone per floor on a good day. They also had microwaves on every floor for the students to use. They also had bowling alleys, clubs, and all types of activities on campus for the students. But I hated the place.

There was not any type of black atmosphere at Pickeville. The classes had forty to fifty people in them, all of the Caucasian descent. I would simply not go to class. I would drink every chance I got. The white folks up there just did not seem to know what to make out of black people.

For instance, I had gotten a job working in the catering department. I was cutting meat for banquets and parties. I had taken off work to go to Racine a few times and the white female over the banquet staff tried to fire me. The situation was crazy.

First off, I had done everything by the book and the white girl knew this. But I just don't think the girl liked me. When the dismissal went down I really did not give a damn about the job, but it was the principle. The white girl had lied saying I had not called in one Friday, and that was why I was fired, oh no. I called the token Negro that the university hired to recruit black students and told him the deal. He was skeptical until I told him I could prove my point. The token then set up an appointment with the girl and me to resolve the issues.

In the meeting she came in with a guideline book for the job cool, I had one too. She started lying. I cut the female off and showed her in her book where I could take time off and not be fired. She got quiet. The token was looking when I issued the coup de grace: I said, "She, the white girl, was prejudiced." Turmoil erupted in the room. The token sat, up the white girl started stuttering, during all of this turmoil I kicked back and folded my hands.

The token asked, "Can you prove this?" I said, "Yeah, I know of white workers who had taken more time off than me and they still have their jobs." The token looked at the white girl and she started crying, saying things like, "I did not mean it."

The token sat back and said, "Well it is obvious you fired him without cause what should we do?" The girl sat there crying into her lap, she could not even look up. The token continued, "There have also been some serious charges brought up in this meeting about race what should we do?" The white female said, "I'm sorry." I waved her off. The spectacle had lost interest to me. I was sick and disgusted by the way the girl carried on. She had been hell on me before, now she went out like a punk. They offered me my job back but I turned it down, hell everybody knows a job ain't nothing but work. I just told the token to take that firing off my record, just in case I wanted to get another gig.

I also developed the knack for stealing up at Pickeville. I had never stolen before in my life, but up there, Lyle and I went crazy. The whites had more than their fair share of stuff, so we helped ourselves to it. Back then *Guess* jeans were what everybody was wearing. The white boys had all of the latest pants and jacket hook-ups.

The white boys were not my size but Lyle could fit their clothes. If I remember right, Lyle was taking their clothes right out of the dryer while they were drying. My favorite place to pilfer from was the liquor store. I wore black clothes all the time. If it wasn't black, it was black stone washed. I also wore a black Russian hat with my Chuck D clock. The whites really couldn't relate to me, nor I to them. So this led to easy pickings when it came to stealing.

The liquor store was a safe haven for us. Lyle and I would get Sam's car and just drive around this boring campus. We would stop at the liquor store and have a field day. We would leave there with fifths of liquor. The lady had to see us taking the stuff but she never said a thing. All we wore was thin Starter jackets who, couldn't see a fifth of liquor bulging out of one of them? So on weekends or whenever we could get Sam's car we had our liquor hook up. The stealing wound up getting plain ridiculous.

One day Lyle and I were riding in Sam's car and Daryl was with us. Daryl was one of the cats from Chicago. I said, "Lets go by the liquor store." They replied, "Man they are going to get tired of us taking their stuff." I answered, "Fuck that." Add in the fact that I was broke and wanted to drink and you get the following scenario.

I went in, and gave the female behind the counter a grim look and went straight to the liquor. I grabbed a fifth of *Jack Daniel's*, a fifth of *Yukon Jack*, and started walking out. On the way out I saw some new *Mad Dog 20/20*, they had a new flavor out. I went outside and handed them the stuff. They was like, "Lets roll." I told them about the *Mad Dog* and went back in. The wine was right in front of the counter so I could not even try to play off what I was about to do, so I just went up to the cooler and just grabbed a bottle and walked out.

As I write this I still can't figure out why she did not call the police on me. Needless to say that was my last time going in that particular establishment to steal. There wasn't any need to push my luck too far. For those who drink, what is the first thing you think about after you get high? Pussy right, well since there were no black women up there, that wasn't an option. This led to food being next on the agenda.

Same principle different business this time it was the Quik Mart. Lyle and I would go into the Quik Mart and microwave burritos and eat them in right in the store. We would also steal pizzas and chips. One night I was walking out eating a burrito with a pizza shoved in my coat when I stopped and grabbed some candy bars for dessert.

I think that may have been too much because the clerk said, "Stop!" I just looked at this fool with a vicious look and said, "What?" The clerk just stood there and I walked out to the car. I walked slow cause I knew if I ran he would call the cops. I left but that was the last trip to that establishment. The stealing got so out of hand, Lyle and I were out in the hall one night trying to figure out how to unscrew the microwaves that were in the hallway. I'm glad that the microwave would not come loose. Our rooms would have been the first checked when they noticed it was missing.

When we weren't stealing or tripping out, Lyle and I would go to keg parties at Sam's house. They knew me when I came in the door. They would usually pass out these little foam cups to the patrons. When I came in they pulled out the big 24 ounce cups because they knew the time. I would go right to the tap and drink down five or ten quick cups. The beer was a weak brand called *Meister Brau* so it took a lot to faze me. I would just sit there and play quarters with whoever was playing. The scene was boring to me because there were no black women in the place.

I definitely was not down with the swirl. For example one night we were out drinking and Lyle and I saw some white chicks shaking their butts. I told Lyle, "Go get the blonde one and bring her over here." He did and when she got over by me she looked at me with a funny face and said, "I didn't think you liked white people." I felt my pride swelling and shame for even thinking about screwing this chick. So I replied, "You're right." I turned around and resumed talking to Lyle like the girl wasn't there. That white girl fetish just wasn't for me.

One Friday they had this set called *Whiskey Fest* over at one of the white jocks' pad. So Lyle, Daryl and I went with some of the other blacks to check it out. I was skeptical cause I had never heard of anything like this, but true to form there was no beer in the house just liquor. We took a few shots and some of the brothers were talking to some of the whites about drinking. I was just watching the scene. The atmosphere led to talk of a contest, quite literally between the whites and the blacks.

I was still minding my own business when the crowd went to the basement. I followed to see what the hell was going on. They had a half-gallon of some liquor called *Red Label* or *Red Flag* whiskey, some hillbilly drink, down there. There was this big ass Caucasian down there who played on the football team. I guess he was their champion. Someone turned and nominated me for the black squad. I was saying to myself, "How the hell did I wind up in this situation?" Anyway it was the white boy and me, face to face. He took a shot and I took one. Me weighing around 180 pounds, and him at about 270. This scene went on until the half-gallon was damn near empty.

Don't get me wrong, the bottle was open before we started, so it was not a full half-gallon to begin with, but it was close. By this time the Caucasian is swaying and so am I. The white boy hollered out, "Its time to go get the *Jack Daniels!*" I replied, "Go get him. Jack's my cousin, now what?" He looked at me and headed up the stairs. We followed. I was confident about drinking *Jack Daniel's*. I knew I could put him down drinking that. Someone produced a fifth, and after two shots or so the contest was over. We agreed we could both drink. It was a stalemate.

They started playing music. They played *Kool Moe Dee*, and the Caucasian showed me how to do his dances. The dances they do at a hoe down I guess, the Potato Digger and the Deer Hunter. I think I showed him the Running Man. By now I was wasted so was this Caucasian. He was wearing a cowboy hat and I was wearing my trademark Russian hat, by the time it was over, he had my hat on, I had his and we were dancing on the floor. He was doing the Running Man and I was doing the Potato Digger. Jessie Jackson would have been proud. I eventually got my hat and left.

Lyle and Rudy, brothers from Milwaukee, helped me get to my room. I took a shower and laid down. Man I was drunk. I vaguely remember Lyle standing over me saying, "Man it's Sunday, time for football and the Raiders are on." I think I got up pissed and went back to sleep. The next time I woke up it was 10:00 Monday morning. I had missed class, slept the whole weekend, and I still felt drunk. What a party.

As I stated before, Pickeville was pretty much a waste and my GPA showed it. I got a 2.21 that semester, my lowest GPA ever in college. Well it did give me the experience of going to an all white school to see how they lived. It also enabled me to look upon those blacks who go to white schools, and sell out with disgust.

It also helped me spit on the weak blacks who go to white schools and come back with white spouses. Traitors the whole lot of them. It would have been easy for me to just grab onto the ways of the whites and sell out. I was damn sure in the environment to do it, but then what? I would not be able to brush my teeth in the mirror. Also, it would have been easy for me to go to screwing white girls but I told you how that went even on an off day, I couldn't do it. Negroes who go those routes are weak individuals who are better off with the whites cause they damn sure are not any use to the Black race.

I hated Pickeville so bad that when we got out for Christmas I knew I was not going back. I tried taking all my clothes with me so I wouldn't have to make that ride. Two things influenced my decision: 1) I was tired of hearing my mother say she sacrificed to send me to school. I knew I would not go back unless I could pay for it myself. 2) I had heard that there was a lot of money to be made in Racine selling cocaine, it was time to roll.

When I got back to Racine I immediately found Wally and Keith to get the scoop on what was happening on the streets. To make sure, I got it from two angles, I tracked down PJ. It all lead me to one conclusion, there was money to be made and games to be played, and in my mind I was *Milton Bradley*. Christmas passed and I was gearing up for the New Year, 1989.

CHAPTER VII
1989

The year jumped off with a bang. I had put a word in Del's ear about me not going back to school. I did this so he could touch base with his uncle, Flyboy. Flyboy was an old school dope pusher who had done time and came out stronger than ever. I knew him cause he knew my father, but I was figuring the man would look out for his nephew. While I was waiting for Del to catch up with his uncle, I'm delaying Mama about school. No one knew I wasn't going back to school except Del. I was trying to stall until I had a hook up so I could roll.

Flyboy told Del to find a spot that we could sell out of. This was cool so Del and I went around looking for apartments that would fit our needs. There was only one hitch. We had to work with PJ and Fats. That was a problem cause PJ and Fats were cool but they liked to play too much. PJ and Fats were already hustling and looked at Del and I as squares. This was one problem, the next was differences in philosophies. PJ and Fats did not think we needed a gun for security in the spot. I thought we may need a 9mm just to be safe. Del, on the other hand, thought we needed a m-16, two nines, and grenades. When we all got together with Flyboy, all of the differences came out about guns, security and the work shifts. Suffice it to say, the deal fell through.

Del felt bad about the whole thing because he knew I had held off on going back to school because I was hoping to get started rolling. He did not realize I was just tired of school, especially Pickeville. By this time the handwriting was on the wall. My mother just told me since I was not going back to school I had to find a place, cause I could no longer stay in her house. I knew that was coming. I had dropped in on my father, and he had already pulled my coat to the fact he had a pad that I could stay at if I paid half of the rent. When I was moving in my father stopped by and reminded me that there was no gas on in the place. Now remember this was the middle of January, in Wisconsin, so you know I could not have that. I went and cut the gas on in my name, the electricity too, just for safe keeping. Now that I had a place to stay in, it was time to get some money.

I went up on Sixth Street to holler at my buddy Wally. Wally had been hustling up on sixth for Bart, a cat I knew from when we were young. I had put feelers out with Wally about the situation before, because I kind of felt the play with Flyboy was going to be a bust. I went down to Bart's spot with Wally, and I touched base with him. Since Bart knew me from when we were young, everything went cool.

I sat up there and watched how they were doing things for a few hours. Later on that evening Wally let me hold his work, I was selling coke. One of his workers named Dizzy, asked how come I was up there selling. Wally cut him off by telling him that Bart said it was cool. That was the last question I heard about me selling out of there.

The way they had the scene set up was slick. The customer would come up the front steps and knock on the door. When this happened we would ask through the door, "What you need?" The customer would reply and slide their money through this hole in the door. We in return slid the dope to them. They did not see us we did not see them, good business for everyone concerned. Also, Bart had scanners and walkie-talkies for surveillance. The workers had to take turns standing outside, or sitting in cars to let the people up stairs, and to know who was coming to the door. I saw real quick that there was no money in surveillance, so I never did it. I was learning fast about the game because I had big plans, and only fools stayed workers. At any given time there were four to five workers in the spot selling. They usually had around two hundred dollars worth of work on them. The only two workers who were over six feet were Kevin and I. This was important when it came to sales.

Out of the two hundred we got paid fifty dollars that was if you didn't know what you were doing. Bart made his bags so fat you could pinch out of them. You could make up your own bags from out of his. So if you were slick out of 200 dollars you could make anywhere from 250 to 300 dollars off of them. Now remember, all you owed Bart was one fifty.

I learned that the second day on the job. Now this may seem like chump change to many, but when you don't have a job and you're broke, two to three hundred a day seems like a million. Plus add in the fact that the spot was booming. Man at that time you could sit there for a day or two and make yourself almost a grand. They were moving a lot of cocaine out of that pink house. As I stated, Keith and I were the only workers with some size on us. So when a customer came to the door it was on.

When there was a knock on the door there was a stampede to the door by the workers to make a sale. We just ran everybody over and made the sale, it was crazy.

By the time I had been in Bart's clique three days I was sick of it. The house was booming but it was too many people there. The spot was doing too well and it was getting hot. Keith had already caught a chump charge on himself for selling outside the joint, so we knew the place was being watched. I told Wally that Bart needed to expand, he should wrap to Bart and convince him to get another spot so we could run it.

The plan worked to a tee. Bart opened another spot right around the corner. Bart opened it to alleviate some of the pressure on the other crib. The situation over at the pink house was so funny it was sad. Nobody was doing security anymore so that was out. Hypes were coming in masses to both entrances. Workers had stopped selling through the door. These dudes wanted a more personal approach with the customers. The place was a raid waiting to happen. I could see this and I was new to the game.

When they opened the new spot I volunteered to work it by myself. I looked at this as an opportunity to get the kinks out of my game so I could master the game. I had no intention of staying employed by no man in a business that was open to all. So when the ball started rolling I was the only worker who would stay at the new spot. The reason being the workers was supposed to send some of the customers to the new spot to get it rolling but they weren't. So most of the other workers went back to the pink house. This was perfect for me. I never liked crowds anyway. This enabled me to get my thoughts together about what I was doing and what I wanted to do.

Eventually the sales picked up that was when the others started coming over there selling. That didn't faze me because all of the customers asked for me, the boy in the Raider coat. Once I could bag pretty good and knew the lingo of the game so-so. I was making plans to get out of Bart's clique. That minion role wasn't for me.

Some of the workers got off on being known as Bart's boy, or washing his car. Don't let Bart take them somewhere and buy them something to eat, they were in seventh heaven, not the dog. My thoughts were fuck you buying me something to eat I can make my own scratch and buy my own food. Fuck your car I can get my own stuff. Basically fuck you, I just need you until something better comes along.

This was the mentality I was developing. I would sit in that apartment for hours at a time. Even when the others came around it would be just me, cause most of them had women they had to cater to. Me it was all about the money.

After the Sandra fiasco I stopped giving a damn about females. I still did as many as I could but that main woman plan had flown out of the window. When more workers started coming to the spot they brought noise and problems. They gave me someone to talk to but the fools kept up too much noise.

There was a family downstairs with kids and these fools would be shooting dice and arguing at 3:30 in the morning. I won't lie I had some fun up there with those fools. We would drink brews, gamble and toot cocaine like Scarface. I tooted regularly but, I made a pact with myself, when I stop selling cocaine, I'll stop tooting.

After about three weeks with Bart it was time to move on. Two things happened to speed up the process. First Eddie and I had gotten cool. Eddie had started off as a top man for this other dealer named BT. But he had fallen out of favor, and now worked for Bart. That man knew the dope game. Add in the fact that I knew some people who would help me get on my feet with cocaine. It was time to go. The second reason was the spot was getting too hot. There were too many people coming in and out of the joint. People were getting careless. The end came on a Friday afternoon.

I was up there serving when Bart came by to check on the joint. Bart parked his Seville out front. Then Lita, his sister, came up and parked his other Cadillac in the front also. These fools were talking and acting like all was fine and dandy. Both of those cars were hot, the police knew whose they were. To top it off RJ came by. This was a cat who at the time was rolling with BT. The man was hot as hell. RJ pulled his hot caddie in the driveway. I gave Bart his loot and turned to Wally and said, "This place is going to get raided." I turned and left.

I was hoping Wally would close the place, hell it was in his name. Wally followed me out and agreed to close the place up. Wally was going by his mom's house so I dropped him off. As Wally was getting out a police car rode by eyeballing us. I looked at him and said, "Man close that joint and stay away from the pink house." He said okay and got out. I told Wally I would come swoop him later to go to the New Yorker and pulled off.

I did not go back to my apartment I went out to my mother's house to chill. I talked to her my stepfather and my sister then went into the basement to relax. I nodded off for a while. I was awakened by Chasity hollering into the basement to pick up the phone. I obliged. Collie, Wally's aunt was on the phone hollering, "They raided the house and caught Keith!" Damn.

The first thing I did was get over on Sixth Street fast. Collie, Wally's aunt, was outside of Wally's mama's house waiting. Collie told me that the police pulled a double raid. They hit the pink house and the new spot at the same time. I told Collie to hop in the car so we could ride around the block. We went around the corner to check out the carnage.

When we got by the old spot there was Keith was being led to the paddy wagon all nice and handcuffed. I slowed down to see what the officers were doing in the front yard but one spun and flashed his flashlight into the car. I sped up and left the block.

By now I knew that the cops knew my car, and the last thing I needed was to be pulled over by some detectives looking to pin a case on me. We went back to Wally's mama's house. Eddie had come over while we were out, he was standing on the porch. Eddie told me that Wally was inside. I went in. The look on Wally's face said it all. Wally looked like a man defeated and betrayed. I just said, "Man let's go get high."

The three of us, Eddie, Wally and I, jumped into the ultimate homeboy car and rolled. We stopped and got some forties and parked outside the New Yorker to drink them before we went in. Eddie and Wally had some dope so we tooted a few bags as we drank.

The mood was somber in the car and it didn't change once we got inside the joint. I ordered *Jack Daniels* for us all. Wally looked at me and said, "They got my brother man." I just looked at him. I wanted to say, "I told you to shut the house down anyway, why didn't you listen?"

However there was no need to rub this in his face. Instead, I grabbed my glass and held it up and we toasted to Keith. I then ordered another round and started checking the place for some broad to go up in. The next day I got up with my stomach feeling upset and nose feeling chalky as hell, semi hung over. I rinsed my nose out. I had picked that up from Eddie, and cracked the fridge. There wasn't anything in there but brew and hot beef polish sausage. I threw a polish in the microwave and cracked a brew and started thinking.

As far as I was concerned the pink house and Bart were over. In a sense the situation worked out fine for me nobody never questioned why I never came back to Bart's clique after the raid went down. Eddie knew the game in and out. Eddie was down to roll with me so I decided to check him out to see where he stood. I went by his mother's house and we rapped.

Eddie was in the same mind set as I, it was time to move on. I told Eddie we should try to get Wally on our team to help us get started. So we went up by Sixth Street to find Wally. He was over at his mother's house chilling. We fed Wally a few questions about the future and his responses were loyal to Bart. We left him sitting on the couch. It was clear to me that it was going to be just Eddie and me to start. We then went by my pad to think about a place to roll out of.

We were starting fresh and didn't have the money to drop on a new apartment. We had to find some fool to let us roll out of their place. We drank on a six pack I had in the fridge. Eddie pulled out some dope. We chilled and tried to come up with a plan that would get us rolling. Eddie came up with the idea of using Twofolk's house. Twofolk was an old school dope fiend who kept hypes at his house. Twofolk usually ran out and picked up dope to bring it to the people who were there in his crib. The setup was fine with me, I coated my finger with the last of the dope inhaled and said, "Let's ride."

In order for this plan to work we had to make sure that Twofolk would allow us to use his crib. When we got over there Twofolk was grinning and smoking as usual. Twofolk said we could come by and make some sales. Bart's spots were play areas where I could stand up on a ledge and look down into the game. Twofolk's house was the pit that I was staring into. That dirty smokehouse was the side of the game that doesn't make the movies, it was hell. I pulled out my Bermuda shorts and willingly went into the inferno thinking I was going to take over. Alas, the dreams of the deluded.

Twofolk's house was a Grand Central Station for dope fiends. There was always someone knocking on his door for twenty dollars worth of heaven. This man was the conningest dope fiend I ever met. Twofolk called us his nephews. Twofolk called everyone who sold dope his nephew. That was part of his scheme to lure you in and get you to drop your guard so he could play you. Except in Twofolk's case he called it, "glazing," this was his term as he beat you out of your dope. Rolling out of Twofolk's pad would come at a price. We had to "look out" for him. This meant we had to give Twofolk a certain amount of dope a day to keep him satisfied. We had a spot now all we needed was some dope to sell. This was not a problem.

Nineteen eighty-nine was a golden time for dope in Racine. Cocaine was everywhere and everybody was selling it. Every fool with a little gumption was walking around with a few hundred in his pockets, made off that "white girl." If you knew the right people you could get a "play" in order to get on. I knew plenty of brothers who gave other people chances to get on their feet. These plays worked well for the brother who gave the play, if it worked out. The reason being, he could get someone to sell his dope and not do anything.

The deal went like this: you got fronted a piece of dope, the size depended upon the dealer you copped from. The dealer would give you the dope and you payed him back more than you would if you came to him with money for a buy. If a brother was about his money he would only get fronted twice at the most. I say this because no matter what weight he started from whether it is a sixteenth or a key, he should be able to save his scratch. This will enable him to either purchase the same weight he was getting fronted, or purchase enough to keep him rolling without any tab to pay.

Those plays hardly ever went that way. Most dudes started off getting fronted and continue until they catch a case and it's over. Eddie and I were no different. We lucked out we got a play from Flyboy. We had run across Flyboy and told him about Twofolk's house, he said he would think about it. We later saw Flyboy walking down 11th street, for what reason I'll never know. The man had the freshest caddy in Racine. We flagged Flyboy down and asked him what was the move. Flyboy told us he would meet us over at Rodney's sister's house later that evening. We were like cool, hell we didn't have anything to lose by waiting so we went over there and chilled.

We sat over there drinking brew and kicking around ideas when Flyboy came by. The first thing Flyboy asked when he came in was, "Is anybody else in the house?" We told him no, he seemed to relax a bit. Flyboy then proceeded to pull out an ounce of cocaine. Flyboy then asked us, "Can you move this?" Eddie spoke before I could open my mouth, "Yeah, hell yeah!" At this point Eddie took charge of the negotiations. I just sat back and watched.

I started to butt in but, Eddie was talking more than a presidential candidate at a campaign rally. I wanted to say, "Man let's start with a half ounce that way we wouldn't be owing nobody a lot of scratch." As I said though, Eddie was chattering like a businessman. There was no way to get my thoughts out.

The way Eddie's eyes lit up when he saw that caine. I now realize that Eddie wasn't thinking about how much he could sell, he was thinking about how much he could toot. The impression he was laying on Flyboy was that he was the brains and I was the brawn. I was thinking cool, let this fool be responsible for the dope I'll just help him sell it. If the play goes bad, well, he copped the dope not me. Eddie wanted to be the man, well I'll let him try on the shoes. So Eddie hammered down a deal with Flyboy about what was going to be the payment plan. Before Flyboy departed I spoke up. I asked Flyboy point blank, "Now you giving this coke to Eddie right?" He replied, "Yes." I said, "The package is Eddie's responsibility correct?" Flyboy looked at Eddie kind of funny and said, "Yeah this is me and Eddie, ain't you helping him?" I said, "Yeah but, I don't owe you, I'm just helping Eddie." Eddie spoke up quickly, "This is my play." He was nodding towards Flyboy confidently. Flyboy replied, "Fine." and left. This could not have gone better if I had drawn it up. I had access to twenty-eight grams and didn't have any debts to anyone. Flyboy left we slapped hands and started bagging.

Eddie had entered into a deal that had him owing Flyboy 1200 dollars. We hurried up and bagged up 1200 dollars worth of dope. This was the amount Eddie had agreed to pay Flyboy. Working with Eddie was an education in itself. The dude could bag dope by eye and still make dime bags equal one tenth on a scale and twenties two tenths. So the bagging went quick, next we had to test the dope. We had to go to Twofolk's house to do that. We each grabbed two hundred in work and rolled out.

CHAPTER VIII

Twofolk's was sitting in his kitchen with his pipe in his hand. I don't think it ever left his hand. The place was semi-crowded with hypes. Eddie pulled Twofolk to the side and told him we had some dope we wanted him to test for us. Twofolk griningly approved to be the guinea pig. Twofolk took the bag Eddie gave him and pulled out a shot glass and some baking soda. Twofolk dumped the contents into the glass added some baking soda and some water. Twofolk then put the stuff into the microwave for ten or fifteen seconds. I was anxious I blurted out, "Is it good?" Twofolk just kept stirring and mumbled, "I see the rock there goes the rock."

I had never seen cocaine cooked before. I looked into the glass and all I seen was this gray substance forming in a cloud. Twofolk got all of this substance onto the hanger. For me this was a learning experience because, I had never seen people cook or smoke dope before, I just sold it. Twofolk held the hanger up for us to see and said, "There it go it comes back good." Eddie nodded and told Twofolk, "Try it." Twofolk grabbed his pipe and a torch, another piece of hanger with cotton on the end. Twofolk dipped the hanger in alcohol and lit it. Twofolk had put a piece of the gray matter onto his pipe the house was quiet.

All eyes were on Twofolk as he applied the fire to the pipe and took the first toke. After Twofolk hit the pipe he closed his eyes and laid back. That fool immediately busted into a sweat. Twofolk opened his eyes with a sly grin and said, "Nephew that's some good dope!" Some of the hypes started reaching for Twofolk's pipe and quickly got elbowed. Twofolk then announced, "These are my nephews they will be here and they got more." That is when the fiends started reaching for their money. Those who did not have any either left to go get some or were shit out of luck. Some started trying to barter to a piece of heaven but that wasn't happening. I wanted cash, skip everything else this wasn't let's make a deal.

We sold out in about two hours. We had given Twofolk about two or three bags to open the door all the way. The setup was nice. We had a spot good and dope, all was well. Eddie felt that I should keep the dope. This was all right with me. Twofolk told us we should be there early in the morning to catch the third shift workers as they get off work. Eddie and I agreed to the fact that we would not pull any twenty-four hour shifts in there. The reason was, there were too many dope fiends in the place. Plus we wanted to go party with our newfound wealth.

The next day I picked Eddie up at around 6:30 in the morning. Eddie was slow-poking around but when I reminded him about the money to be made he got his act together. We got to Twofolk's house around 7:15. Twofolk was standing in the door waiting. Twofolk said, "Nephews come on in, I told them you was coming." His kitchen was full of people who looked like they had just gotten off work. The scene was crazy, most people want to go home and sleep after third shift. These fools wanted to give me their money to get high. Well, if they wanted powder well Eddie and I was Johnson and Johnson. Our powder was much stronger than baby powder.

That morning alone we each boomed of around two-fifty in bags. Around eleven o'clock Eddie told me he was just about out he needed more dope. I had never bagged dope so I was just going to pick up a piece and bring it over for him to bag up. I was happy as hell. School was as far from my mind as Sirus B is from earth. I went to the pad and got the dope out of my Stacy Adams, I kept the dope in my shoes, and grabbed some paper. I folded the paper into a football shape and shook out a nice piece into the paper. I put the rest back into my shoes and rolled. When I got back Eddie was in the doorway, he had sold out. Eddie bagged up the dope and we were back in business. That day we sold about a grand between the two of us. We settled into Twofolk's house nicely. We set up a basic routine; I would go pick up Eddie and we would go by Twofolk's house and roll. One day I mentioned to Eddie that I needed a television set for my crib he said, "Cool we'll see what happens." I forgot about it.

Later I walked into the house after going to the store for beer and stopped. Eddie was sitting at the table tooting some powder and Twofolk was putting a piece of dope on his pipe grinning. Between them was a brand new television set and iron still in the box. Eddie looked up and said, "Dude only wanted a forty piece for both." Eddie went back to tooting. I thanked him for looking out for me.

The iron lasted only a few years but the television is sitting in my front room right now! Eddie and I were doing all right. Only two weeks ago we were working for Bart now we were moving ounces. I cannot recall how we paid Flyboy for the first ounce but we must have. Because we met Flyboy again at Eddie's sister's house and he handed over another ounce.

By this time rolling was my life, basketball was a thing of the past. My life was; money, dope, liquor not necessarily in that order. Eddie liked to toot so by us being partners he had to pay me when he tooted a bag. If Eddie tooted a twenty he owed me ten dollars. The business was good. We got cool as hell cause we spent so much time together. Eddie's mom knew me well, she was nice. Starter jackets were still in at the time. One day Eddie and me was up at Lafayette center when PJ and Fats busted in. They came in wearing brand knew UCLA jackets. We looked at them and I said, "That shit look fresh as hell." The following Saturday Eddie called me over my mom's house from the mall. Eddie said, "They got gray Raider coats out here! I just bought me one!" I asked, "Do they have any more?" He replied, "Yep!" I said, "Pick me one up then." Dude was hesitating too long on the phone when I said that. So I said, "I'll be out there." I hung up and left rushing to the mall. When I got there I headed straight to Fanfare, the store they were in, and went straight to the counter. I asked the dude who was working, "I heard you have gray Raider coats where are they?" He pointed to the front of the store. In my haste I had walked right past them. They had two left a large and a medium. I told dude, "Pull the large down." Dude looked at me funny then pulled it down. I realized why he was looking funny, he was looking at my attire.

I had jumped into some Puma sweats and just threw on a coat and hat. I was looking like I was broke or something. I did not even bother to try it on, I said "I'll take it." The man went back up to the counter and asked looking at me skeptical, "Will this be cash or charge?" The idiot thought I was broke or something. I pulled out a horse collar, bankroll, and said, "What do you think?" That mans eyes lit up, "Yes sir cash it is. Will there be anything else?"

I was in control now I grunted, "Give me two Raider hats. A black one and a white one to go with it." I felt petty satisfaction as I watched the buffoon jump like a steer that been prodded with one of those cattle prods. I was fronting now, going through my money pretending to count it enjoying the envious glances I was getting from the other fools in the store. I heard a voice say, "Man look at all that money!" Uh-oh it was my sister with her friends. Mama and my family didn't know what I did and I damn sure didn't want them to find out. They thought I was broke and I intended to keep it that way. Chasity was standing there watching the dude put that coat into the bag with a questioning look on her face, I had to think fast.

I knew where this info was headed straight to mama's house and I damn sure did not want that to happen. Some of my friends didn't give a damn about what their parents thought, I did. I had no choice I had to lie. I grinned and said, "Hey, what's up?" Chasity wasn't buying it she said, "Where did you get all that money from?" "Is that your coat?" I replied, "Yep, it's mine." To add emphasis I paid the man and grabbed the bag and started walking away, she followed. Now it was time to lie.

I told her I had a girlfriend in Waukegan. The Waukegan girl had gave me the money for the coat, and the other scratch. Chasity looked skeptical but she knew I had a girl I knew in Waukegan so she was kind of going for it. I capitalized on her indecision I pulled out ten or twenty dollars and gave it to her. I said, "This girl in Waukegan will be giving me money all the time but don't tell Mama okay?" I added, "She is rich." That seemed to go over okay with her. Chasity walked away feeling proud that I was her big brother. Little did she know the money I gave her was straight out of some smoked out fool's hands, for a piece of heaven. I started walking out of the mall O seen Eddie. He asked, "Did you get it?" I said, "Yeah." I noticed Eddie had a few bags so I asked, "What about Flyboy's loot?" He replied, "We straight." "Well fuck it." I thought. It was his butt on the line anyway. Eddie pulled his coat out the fool had bought an extra-large. I laughed at him.

I knew the coat was going to be too big for Eddie and I had bought the only large in the store, he was screwed. The girl Eddie was with then said something that made the smile fall off my face. She said, "That large is going to be too tight on you." Damn, she was right I had gained some weight since the last time I bought a Starter coat. I thought fast I told Eddie, "Give me the XL and I'll give you the large." Eddie was cool with it so the situation worked out. We exchanged coats and I told him I was leaving, I still had some bullshit on and the place was filling up.

As I was walking through the mall, I passed several hustlers out there spending their dirty money. I saw Keith out there buying his girl some tennis shoes, I laughed and kept stepping. I thought to myself, these cats are fools. I wouldn't give a chick a bite to eat, much less spend my hard earned dope money on a female. To me they had it backwards. These fools believed that dope money was easy money. They felt that if they worked a job they would not give a female their scratch. I felt, dope money was the hardest money to make.

For one you risk everything to make it. You gamble your freedom on every sale you make. You never know when a police informant or undercover cop is the person your selling to. Even worse lets say the spot you are rolling out of gets raided. At the time this happens you have five or six hundred dollars worth of bags on you that you can't flush down the toilet, oh baby!

Another way to look at it is on a job you get off work after eight or ten hours. If you are a good hustler you're on the job twenty-four hours a day seven days a week. You work twenty-four hours a day to keep from working eight.

The last and major factor was you never know when you might get killed. You never know when some punk is going to push your cap back. It could be that fiend you shorted or some jealous punk who wish he had your hand. So in my book if a chick wasn't out there elbow to elbow with me selling dope, she wasn't getting zero but the price of a condom.

Eddie and I made the scene with our new coats on. This solidified the rumors around town that I was rolling. We used to hang at the New Yorker, that was the spot. I would go there any day of the week to mellow out. Most other hustlers would go to other places that had a more underworld type atmosphere, not me. I went to the New Yorker cause it had a more booghie clientele. The owner Ron was cool so it was my chill spot. I would go by the crib chill and listen to Superfly and drink brew and think. Then I would usually toot a bag or two then head for the New Yorker. I could go in there buy the deejay a few drinks and he would play Curtis Mayfield in there.

I guess that place was my therapy to try to get my head together. On the off nights there was never any women in there except for this old broad, who I tried to bone damn near every time I went in there. One night Del came in there with me and seen what I was trying to do and he just shook his head. He said, "Man that's Felicity's mama." I replied, "I know but she look three times better than her daughter." I knew Felicity because I had been over her house before trying to freak her. That was when I first seen her mother. I really didn't give a damn about the situation hell if her mother would let me I would bone her.

One night I was sitting in there drinking thinking about my position. I was now able to bag dope by eye. I also knew all the prices for the various quantities. It was time for me to go out on my own, get my own play.

One reason was Eddie. Eddie had started wanting to keep the dope at his house and lord knows he tooted too much. I could see the handwriting on the wall, the boy was messing up. Eddie was spending money and tooting too much dope. Eddie wasn't paying Flyboy though. I wasn't any help I was spending and tooting too, but I felt if Eddie did not give a damn why should I?

I had made it clear in the beginning to both of them that Flyboy was giving that coke to Eddie, it was his play. It really was not a loss to me.

Another reason I felt this way cause Eddie had started acting flaky about the dope. Eddie had copped another ounce and didn't tell me about it. Which was fine by me it was his business anyway. Add all of this together and by the time I left the New Yorker Eddie was a thing of the past to me. It was time to roll solo.

The next day I tracked Eddie down over his sister's house. I quizzed Eddie about the dope and he was vague about the subject. Eddie was sitting there tooting away. I just shook my head. I did not let Eddie know I was cutting him loose I just left Eddie sitting there powdering his nose. I think the main reason we parted ways was the fact that Twofolk's house had gotten raided so we did not have a spot to move the dope. Idle dope in Eddie's hands meant toot time.

I don't want you to get the wrong idea I tooted a lot too. The difference was my head was not on the line for payment on products received. If he busted open a bag and shared it I made sure I got my finger in it. I sat there for a few minutes then I rolled out. The next time I saw Eddie I was making my own scratch.

I left Eddie's sister's house and went to my pad. I needed some loot fast. I was down to a couple of hundred dollars and I did not want to go into that. I tooted one of the bags I still had from my partnership with Eddie and rolled out. I had to put some feelers out now that I was out of work. I hollered at my boy Del his agenda was all screwed up. Del was trying to cater to a female he got knocked up and hustle at the same time. One reason Del wasn't any use was his source was his uncle Flyboy. After the deal with Eddie, I was not going to press my luck. I went by Sixth Street to holler at Wally and Keith.

Keith had made bail and was waiting for his trial, so he was laying low. Wally had his head so far up Bart's ass that I think he thought I was a traitor cause I had left his clique. I talked to him but his only idea was to go back to work for Bart. I looked at him and thought; man this dude is crazy. I kept those thoughts to myself and drunk a brew with them and left. I was rolling around burning gas when it hit me, let me go check out my boys PJ and Fats.

These dudes were a trip. They hung up at Church's Chicken damn near 24-7. That was where they got their hustle on at. The fools sold dope and ate chicken all day. Sure enough I rode past there they were sitting in one of the booths chilling. I parked and went in. When I hit the door I said, "What's up?" These were my guys but I didn't kick it with them as tough because I was rolling with people they did not care too much for. Sure enough they let me know it. PJ said, "Look the nigga finally got time to come around us now. Wally and Bart must have put him down or something." Fats said, "Naw it's Eddie." PJ cut him off, "Yeah Eddie must be fucking off or something to bring you up here." The talk was foul but it was true. I did not kick it with them as much as I once did. The reason was they didn't do anything. They did not drink, smoke weed or toot. I was doing all three so why bring bad habits to people? That was how I saw it, but I didn't let them know my reasons. I said, "Man, you know I'm still down with the PJ posse." That was the name of PJ and Fats clique the previous summer. They laughed and I sat down and shot the shit with them. As we sat there I watched some of their minions catch sales in the lot. I had to give it to PJ and Fats they had their hustle down. They had all of these little fools who sold for them. PJ and Fats were not paying them because the idiots just wanted to say they were down with PJ. It was really crazy cause everybody knew, including the police that the stooges were selling dope.

The minions sold in two places, either at the chicken shack or in front of Fat's mama's house around the corner. I asked PJ if they were booming cause I needed work. He said, "We doing a little something but we damn near out." We kicked it some more and he told me, "Come swoop me tomorrow and we'll go try to find some work." I told him cool and left.

I stopped by the store and grabbed me some brew and went home to chill. I had to rest up cause I knew rolling with PJ and Fats was going to be different from what I had been used to. As it turned out different was just the beginning.

I hopped up the next day and put my clothes on and went by PJ's house and picked him up. We drove around town and PJ gave me the rundown on his hustle. PJ said that he was short on work and had to find some quick. I agreed because I was in the same boat. The one obstacle we both had was we were both tight on money. In order for us to get on someone was going to have to front us some dope.

PJ and Fats had shitted on damn near everybody in Racine as far as paying back people who fronted them. I look back on that scene and I'm glad PJ and Fats weren't in Detroit trying to pull that. Somebody would have found PJ and Fats naked in a field somewhere with bullet holes in the back of their heads after one week of their con. Good thing though they were in weak Racine they got away with the garbage they pulled.

As we were talking I was throwing names out of people we both knew who were on top to see PJ's reaction. All the bridges were either burned or on fire, PJ couldn't catch a play if he was on Broadway. PJ then said, "Lets go by Fat's house." PJ was cool about the situation he probably had a piece of dope out on the streets and also PJ lived at his father's house. The man didn't have any bills. Me on the other hand, I had to pay my half of the rent plus the utilities. I had to come up with a plan fast.

CHAPTER IX

We went by Fat's house. This was like walking into a loony farm. This scene was a stone trip. Fats and his brother Big K were laying around in their draws in the front room. Their sister just walked in and started talking like this was cool. This was ridiculous. I nudged PJ and asked him, "Man you be here all day and this is how these fools act?" PJ replied, "Man you ain't seen nothing wait until Fritz, they daddy, come in." I just sat back and watched the show. Words do not do this picture any justice, trust me.

Fats was going to the door every fifteen minutes looking out checking on his workers, still in his draws. Big K who was around 250 to 300 pounds was talking loud as hell cussing at his sister. I was tripping on the scene, I looked at PJ he was loving the banter. I guess PJ had discovered his own personal comedy show. PJ would jump in their conversation and talk loud and cuss like Big K and his sister. Hell PJ was fitting in so good I was wondering if he was going to pull off his pants and sit in his draws. I was tiring of the scene so I told Fats, "Come on man so we can go find some work." Fats was like, "Cool let me take a bath and we can roll."

This was comedy classics in its purest form. The problem though was the fact that the dumb workers kept coming to the door every five minutes. This was trouble in my book. Big K kept telling them to wait outside and to be cool they weren't listening to him. The setup was a raid waiting to happen. I was relieved to see Fats go into the bathroom and start running water in the tub. Then the last sliver of reality came apart in the house Fritz walked in.

The first words out of Fritz's mouth was, "All you mudda fucka's get out my house!" That was all it took for me, I was rising up off the couch when I looked at PJ. PJ was still sitting there laughing. Big K said, "Man you don't have to go nowhere." I was puzzled when Big K said, "Fritz shut up!" I sat back down in a daze this scene was killing me. Fritz just looked then went and sat down, mumbling to himself. Fritz then shouted, "This is my house keep them mutha fuckas away from here with that shit!" Fritz had to be referring to the workers selling dope in front of the house.

Fats walked out of the bathroom with a towel wrapped around his fat butt and said, "Fritz ain't nobody messing with your house, damn man!" He then turned and went back into the bathroom. Fritz just looked and sat back in the chair with his shoulders hunched.

The whole scene had went from funny to lunacy, I had never seen black people like these before. I looked at PJ, he was soaking all this insanity up, loving it. Fritz sat up in the chair and hollered, "How come didn't anybody take out the damn garbage?" Fritz's answer from his offspring was, "Shut up Fritz!" I felt sorry for the old dude. Fritz seemed a broken man with no control in his own house. Fritz then said what I was thinking I would do if I were he; "Damn it! I'm going to get my Winchester and kill all the sons of bitches!" I had to laugh because of the type of gun the old man was talking about using. The look on his face though was nothing to laugh at. Fritz looked like a man on the verge of snapping.

I told PJ, "Lets go, if this fool get to shooting our asses is going to get capped!" PJ sat back and said, "Relax, dude ain't going to do nothing. Fritz always saying stuff like that." I was still ready to get the hell out of there thankfully Fats came out of the bathroom dressed to go. We got up and walked out the door. I felt like a black Jack Nicholson in, *One Flew Over The Cookoo's Nest*. Later on I pulled PJ to the side and asked, "How in the hell did he stay over there so much?" PJ's answer was, "The shit don't bother me." I just looked at dude in awe and thought; "He doesn't even drink."

As we got into the car one of Fat's minions ran up to the car panting and said, "We almost out." Fats said, "I know, I'm going to pick up some work now." The minion went away happy. The first words out of my mouth were, "Where are we going to find some work?" Fats suggested, "Lets go check out Sly from chi-town." Sly was new in town and he had three partners. They all wore Cincinnati Bengals jackets. Sly was cool and I was damn near desperate so I replied, "Let's roll." We went over by his spot and true to form Sly was looking out of the front window of the spot in his Bengals coat.

Sly waved us to the back door where we went in. Sly asked, "What's up?" We talked awhile and the conversation led up to the fact that we needed a play to get back on. Sly was cool about it and told us to follow him into the next room. Fats fell back PJ and I looked at him he replied,

"I'm straight." So PJ and I let Sly know it was PJ and me who needed a play. Sly gave us two sixteenths.

For those of you out there not familiar with dope weight terms a sixteenth is one point two grams. It may vary. It depends upon the type of play you get. The sixteenths were fat so it was close to an eight ball, three point two grams. Sly told us all we had to do was give him back a C-note. I looked at it I could tell we could bag around three hundred and fifty dollars up from them. It was not much but it was work. We grabbed the dope and rolled. Fats wanted to be taken home so we went and dropped him off at home. PJ had a scale at his house so we went by there to bag the dope.

I could have bagged it up by eye but I just went along to see what PJ's program was. As we were bagging up the dope I was quizzing PJ on the game. The way PJ had gotten on was by getting some golden opportunities from people. PJ and Fats had been getting half ounces from a dealer named Rollo. Rollo was only asking for five hundred in return. I couldn't believe that, at the time if you bought a half-ounce it would cost you from $450.00 to $500.00. This was the play Rollo gave them on a front tip, unbelievable. Of course though, PJ and Fats had messed the play up. I asked PJ how they managed to mess that up he said, "We gambled the money away." PJ then gave a list of names of people who had given them plays and they had screwed, I just shook my head. I knew one thing though I was determined to make sure Sly got paid. I did not want any violence rained down on my pretty head. The play was nice we bagged about three-fifty, which meant one-twenty-five apiece, after we paid Sly. Now we had to sell it.

I asked PJ, "Where should we go to sell this coke?" PJ looked at me like I was crazy and replied, "Go by Fat's house." I was skeptical but I drove over there anyway. When we got over there PJ took the dope. PJ then called two of the minions to the car and gave them 175 each in bags to work. I was in a panic I said, "What if they mess up?" PJ replied, "Man chill, they will work the dope." I replied, "It ain't enough dope to pay anyone to sell it." "Dude relax." PJ grinned, "We ain't going to give them shit, maybe ten dollars." I just shook my head. This dude had the sweetest deal in Racine. PJ had people who would sell dope just to say they were down with PJ.

I parked and we went into Fat's house thank God he was dressed, so we just rolled out. We went by Lafayette center to holler at some young girls and talk trash. We left and rode around awhile. When PJ said, "Go by Fat's house to see what is going on with the workers." We pulled onto the block and sure enough they were out there running like flies to shit. When they seen the car they headed towards it.

PJ rolled the window down and said, "Meet us up at Churches in fifteen minutes." I drove up there and got out and went in. Fats and I ordered some chicken, PJ went to Total to get some candy. The peons came in and asked Fats, "Where PJ at?" Fats said, "Chill he'll be in here in a moment." Fats and I was eating our chicken and those peon eyes were glued to our chicken. They must have been hungry, I looked at Fats he was eating and ignoring them. They weren't my boys so I kept eating.

PJ came in and the two of them went over to him. I seen money change hands and then more talk which lead to PJ going up to the counter. PJ ordered some food paid and walked over and sat down with Fats and I. PJ gave me my piece of the loot and said, "I had to spend ten to buy them some food." Hell it did not bother me. I was elated on the inside, they had done all the work and all it had cost me was; a three piece with mashed potatoes and a coke.

We finished up and I said, "Let's go pay Sly." We left and went by Sly's spot. We paid Sly and he said, "I knew y'all was cool." I asked Sly what he had. I wanted to see if we could get another play. Sly said he was low but he pulled out a few fat sixteenth pieces. By this time another one of Sly's partners came into the room. I asked Sly if we could have two on the front tip. Sly got a funny look on his face and replied, "You know I can't do that." Sly's partner butted in and said, "No loot, no dope." I felt the tension in the air so we just told Sly we would get back with him. On the way to the car Fats said, "Man you should have pulled Sly to the side and hollered at him." Fats was right so I just grunted, "Yeah."

Rolling with PJ and Fats was cool but, it was time to move on. PJ and Fats didn't share any of my vices such as drinking or tooting, or even smoking weed. Hell they were squares in a sense. PJ and Fats main thing was to crack jokes all day and do silly stuff. For example they would call people to the car then pull off on them. Don't get me wrong, I loved that joke but some of the other things PJ and Fats did were down right degrading. When I dropped PJ and Fats off at Fat's house I knew I was through rolling with them. I had come to the conclusion it was time for me to get my own plays and get my own business started. The sole proprietor was going to be me. It was time to get down for real.

The first thing I did was put feelers out about the type of plays dealers were giving. I knew the plays were ranging by dealer. Some were fronting ounces and asking for fifteen hundred back. That wasn't a bad deal but I knew others who were giving the same play but only asking for a grand to twelve hundred back. Another factor was who was hot and who wasn't. Some cats were way too hot to be dealing with. What I mean is the cops had an eye on them. BT was giving up some good plays but he had one foot in the pen.

Another player I knew was Clean C. I had known him all my life but he put too much cut on his dope. I went to Rollo. To me Rollo was the smartest dope man in Racine at the time. I remember Rollo got busted one time at the mall. The police had him. They threw dude in the car and drove his Lincoln off grinning and laughing. Up until that point Rollo had all kind of flashy gear. Rollo wore leather outfits, tight Lincoln, the works. After that incident Rollo didn't flash anything.

I think Rollo beat his case. Whatever happened dude was very low key. If you just looked at Rollo you would swear he was broke, he would just wear some bullshit clothes around town. Rollo even started driving this raggedy brown van around to complete his disguise. That was what made Rollo so smart. Rollo knew how to play the game to keep the heat off of him. I knew Rollo but not in a way to get a play I had to find a way to get in good with him. The opportunity soon presented itself.

I was over Clean C's pad chilling with him one day when he ran out of dope. Clean C needed some dope to take him until he got his package. I told him I could get an ounce for nine hundred dollars. Clean C was hesitant and gave me a grand just in case. I told him I would be back with the dope and left. I went looking for Rollo. I had an idea where I could find him. I went up by Total. Sure enough Rollo was up there kicking it with PJ and Fats.

I parked and went where the three of them were standing at and talked with them for awhile. Then I told Rollo to let me holler at him. Rollo was cool but I knew he had to be wondering what the hell I wanted. When we had gotten by my car I told him, "I need to buy an ounce." Rollo looked at me and asked, "What makes you think I have one?" I played it cool and said, "I don't but maybe you can direct me to someone who does." Rollo then asked, "How much you got?" I said, "Nine hundred dollars." Rollo was cool with it he told me to meet him around the corner in fifteen minutes. I went back over by PJ and Fats and kicked it with them then made it around the corner to handle my business. Rollo was around the corner I pulled over and he hopped in. Rollo asked, "You got the cash?" I replied, "Yes." Rollo then pulled out a bag with an ounce in it. I could tell it was an ounce by the look also it wasn't all powder there was some big chunks in it. Rollo said, "It is more than an ounce cause I want you to come back." I just flat out told Rollo the dope wasn't for me it was for Clean C. Rollo looked and said, "Well you can take a piece out for yourself." I was appalled at the suggestion.

I still believed in honor so I could not do that to my boy. Plus, Clean C trusted me. I told Rollo, "Naw man dude trusted me so I'll give him what you gave me." Rollo nodded then asked, "Are you working for Clean C?" I told him no I wasn't. Rollo then asked, "What are you doing then?" I told him I was in between hustles and trying to get back on my feet. Rollo then hinted that I could check with him later about some work. I let Rollo know that I might but I had to roll now to get this man his dope. Rollo got out and I pulled off.

When I got to Clean C's pad I dropped the ounce on the table he took the dope and placed it on a scale. While Clean C was working the settings he said, "I know you pinched out of it." I replied, "Nope, it is all there and more, Rollo gave me a play." Clean C nodded and said, "Yeah but I bet he charged a grand though." Before I could answer his uncle Toddy blurted out, "If Rollo didn't Frank is going to say he did to keep the hundred." I squashed that lie real fast by throwing the money onto the table and grabbing a brew.

Clean C looked at the money then at the scale that was reading twenty-nine grams and gave me a cool look. He said, "Man I'll give you a piece for your time." I replied, "Don't sweat it, that was a favor to help out an old friend." "One day I might need a favor from you." Clean C nodded and gave me dap and looked at his workers and said, "Let's get this cocaine bagged up." I sat down and sipped on my brew. I knew I had gained favor in Clean C's eyes and could count on him if I needed him. I also had made contact with Rollo and had opened the door to his snow kingdom. I was set my troubles were over.

A few days later I hooked up with Rollo. We talked and Rollo fronted me an eight ball. I had to start small in order to build up Rollo's trust in me. Rollo had heard the stories about what had happened with Flyboy's loot and did not want to be burned. I took the dope and told Rollo I would see him in a few days with his scratch. I had to find a spot to get it on. Twofolk's house popped into mind.

I went over Twofolk's house to see what was going on over there and he said, "We back open nephew." Twofolk had some other cats in there selling so they were his nephews also. I pulled out a bag I had brought for Twofolk to sample for me. I pretended like I needed him to test it. To see the how good it was. I already knew it was good because when I was bagging it I could tell it was good by the color and texture. Rollo had told me I could hit it with some cut and double it. That was never my thing so I just bagged it raw. Now it was time to see if it was as good as it was billed.

Twofolk's eyes lit up when he opened the package. He hurriedly emptied the contents into a shot glass along with some baking soda and

60

water. Twofolk placed the concoction into the microwave and looked as it cooked for ten seconds. As always there were fiends in his house and they were watching the proceedings with curious masks on their faces. I was curious too but didn't show it. Twofolk pulled the shot glass out of the microwave. Any fool could see the rock forming in the bottom of the glass. I kept cool but Twofolk had started sweating on his forehead and he was grinning. Twofolk picked up a stem and stirred three or four times and said, "Ohh nephew this is some good dope it came back good!" He then slid a rock out that looked like a thirty piece. I tripped cause I knew I had only given Twofolk was barely enough to be considered a dime bag. The fiends wanted a piece of Twofolk's dope he then got serious. Twofolk hollered, "Get back my nephew brought this for me so stay the hell back!" Twofolk then looked at me and said, "It cooked up good but that don't mean it is all good." I said, "Fire it up." Twofolk grabbed his pipe grinning.

Keep in mind that Twofolk had been smoking for years and it took real fire dope just to make him sweat.

Once that fool put that fire to his pipe and inhaled a miracle happened in dope terms. That fool's head dropped and Twofolk slumped and fell back into the counter. Twofolk was slumped like a dead man. I shook the hell out of him intensely calling his name, "Twofolk, Twofolk!" That scraggly fool looked up and got his bearings and grinned and said, "That's some gunpowder nephew." I looked at Twofolk and this fool was drenched in sweat. Twofolk said, "That coke fluttered my ticker, but it is some damn good dope! Coke like that has to be straight off of the key!" Twofolk was talking about a kilo of dope the ultimate weight you wanted to be moving. That was all it took. The fiends started calling me the boy with the gunpowder. The fiends knew if the dope could stagger Twofolk, it had to be some good dope.

That is when everything started going downhill fast. Oh I was making money but my life was turning into shit. This is an example of how I was living. Get up and get by Twofolk's house at around 7:30 to catch some sales. At around 9:00 I would either walk to the store or get some hype, to get my morning drink. That was Cool Breeze wine passion fruit, I used to drink that cheap wine like Kool-Aid. I would drink until 11:00 then get some fool to go to Pinnichio's, a burger joint, to bring me some food. The usual meal consisted of two double cheeseburgers and two fries. Washed down by a fifth of Cool Breeze wine.

I would just sit in this raggedy house around a bunch of pipe heads. After I ate I would let my food digest then send for my first round of *Old English 800*. I would periodically make dope runs because I never sat over there with more than three hundred dollars in bags on me. It was still a dope house.

I saw some wild things working that month in Twofolk's house by myself. For instance Twofolk was what you would call a professional dope fiend. People would come to Twofolk's house wanting to learn how to smoke this was something he would willingly teach. This is one of the reasons I never got bored. When a student would come in wanting lessons Twofolk would come and tell me and I would gladly give him a dime piece to get them enrolled. This would be like investing in a sure stock tip because once they got started they would spend all the money they had on them. That pipe would grab them nine out of ten times and they had gotten the only freebie they would get out of me. This was a money making machine. Hell I started telling people who were buying cocaine to toot, "Why toot when you can smoke?"

The first was the wildest day of the month. Mothers would be in there with money blowing it on cocaine to enjoy their miserable lives. They didn't give a damn about the fact they would be broke for the rest of the month. Since they didn't care I didn't give a damn either, I wanted the money.

One day the landlord came by. I was in a panic because he was white and I didn't want to catch a case. I went into the back room before he saw me and hid my dope under a raggedy bed that was in there. I heard Twofolk calling my name and I thought the fool had went crazy yelling my name in front of this white man. Twofolk came into the room where I was at and asked for a dime, I looked and gave him one wondering what the hell he was doing, hoping he wasn't setting me up. I waited about ten minutes then decided to go into the kitchen to see what was going on.

When I got in there I did a double take. That fat trick was sitting there in just his T-shirt and pants smoking that glass dick! I looked at Twofolk and grinned relaxing. The landlord had collected rent from his other properties that day and had stopped by Twofolk's house to donate it to me, reparations baby!

The craziness in my life was not only limited to the dope house the madness followed me when I left there too. One Friday I was getting ready to leave Twofolk when Del stopped by. Del was going by the New Yorker that evening and wanted to know if I wanted a ride. I told Del to stop by the pad around 10:00 and swoop me. He left. I caught a few more sales and I left. I stopped by the store and grabbed me a six of *Old English* in the tall cans to go along with the two fat joints I had in my pocket.

I got home bathed and dressed and just sat back and chilled. Del came and for some reason I just wanted to chill alone so I told Del I was busy I would meet him at the New Yorker. After Del had gone I put on my *Curtis Mayfield* album and blazed up the joint. I was drinking brew and smoking the joint when I had a taste for some *Jack Daniels*, so I pulled out my stash bottle and took a few shots out of that.

By the time the soundtrack got to *Superfly* I was good and buzzed. I had played *Little Child* about three straight times and was feeling fine as hell. I had drank five of the six brews and knocked back four or five shots of *Jack Daniels*, now it was time to powder my nose. I tooted a fat twenty piece and started on a ten piece. I was wired to the tee, it was time to go. I finished the ten piece and rubbed the last bit on my gums and rolled.

I hit the New Yorker feeling good as hell. When I walked in the joint I spotted two or three victims to relieve the tension in my balls. I knew it was going to be a good night. Del walked up and I gave him dap and told him some lie about why I wouldn't let him in. The main reason was I was getting high, and I didn't want Del around cause he didn't toot or smoke weed. Del didn't give a damn, he asked, "What you drinking?" I replied, "Nigga you know I drink *Jack Daniels*." Del ordered me a shot and I knocked that off. I was felling good and they played a jam. I think it was *Groove Me* by Guy, I had to dance. I grabbed Liza, Wally's girl, and headed for the dance floor.

As I got on the floor I remember clapping, and starting to sway with the beat when, bam! The scene was like in the movies. I could see myself standing there while everybody else was dancing. I felt my heart flutter and I remember thinking, "Damn, I'm going to pass out!" I had done too much dope and was about to pay for it! Then my pride kicked in and I thought, "If I fall out in this joint I'll never hear the end of it, I've got to focus." So I started willing myself under control but the drama wasn't over.

The New Yorker didn't have a strobe light at that time, I'm sure of it, but I did. I swear my vision was blinking on and off like a strobe light! Now keep in mind the people around me are partying like there is no tomorrow, and I'm in the middle of the floor tripping out! When the strobe effect started happening with my vision I wanted to scream, but once again my mind kicked in. It told me, "Keep cool and keep dancing." So dance I did like never before!

The deejay mixed in *Rebel Without A Pause,* and PJ was in the house so he hollered, "Frank!" he was letting me know we would do our little routine we had for the break down. My mind kept telling me, "Just keep dancing and you won't die or fall out." I was a dancing fool for the next couple of songs. I don't even know if I had a partner or not. I remember thinking while this was going on, "I can't fall out! I would be a disgrace to my mother!" I danced harder on that thought. By the time the dee-jay slowed it down my vision was back to normal. My heart on the other hand was racing like a damn Nascar or something!

I went and sat by Liza at her table. Liza was cool, so I told her how I was feeling. She just shook her head. I ordered *Jack Daniels*, but I did not have a taste for it. My leg was shaking so bad it was vibrating the table. The rest of the night was a blur to me. Wally and Eddie was in there that night. I hooked up with them when the place closed. I don't think I even really talked to any females about no cat. I was paranoid that I'd fall out on top of them. Now don't get me wrong if I have to go, I'd rather go between some woman's legs. But at that time I wanted to stay on this small planet. This is why I hooked up with Eddie and Wally. They were tooters, and they may have known some way to get me down off of this high I was on.

We went by Eddie's sister's house. I was still racing on all cylinders. I remember Eddie saying, "Man, you have too many drugs in your system." I had told them about my consumption of drugs and Wally nodded his head in agreement to the statement. They were sitting in the living room tooting cocaine off of a plate. I remember looking at the cocaine on the plate and saying, "Yeah, I've got to give up the weed. I'll just stick to liquor and coke." Another time I had messed up some money and I needed a quick play to pay off Rollo. So I went by Clean C's pad to see how he was laying. Clean C gave me a play on a quarter ounce. It was an all right play so I took it. I knew Clean C's dope was not as good as Rollo's, so I bagged it and gave it to some young cats who wanted to work for me. I then went by my mothers house. My sister hollered pick up the phone while I was in the basement chilling. When I did it was one of the workers. He proceeded to tell me the dope did not come back and the hypes were mad. I knew Clean C put a lot of cut on his coke, so I went by Twofolk's house to see what was wrong.

Twofolk met me at the door looking vicious, the dude was wound up! As I walked past him all the workers rushed up to me talking at once. I waved them off and turned to Twofolk. Twofolk said, "What kind of game you playing nephew?" I told him.

I didn't know what the hell he was talking about. Twofolk must have believed me, cause then he came up close and whispered, "Where did you get that dope from?" When I told Twofolk it was Clean C, he visibly relaxed. Twofolk knew about Clean C and his dope, so he knew I was not trying to put game on him. Twofolk then said, "Nephew, that dope didn't come back at all." We went into the kitchen and a few fiends were in there looking cagey. I guess they had bought some of the bad dope. I told Twofolk to cook up a bag. I had taken the rest from my workers. Twofolk did and sure enough there wasn't anything in the bottom of the glass. I was pissed but I didn't let anybody see it. I pulled out the rest of the dope Rollo had given me and told Twofolk, "Cook up a piece of this." Same process, different results, the rock was waiting in the bottom. Twofolk was grinning he said, "Nephew, this is what I'm talking about." I said, "Break it and put a piece on all they pipes." Twofolk looked hesitant but I nodded him on. Twofolk did and they blazed up and broke into sweats. I knew all was well then with the hypes. My workers on the other hand were a different story. I didn't have enough dope for them to get paid, cause I was already short on my payment. The workers were looking pitiful, so I divided up the rest between them so they could make some scratch. I was just going to have to get Rollo to front me with me owing him about a hundred and fifty. I knew Rollo would, but I did not want to get in the habit of falling behind on packages. I took the bullshit dope with me. I stopped by Clean C's house to give him the dope back but he was gone. I left a message for Clean C to get back with me about the dope and left. I grabbed a six of tall cans and went by the pad.

Eddie and Keith stopped by later on that evening. They brought some beer with them we rapped and Eddie had some caine he was sharing. I broke out my stash of *Jack Daniels* and we drank on that. Eddie and Keith wanted to know how I was doing. They did not know I was broke. I said, "Let's really toot." I busted out the bags of the bullshit dope and set them out on the plate. I mentioned it was some of Clean C's dope and it wouldn't sell to smokers but it tooted fine. They didn't give a damn, by the time it was over we had drank two twelve pack finished my stash of Jack and tooted all the bunk dope. That bunk coke went straight up our nostrils.

A few days later I seen Clean C, I told him about the dope. Clean C asked, "Where is it then?" I told him I had gotten rid of it. Clean C did not say anything. As I look back on it Clean C had to know the coke was bold. That was probably why he gave me a play on it anyway.

CHAPTER X

As they say, "All good things must come to an end." My career as a dope man was winding down. The grind from being around a bunch of dope fiends was starting to get to me. A few times I had given up too big of a play and beaten myself out of scratch. It was also getting hot at Twofolk's house. One day I was over Twofolk's house standing in the doorway chilling. I was waiting on some fiends to come buy this candy I was selling when I saw this long black van inching up the block. I flashed through my memory files and remembered that the police usually raid in a van, a black one! I had about four hundred dollars in bags on me and the van was two houses away inching like something was about to jump off! A funny thing happened, I got calm as hell! I thought, "Well I'm about to go to jail fuck it." I didn't have any fear because I knew the risks of the game and I was willing to accept them.

I stood there in the door waiting for this to happen. The van was too close for me to run so I just stood there. Lady luck must of noticed me and said, "Ooh he fine!" Because just as I was about to throw my dope into the kitchen with the fiends, the van went past the house! There was a man with a baseball hat on driving but he was looking at a house two houses down, so they went past the spot! The brake lights flashed and someone popped up and pointed back at the house I was in. The driver sped up and turned to make the block. I hollered, "Twofolk you better shut down the police are riding!" I didn't even wait for Twofolk to reply I vamped.

I knew they were making the block and I had about thirty seconds before they came back. I ran down the street and cut through a yard and came out on Martin Luther King Drive. My car was parked two blocks back the other way. I had to put some space between me and Twofolk's house. I was about to run over to State Street when lady luck shined on me again. I looked up and Del was driving up the street, man I was glad to see him! I flagged him down, and hopped in the ride. I told him to, "Hit it! I just missed a raid!" Del didn't have to be told twice because he had some dope on him.

We went up by Total and Del asked me, "What happened?" I laughed and ran it down for him. The way I saw it the driver drove past the house that they wanted to raid. That was why the other fool was pointing back at Twofolk's house. Instead of hitting reverse the driver must have panicked and just made the block instead. Who knows, I really didn't give a damn as long as I exited stage left. Del shook his head and said, "You a lucky man." Tell me something I didn't know. We got some beer and went by my pad.

Del told me he had some work he wanted to move. I told Del I would help him. I figured Del could come by Twofolk's house with me.

Later on I had Del drive me to go get the ultimate homeboy car from over by the dope house. True to form as we rode past you could tell they had gotten raided. The screen door was torn off and hypes were just wandering the block in front of the house. I told Del to stop and went in. Twofolk was sitting in the front room staring at the wall. I asked Twofolk, "Are you closing down?" He replied, "Just tonight, we'll be back open tomorrow." Twofolk then asked for a piece to calm his nerves. Twofolk looked nervous so I gave him a twenty piece and left.

I also told Twofolk Del was coming with me to catch some sales. Twofolk was cool with the idea. I was feeling good. I had missed another raid. I was invincible, I strode down to my car feeling fine as silk. I never stopped to think that I had just missed a free ride to the joint. Plus to this day I never thought, "Why the hell did they let Twofolk go?"

My career ended just like it started me working with Wally. I went to go get my package from Rollo one day and he met me with Wally in the car. I thought to myself, "That's odd" but I didn't say anything about it. Wally was Rollo's brother so shit who was I to say anything. Well come to find out Wally was getting a play from Rollo just like I was. Wally was there to pick up his work. Rollo then pulled out an ounce and said, "Can you work this?" I thought it was mine I said, "Yeah, the whole ounce?" Rollo had never fronted me more than a quarter ounce in the past. This was a breakthrough. Rollo replied, "No just a half for you and a half for Wally."

I was still cool with the play cause I would be able to bag fifteen or sixteen hundred with my half. I could clear a thousand at least after I paid Rollo. Wally was also happy with the play. There was one problem, it had to be cut in half. Rollo had brought one whole ounce instead of two half ounces. Rollo must have read my mind cause he said, "Can you two divide it up." I didn't want to be bothered with Wally. But he was still my boy so I said, "Yeah it's cool."

After we left Rollo we went to my apartment to divide up the ounce. Right off the top the deal went bad. As we were emptying the dope onto the plate and weighing it the doorbell rang. I had to go see who was at the door and left Wally weighing the dope. When I came back Wally had it all on the scale he said, "The ounce was a eight ball short." I shook my head inside I thought, "Rollo never makes mistakes with dope."

I shrugged those thoughts off because I knew this was Wally, my boy. I had known Wally for years he wouldn't beat me. Well I won't say he did or did not. But I later mentioned it to Rollo and he replied, "You let Wally beat you out of the dope, I gave you all more than an ounce." Oh well.

Wally said, "We can move this together, I can sell most of it out of Bart's house." Laziness is the death of a dope man and it killed me, I said, "Cool." I was very lazy by then if Wally hadn't of offered to move it I was going to drop it off with my workers. Plus Twofolk's house was a damn near inferno with heat, so I figured it would work out fine. One play with my boy would be all right. We bagged up about eight or nine hundred and still had a big piece left, I was happy. Then I made the mistake that would put the nails in the coffin as far as me rolling was concerned. I let Wally keep the dope. As I look back upon it that was the best thing that could of happened to me but in 1989 I didn't see it that way.

Wally was risking his ass there was no doubt in that. The reason being Bart's workers were only supposed to sell his dope. I was basically back to hanging on Sixth Street again. The business went fine for about two days. Wally had moved seven hundred of the work and he gave me my split. This is how people's money gets messed up. I put the loot in my pocket like it was mine. I should have told Wally to give me five hundred and went and paid Rollo half of the grand we owed him. But it was not to be. We bagged up the rest of the dope it was more than two thousand worth of dope left. We had enough to pay Rollo and make a little scratch for ourselves.

I had already came to the conclusion when we finish this the next play I got would be on my own not with Wally. Once again I left Wally with the dope, why I'll never know. Common sense would had me take at least a grand for myself but my senses at the time were not common. I guess subconsciously I was ready to quit because I may as well had flushed the dope down the toilet.

The next day I kicked it with Del so I did not get the chance to holler at Wally. When I did catch up with Wally the day after I was in for a shock. I saw Wally on Sixth Street in front of his mama's house with Keith. I got out and walked over to see how we were progressing. Wally told me, "I got ripped off at the hotel last night." I was stunned and I asked, "For how much?" Wally replied, "All of it, the whole two grand." Wally proceeded to tell a wild story about hiding the dope by a car. When Wally came out the dope was gone. I had stopped listening to Wally's speech, I knew I was screwed. I owed Rollo five hundred off of that package and some change off of a previous play. In the distance I could have sworn I heard a fat lady singing.

Wally must have seen the look on my face because he said, "I'll make it up at Bart's." I had to laugh at this. I realized the situation had left me in a position where I had to hope Wally could do it. Keith was just sitting there shaking his head saying, "Wally done messed up again, Wally done messed up again." I was in total agreement with that statement. Wally pulled out a bag of dope and offered it to me. I tooted a few times and passed it to Keith. I then said, "We have got to dodge Rollo until we can get him some of his loot." Wally nodded and said, "We'll give him a piece Friday, so we can buy some time." I gave them dap and asked, "Are you going down to the pink house?" Wally said, "Yeah, I'm headed down there now."

I walked to the car and drove away. I was hoping Wally could do it but deep down I knew I was screwed.

For the next few days I went by Sixth Street and hung with Keith. I could lay low over there plus keep in touch with Wally. Every so often Wally would come down the street and give us a bag or drink a brew with us. Wally would say he was doing all right. All I could do was hope he was and wasn't lying.

Friday came and passed and we did not make the payment I can't remember why we didn't but we didn't. Time was going by and we were not getting any closer to paying Rollo. I was getting sick of ducking and dodging Rollo but I had no choice. My money was low and I had no dope to roll to make it back up. I was in a bind, plus I was tired of the game. I was thinking about getting out. Before I could do that I had to get my debts taken care of.

I went by Wally's mama's house one day to see what was going on. Keith told me Rollo had just left. Rollo was pissed about his money. I asked Keith did he stall him or play him off. Keith gave a vague answer, I went and sat on the couch. As I was sitting there the doorbell rang. Keith got up and looked out of the window and said, "It's Rollo!" I said, "Tell him I'm not here." Rollo was the last person I wanted to see. So I sat back figuring Keith would blow dude off, wrong. I looked up Rollo was standing in the doorway. My mouth would have dropped but I stayed cool. Rollo said one thing, "Where my money?" My only reply was, "Wally is working it. We'll get it back to you."

My mind was racing cause I didn't know where the hell Wally was or how much he had saved. Another thing that was messing with me was Keith was supposed to have told Rollo I was not there! What kind of play was this, what if the dude had of came in with a gun? Rollo said, "Frank don't lie to me about my money. I gave y'all more than enough to pay me." That verbal jab stung me cause I knew Rollo was right and the reason I was short was because of another fool, and my own mental blindness. I said, "You did and we are going to pay you we need a little time." The sad part is I really wanted to pay Rollo because he was cool.

Rollo looked and asked, "Where Wally at?" I told him Wally was down the street moving the dope. Rollo shook his head and said, "Have my money in the next few days or somebody is going to be selling ass to get me mine!" And walked out of the room. I heard the door shut. Keith walked back into the room I asked him, "Man why did you tell Rollo I was here?" Keith started to lie but I waved him off cause it had clicked in my head. Keith and Rollo were brothers they had the same father. That was the answer. I got up to leave and said, "Tell Wally it is on! I'll catch up with him tomorrow morning to rap with him." Keith asked, "Where you headed?" I walked out of the house.

I went to the New Yorker to think about the situation I was in. I realized then that I was in a trick bag and it was closing fast. One thing was for sure. I wasn't taking any ass whippings. That was out. I'm not saying I could beat dude or anything like that but those ass whipping days had past. I had no intention of repeating such foolish times. I was feeling nervous. It was like I was being forced to take some action I didn't want to take.

I was not worried about what Rollo would do to me, it was what I might have to do to him. I was thinking I was going to have to kill somebody. It was too easy for me to get a gun, and as I stated, Mama had stopped whipping me in middle school. The reason I was nervous was not the fact that I may have to take a life. It was I might not be able to get away with it. Racine was a little town and news spread fast. I was also broke and did not have the scratch to go on the run. Twenty-five to life was not an option either.

I sat and drank a few Long Island Ice Teas and came to one conclusion, the truth needs to be told. Rollo was cool. I really did feel bad about his money getting messed up because he trusted me. I felt I let Rollo down. Rollo deserved the truth. I also could see why Rollo would be upset about us dodging him. If Wally could not come up with the scratch I would just go tell him the facts and let the cards fall where they may.

I was tired of this dodging game it was for females in my book. One thing in my favor was the fact Rollo had to see I had taken about a two

70

thousand-dollar loss myself off of the deal. Plus I only owed Rollo five hundred from my half of the ounce, I would work that off in no time. I downed the last of my drink and rolled. I felt better because I could see some light in that trick bag. I saw Wally the next day and he was evasive about what we were going to do about Rollo's scratch.

One thing I noticed was Wally had dope, a good size piece at that. Wally then stated, "We'll take care of Rollo as soon as possible." I nodded my head, but I already knew what I was going to have to do. Wally was leaving going back to the pink house to roll some more. Wally said, "Come get me and we'll go to the New Yorker tonight it's Friday." I told Wally I would because I was definitely going even if he wasn't. I swung through to get Wally at around 11:00 that night. Wally was dressed and up beat. Wally said, "We'll be able to take care of Rollo next week." Wally was grinning like a chess cat. I knew Wally had been peeling dope from Bart for weeks. One reason was Wally always had some dope. I guessed Wally had taken Bart for a big piece this time. Wally confirmed my thoughts by saying, "Man I glazed Bart hard tonight." I just shook my head and said, "Man you better quit while you ahead." Wally looked at me and said, "Bart trust me we tight!" Wally started explaining but I stopped listening.

We hopped in the car and went by the store to grab some forty ounces to drink in the car on the way. We parked outside the New Yorker and guzzled the forties looking at the women going in the joint. I mentioned the fact that we ought to tell Rollo the deal. Wally shook that off and said, "We'll be straight." I looked at Wally and took the bag of dope he was holding out to me. I tooted strong and said, "Yeah you right." I knew what I had to do. I was going to have to face Rollo my damn self with the truth.

After we finished tooting and the forties we went inside. I leaned over and told Wally, "It is some females in here tonight." he grinned. I walked over to the bar and ordered Jack for us both. I gave him his and knocked mine off and looked around the club to see who was going to be my victim for the night. I noticed Bart and two of his workers walked into the joint.

I didn't pay them any mind I was too busy trying to find the finest female in the joint, I always did like top shelf. I told Wally, "I'll be back," and went to dance. I went past Bart I said, "What's up?" He said, "Nothing much." I kept walking and stopped by some people I knew and started talking to them. As I was talking to them I seen Bart talking to Wally, I didn't pay it any mind. I eventually talked myself into a dance with a female at the table, so we headed to the floor. We danced I was having a good time. As we went off the floor things changed.

As I was leaving the floor I saw Bart standing on the edge of the floor with a serious look on his face. I took note of this but I didn't pay it any mind. I hadn't done anything to him. I also noticed his workers were looking crazy like they were waiting for the word to jump on some poor sap. I kind of felt sorry for the poor fool they were looking for because those fools were crazy. As I went past Bart he said, "Frank let me talk to you." I said, "Cool, it's loud out here let's go into the bathroom." Bart waved his boys off and we went into the bathroom.

The first words out of Bart's mouth were, "Do you have my dope?" I was shocked so I replied, "Man I haven't even been down to your spot, how could I have your dope?" Bart said, "I know" I cut him off. I asked, "Man what's up?" By now alarm bells were going off in my head, it was getting tense. Bart said, "Man I know you left to do your own thing," I interrupted again by saying, "Yeah, and I left with a clean slate." Bart's reply was, "We've been having dope missing and Wally said you have it." Oh baby! That was why those fools were out there looking crazy, I was the fool they were going to jump on!

On the inside I was tripping on the outside I was cool. I said, "Man you bullshitting me." Bart said, "No, the man said you have it or he left the dope with you, something like that." I had stopped listening because my mind was clicking on all cylinders. My boy had tried to put dirt on me and the only thing that was going to save my ass was what I said in the next few seconds. I then said, "Let's get Wally's ass in here so we can clear this shit up, I haven't had any of your dope since I left! I sure don't have any that Wally has supposed to have given me." The situation was pissing me off. I wasn't mad at Bart I was pissed at Wally, he had lied on me. Bart said, "Okay." We went out of the bathroom, I looked all over the bar with Bart following and didn't see Wally. That cat had left. That really burned me up. I turned and looked at Bart the next move would be up to him. Bart looked at me and said, "Frank your boy ain't your friend. He done put dirt on you and left your ass to pay for it." I stood listening tense because I didn't know what he was going to do. I didn't know if Bart believed me or was he just going to sic his boys on me.

We walked over to a corner I said, "Bart no bullshit I haven't messed with your dope." Bart said, "Man I believe you. I didn't think you had the coke that is why I asked you before I made a move on you." He continued, "That fool Wally did this. Frank he ain't your friend." Bart gave me dap and said, "It's cool." As Bart turned to leave he said, "You making money now, you too big to come visit us?" Bart said that grinning my reply was, "Man I'm damn near broke." Bart shrugged and said, "We'll stop down sometime." And walked away.

I went to the bar and sat down and ordered a double shot of JD. When it came I knocked it off, the little broad I was dancing with earlier was looking at me hard. I didn't even look twice at the girl, I had other fish to fry. I got up to leave I had to find Wally and see what kind of game he was pulling.

I rolled down Racine Street looking for Wally cause I knew he was walking and couldn't have gotten far. On a hunch I stopped at Lee's place to see if Wally had went by there. Guess who was sitting at the bar having a drink, Wally. I wasn't mad at Wally I just needed to find out what the hell was going on with him.

I sat down next to Wally he looked up and I asked, "Why did you leave?" Wally said, "It was too packed in there I needed some air." I looked at Wally and in my head I chalked him up as a loss. Wally was all messed up. I also knew I had to clear my slate up with Rollo cause Wally was headed to hell in a Ferrari and I wasn't going to be a passenger. I felt sad for Wally I think the dope was getting to him. I ordered a shot of Jack and knocked it off. I then asked Wally, "Are you straight man?" He said, "Yeah I'm cool." I left and went back to the New Yorker to finish off my night. The honey was still in there but she was playing hard to get since I left so abruptly. In the end she listened to some lie I told and exited with me.

CHAPTER XI

The clock was ticking and I did not want it to expire on my black ass. I went by Sixth Street to see what was up with Wally and Keith. As I got out of the car I saw Wally standing across the street so I waved. I looked at Keith he had a serious look on his face. I glanced back at Wally who was coming across the street. Then I looked again, Wally's head looked funny. I saw why his head looked funny. It was swollen. I said, "Man what happened to you?" "Nothing." Was Wally's answer. Keith blurted out, "Them niggas jumped on him!" I remembered what had happened in the New Yorker so I asked, "Bart?" Wally said, "No." I said, "Let's go get them!" After all through thick and thin Wally was still my buddy in my mind. Keith said, "It was Bart's workers."

It dawned on me Keith didn't have to say any more. Bart had his workers peel Wally's head. I then asked Wally, "Man do you want to go get them niggas?" Wally replied, "No, it wasn't no big deal." I looked at Keith he had a disgusted look on his face. Wally continued, "They did this when Bart wasn't there." I guess in his mind that made it all right.

I was thinking Bart knew cause those dudes wouldn't piss without his permission. Wally started walking down the street. I said, "Where you going?" Wally replied without turning, "Down to the pink house." I hollered, "You still going to mess around down there?" Wally kept walking and said, "Yes." I looked at Keith he just shook his head. Keith got up and walked up the stairs to the house and said, "That dude got his head up Bart's ass for sure!" I stood there speechless alone, watching Wally go back to slang dope for the people who beat his ass. "Damn I need a drink!" flashed through my head.

My dope career was officially over. I was broke and on the run dodging Rollo. I wanted to face Rollo with Wally so the truth could come out. This happened one night when we were leaving Smitty's bar. Keith, Wally and I had just pulled off from the bar headed down Mead Street. When a car following us started flashing it's lights and blowing the horn. Keith said, "It's Rollo." I was nervous but relieved, now the truth could come out into the open.

We pulled over and got out. The first words out of Rollo's mouth were, "Where is my money?" I stood back and said, "We took a loss, tell him Wally." Wally looked his half brother in the face and said, "Someone stole the dope from me." I kept my eyes on Rollo to see how he was going to react to this news flash. Keith had his eyes on him too. Wally proceeded to tell the story about the motel and how the dope was gone when he came out. Rollo looked at him then at me and asked, "Frank you believe that?" That was the one question Rollo could have asked that I was not ready for. I mumbled, "Yeah."

Rollo just looked at me as if he was wondering how stupid I could get and said, "Y'all played me once but it won't happen again. I am through with you!" Rollo then walked to his car and drove off. On the inside I let out a sigh of relief. I knew I was wrong. Rollo had trusted me with his product and I had messed up. That was the official end of my career as a dope man. From that point on, things started going to hell fast. Bart's house got raided, again. I didn't give a damn but Wally did. I was talking to Wally one day and he seemed worried about Bart. I guess Wally could feel what was going to happen. Right around this time the police did a major drug sweep of Racine. Del was selling off and on in Twofolk's house cause he needed money for his kid.

One day I was chilling with Del over Twofolk's house. I borrowed his car to go get something to eat. I went up to Churches and laughed with PJ and Fats while I was waiting for my order. I looked out of the window and guess who was running up to the door, Del. Del came in. I grabbed the food and went over to talk to him. Del was nervous looking and said, "The police are raiding Twofolk's house!" I felt a funny twinge but I ignored it, and said, "Come on!"

We left and rode back by the house and sure enough the door was hanging off the hinges. A few hypes were outside and they beckoned me in the car. I sped up and left the block. "It was getting crazy." I told Del he readily agreed.

One day I was looking out of the back window in my apartment and seen some cop cars in the alley. I thought, "Oh shit, they coming for my ass!" I felt that funny twinge again but ignored it once more. I had odds on my side for one the dude down the block was a big time dope man. Two, I had never sold dope out of the pad. I had bagged and tooted in my place, but no sales. Just to be safe though I left. I went and picked up Wally and Keith.

As we rode through town we seen cops everywhere, they were locking Racine down. Keith asked me did I ever get some bags he had stashed in my seat out. I told him no, I didn't know there were any in there. Keith then proceeded to tell me about how he put some bags of dope in the seat when he went to jail one night three months ago. I remembered the night but not the dope. We pulled over and snatched up the seat, sure enough there was four bags under there! I just shook my head.

If the cops had pulled me over and searched my car I would have had a case. I would have been facing a felony possession with intent to deliver for some dope I didn't even know about. I would have owed it all to my friend. I told Keith, "Man, give me a bag." He did and we wound up tooting it and the rest of the bags. I guess in my sick head that made it okay.

While we were chilling Wally mentioned the fact that he was going to Bart's trial the next day. I said, "Man I wouldn't go down there." Wally said, "I'm just going to hear what type of case they have against Bart." The scene felt funny to me and I replied, "Okay." We went and grabbed some beer and chilled. That was the last time we kicked it together.

The next day Wally went to watch the proceedings. While Wally was down there worried about the next man they arrested him. I heard the news and went by Sixth Street to check with Keith about it, he was sitting outside on the stoop. Keith just shook his head and said, "They picked Wally up in the hallway while he was waiting on Bart's arraignment." We talked awhile longer.

I noticed the police kept riding up and down the block so I told Keith I would stop by later. As I drove away I seen a police car in the rear view mirror and wondered was I the next person slated to be picked up. I knew if I went to jail for dope there was no help for me. Mama wasn't going to help me. I didn't have anyone else with the type of money I would need to beat a case. I knew if they picked me up on a dope case, I was through.

I went to the crib and chilled. I was out of dope and was on the verge of bankruptcy as far as money went. It was getting kind of hectic. I thought about Wally. Wally and I had made a lot of sales together. What if Wally dropped my name or something? I felt that twinge again, this time I could not shake it. The twinge was fear. For the first time since I made the decision to roll I was scared.

Del came by with a twelve pack. Del gave me a run down on who had been picked up and who wasn't. I really didn't feel like drinking so I listened and thought. When Del finished talking I told him I would get back with him and showed him the door. I kicked back and started scheming. I knew what I had to do. I was just hoping time wouldn't run out on me before I could make it happen.

The next day I went to Mama's house and called Willyfarce to see if I could get reinstated. The answer was yes. When I left I was on the Dean's List so it was no problem. I needed money to go back to school, no problem. The following day I called Parkside University and talked to a brother who did financial aid for students.

It was time for me to use my father status for my benefit. This brother would hook it up where I could get Pell grants and loans so I wouldn't have to ask Mama for money. I did not want to hear that song about how she was paying any more. By me having a child I could file independent and that was all I needed to get the scratch to get me back to school, out of the state.

My plan was hinging on the fact that I did not have any type of record. I wanted to be able to show, if I got picked up, that I was getting my life together. I had talked to the county and gotten my old job back so in a sense I was going legit. My old supervisor had told me I could start May 15th. This was right on time. In the eyes of the judge I was a college student working to go back to school. Instead of a deadbeat dad looking for the next hustle. There was one more thing I had to do I had to get clean.

When I started rolling I had made a promise to myself that I would only toot as long as I sold dope. Well the end had come so it was time to give up one of my favorite pastimes, tooting cocaine. This was actually no problem, in May 1989 I tooted my last bag. I got my last drain and waved good bye to that white whore. I haven't tooted or even thought about it since then. Giving it up was quite easy because of the pact I made with myself.

One day after I got all of the things I needed in order, I sat back and thought about what had happened to me. I knew the reason I dropped out of the game. I had lost the edge. The no-fear attitude I had when I first started rolling was gone. I could no longer ride by the police with five to six hundred dollars worth of bags on me and act like I was clean. The, "I don't give a damn," attitude was gone. This was death to a dope man or any criminal for that fact. This is what killed my career. Now I just had to make it to September when I could leave and go back to school.

Somehow Keith wound up in jail so I really felt like I was treading on thin ice. To top things off the landlord was kicking me out of the apartment! This was really messed up he claimed I made too much noise. I was never there except late night. I tried to explain to the landlord I was going back to school and had a job. Dude was not trying to hear that line. I had to go. The only place I had left to go was back to mama's house.

This was real messed up but it actually worked out in my favor. This move got me out of the area I had lived when I was rolling. People who may be looking for me for street reasons would think I had moved or been locked up. Chuck and Mama let me move back in which was cool. It was time to play the waiting game.

I knew that if I made it back to Willyfarce I would be straight. I steered clear of a lot of my old hangouts. I also did not look to hard for the associates I once had when I was rolling. I had big plans and the joint wasn't in them.

I remember stopping by Liza's house to see how she was doing. I also stopped by to see if Liza had heard anything about Wally and Keith. Liza made the statement, "I bet you wish you was down there with Wally and Keith, in the county jail because you miss them." I laughed it off. In my mind I was thinking, "Fool you crazy!" I didn't want any part of jail that was why I wasn't running down there to see them. I knew though that I was going to have to go down there at least once to holler at them, after all they were my guys.

The main problem was I wasn't sure if the police wanted me. My thinking was they might have a case on me. If this was true then they were going to have to come find me. I wasn't going to say, "Here I am. Come lock me up Mr. Policeman." In my view visiting jail was saying just that very thing. As they say though I had obligations.

The Sunday I went down to the jail it was packed. I had to wait to see my boys. The scene was flat out crazy. There were women down there with kids. Dudes were up pacing the floor. I was anxious as hell. When I looked at Liza though she was calm as hell. I guess Liza was used to the scene from being with Wally. I just chilled and looked around the hallway.

Females were made up to look good for their man. Some cats were there putting money on the books for they boys so they could buy candy bars. As I sat there I wondered if I took a fall would anybody come see me. The females I boned were just hit and run so that was out. My boys were in jail so they were not an option. I think the only person who would come would be my mama. I remember thinking if I got locked up I would not even come down for visitors.

I finally got in to see Wally and Keith. It was a waste of time. There was a guard there and we were separated by this thick piece of glass. We also had to talk on a phone to one another, it was pathetic. I was glad to see Wally and Keith but also sad because of how I had to see them. As I walked out of the jail, I knew I would never come back down to see them again. It was not because of the fear of being arrested. It was because I did not like the glass separating us.

That summer passed with me growing more and more relaxed as the day to leave Racine got closer. The police picked up a lot of people that year.

The only people that I ran with who caught cases was Wally and Keith. PJ and Fats were still doing their thing. Del had quit and enlisted in the Marines. Even Eddie was still somewhere tooting on the streets. I guess Wally and Keith were just unlucky when it came down to police and jail time.

Del enlisted in the Army to get away from Racine. I'll never forget the day Del came by talking about he was leaving the next day. That fool had enlisted and asked to be shipped out as soon as possible. I told Del, "Now you know we have got to go celebrate, let's roll." We went down to a tavern owned by my father's uncle. My father was down there and he liked Del so he joined in on the celebration.

My father told everyone and soon everybody was buying Del drinks. Del was drinking and he was hyped. Del was telling everyone he was going to be a killing machine. After awhile somebody talked Del into taking triple shots of Old Crow, oh baby! This was past wild, my father was yelling, "You a soldier you can do it!" Del was yelling, "Yeah, yeah!" and downing shot after shot. Del was buying off into that Army thing tough. For some reason I did not join in on the shots but Del kept going. I said, "Man let's roll by the south side and see what's happening over there." Del agreed. I told my father I'd catch up with him later we left.

Del was hyped, he was saying, "Man I'm high as hell!" Dude started the car and we shot off like a rocket up Twelfth Street. Del was feeling his liquor. Del started cranking the system hollering about how glad he was that he was leaving Racine. All while Del was talking he was driving fast as hell. I told Del to swing by Clean C's house to holler at him.

When we got there Clean C wasn't home. We left to go to the gym. Del was hyper as hell. All while Del was driving he was talking a mile a minute and getting rubber at every stop sign. We got to one stop sign and Del was nodding his head singing the lyrics to *Gangsta, Gangsta* and sped through it and hit a truck dead broadside.

The aftermath was ridiculous, Del sped to the curb with his eyes all bucked out. The car wasn't damaged the rubber on the bumper was knocked a loose. The other car was dented just over the rear wheel well. I told Del to tell dude he would pay for the damage and leave, no police. I was hoping Del could get his information and get in touch with the guy later. I knew Del didn't have any insurance. Plus Del was drunk as a skunk.

The other driver didn't want to have any part of that. This lead to Del getting mad. Del started screaming at the man, "Take that offer or don't take shit!" I had to calm dude down. I then told Del to tell the police that he was alone I didn't want to be bothered with what was going on. I heard the sirens and started walking away. I saw Clean C riding down the block I flagged him down to catch a ride. I told Clean C what was going down and Clean C said, "I'm headed to Kenosha, you rolling?" I told him, "No, drop me off at the crime scene."

When Clean C dropped me off Del was talking to a cop. I don't know how the hell Del did it but the cop let Del go. The cop just wrote Del a ticket and let him leave. Del smelled like a whiskey bottle. Well I didn't trip. I was glad the cop didn't arrest Del. The police left Del came by the car and I said, "Let's go to the liquor store." Del hopped in and opened the door, about a minute later I was buying four forty ounces at the liquor store. The party didn't stop cause a because of a little accident.

After Del left I just basically worked and chilled out. There was only one thing of interest that happened to me. I got into an accident while on the job at the county.

One day I was riding shotgun in one of those big county trucks. This old fool named Peter was driving when a little Pinto or Escort crossed the yellow line and hit us. I was shook up from the impact. The driver of the car was pretty messed up though. The ambulance took her away. This accident would pay off in the future. Other than that incident I was just burning daylight until I could get out of Racine.

I remember getting back down to Willyfarce thinking, "Damn I got away! I made it!" But did I get myself together and give up the liquor? By now I think you know the answer, if I had I wouldn't be writing this book.

As far as classes were concerned that was never a problem, I think I had a 3.2 or something that first semester back. I was no fool. I was taking care of business because I was determined to graduate in eight semesters, four years. To me it didn't make sense to go five years or even four and a half for a four-year degree. The math just didn't add up. So as far as the books went, I was straight. But socially I was a man out of place.

I was an old man in a young adult's body. I had grown used to drinking every night and hanging out until the morning. I was street poisoned to the max. I used to look at the students going back and forth on campus attempting to hold their butts tight and shake my head in disgust. They were already grooming their behavior to appease white folks.

Some of the people I came into Willyfarce with were coming back from internships where they worked in the business world. They were looking forward to getting their degree. They wanted to get back to corporate America. These people wanted to run to the whites and say, "Look boss I's educated too." Me I needed a place to cool off to keep from going to prison and escape from the sink hole named Racine. That corporate America scenario never crossed my mind. Fuck corporate America, hell fuck

America period. I needed a place to get my head together and lay low college was made to order.

The one thing my street training had really affected was how I interacted with women. I was used to females who hung at bars and chased after dope men. These women had sex on a whim. They did not play when it came time to bone.

Down at good old Willyfarce. The dudes there were catering to females! It didn't make a bit of sense to me because the females out numbered the dudes at least five to one! There were four dorms on the yard. Two and one half of another dorm was for females you do the math. These tricks were down there begging for sex. I was used to just dropping a few lines and it was on. Down there though they played different. I guess it was because you were dealing with girls of high morals, yeah right. I knew females down there who were nastier than dope fiends who were strung out and feigning for a hit.

I had seen the picture from both sides of the track and it was the same damn race. The so called hood rat in the club was more real than the fake wanna be white pro Negress. If you are wondering why I felt like that it is because it was true.

There was more fucking and sucking going on down there than an orgy! So I felt let's keep it real. You fucking I'm fucking lets fuck, case closed. I just never seen the need to be phony about sex. A whore is a whore no matter if she has on a mini skirt or a business suit that's it. Just like on the other hand a dog ass brother is the same no matter if he's wearing sagging jeans or a damn Armani suit.

One good thing that was going on down there was PFA. PFA had grown since I had left the yard. They had about ten brothers and some sisters. I remember talking to Len back in the summer about this and tripping off of this info.

One of the first things Len and Dontae did when I got back on the yard was introduce me to my brothers. My mouth dropped. These dudes were nerds! The females were ugly as hell. That's just what I get. When I first heard they were females in the clique my first thought was what type of freaky things I could make them do. Wrong these girls were ugly. Liquor couldn't even make them right. The dudes were weak as hell. I remember looking at Len and asking him, "Why did you let these weak ass fools in?"

I was still Frank and I had a lot of partners around the yard. I would be chilling with some of them and one of them weak ass dudes would walk by with a PFA hat on and they would say, "Isn't that one of your PFA brothers?" They would say that with a smirk. That would burn me up. As I look back on it these fools wished they could have someone pledge their name and be proud to wear their initials.

I could understand the fact that they were nerds but they didn't even try to act cool. These tricks had cars but Len and I would have to catch other people to get a ride to town. If the fools did go to town they would speed off and not tell us. Weak things like that. We weren't trying to dictate their cars or anything like that but if we are supposed to be brothers then let's act like it. To me this was insulting because the square punks should have been paying me to wear my name! No other group would have them because of their ho-cake ways.

I have to admit though they were into PFA. As I stated no other group would have they ass so they put a lot of time into mine. They even created bylaws. One of the brothers created a shield for the clique. They did some good things organization wise.

As I look back on it I should have never went back to Willyfarce, as far as PFA went. The clique would have blown up with my name on it. When I came back down there people who knew me would point me out. I know it had to feel funny to the brothers to be wearing my creation with me there. If I was gone I guess the existing brothers could play it off and paint some scholarly picture of me to recruits. With me there they seen the real me, a fool drinking Mad Dog wine in the hallways.

If I had of went back to Willyfarce and been a model student, head of SGA and things like that, PFA still would have blown up. That would not have been Frank though. I could give a damn about SGA or the PGA for that matter. I was just down there to buy some time until I could find out what the next move was.

As the year went on the relationship kept getting worse between the other brothers and me. It just boils down to the fact the Negroes were just not cool. The situation reached critical mass one night we had an interest meeting for recruits.

We had taken a guy over to these apartments to see if he wanted to be down. I was good and high from drinking with the Twins. I was just sitting back listening to Dontae run down the scoop on what we were about. I got up and went to the refrigerator and discovered there was some microwave chicken in the fridge. Naturally I started helping myself. While I was doing this I would blurt out statements like, "Yeah your weak ass is mine!" And, "You a pussy you can't make it!" Things like that to see if the cat was weak or not. As I look back I was being an ass but skip it I was PFA number one. I could do what I wanted.

Dontae finally got fed up and said, "Forget him don't pay him any attention he's a fool." I froze, skip some chicken, this fool had gone too far!

The room got quiet, I walked over to where Dontae was sitting and said, "Man take that shit back." I didn't yell or anything, I was calm. Dude must have realized he had messed up. I could see it in his eyes but the weak bastard had heart. Dontae's reply was, "No," or "Fuck you." Something like that. Whatever he said it was wrong. I fired on his punk ass.

I'll give it to Dontae though he got one lucky punch in that hit me in the nose. But when it was over Dontae's ass was balled up and I was measuring him for punches. I had to laugh later because the liquor messed my aim up and Len said I was missing Dontae and hitting the wall. All this chaos happened in front of a prospective pledge. Needless to say the guy did not join PFA.

Another time we were pledging a girl's line and shit hit the fan. I was known as the one who went overboard all the time so the brothers kept me away from the pledges. The brothers had been telling me about this female who was bullshitting the sisters around. The sisters wanted to drop her. They turned the situation over to the brothers to handle. The females wanted some satisfaction before they dropped her. They wanted revenge for being played.

Usually I would have been ready to give a pledge hell. But this time I had the feeling something wasn't right. As soon as the sisters brought the chick into the room all hell broke loose.

The brothers started pushing the girl around and hollering in her face. Dontae who had always remained cool had lost his mind. Dontae was yelling and pushing old girl up against the wall. The pledge was trying to rattle of the history she had been told. But the brothers were out of control. I was sitting there watching this debacle spellbound, I was thinking, "They say I'm the crazy one!" The climax came when they had the chick doing pushups.

The pledge was doing the pushups like females do them. The girl was in a doggy-style position pushing up. My main man Len, Mr. Calm and cool, was behind her hollering. While Len was yelling he was boning her with a dictionary! Now I don't mean literally but Len was shoving that book between her legs like it was going to bust a nut and spray words all over the place! That's when I snapped out of the shock I was in.

I realized the hazing had gone too far. I was a junior I did not want to be kicked out for something like this. To stop them I hollered, "Man get it together!" Len looked at me and then at the dictionary sheepishly. I looked at Dontae he just shrugged his shoulders and sat down. I asked the pledge, "Are you Okay?" This girl was all messed up she didn't reply. I knew right then we were in for it. I told the pledge to go outside to pull herself together. She left the room.

I turned to the brothers and asked, "Boys you know campus police is coming don't you?" I continued, "Y'all messed up now it is time to do damage control!" I said, "Get Freda, the head sister, to write old girl in." This would have made her a HOE this was what the girls were called. The brothers disagreed with me. I said, "Fine then." I turned to open the door to talk to the pledge and guess what she was gone!

That quickly pushed the brother's minds into gear! Dontae ran and told Freda what had happened. When Freda heard she went looking for the pledge. Guess where Freda found her, the damn police desk! Freda came back up and told us about it, you could have bought us for a dollar. I told the brothers to get their lies straight because it was going down!

I knew ML, the head cop, was on his way up here right then. ML wasn't going to be playing around either. I knew the light-skinned faggot did not like me. I told the brothers to keep me out of it.

True to form when ML came to the room the first words out of his mouth were directed to me, "What was your role in all of this?" I think the high yellow sissy was disappointed when the brothers told ML I had little to do with the affair. The pledge even told him and Yackov, his booty buddy on the force, I didn't touch her. I don't know why but ML didn't pursue the case any farther. The incident was squashed. I was relieved. I didn't need any hassles down there in my safe haven.

Hazing people was not always bad. The best time I had pledging a line was pledging this fruit named Julian. To make a long story short Julian's brother was a PFA already so Julian wanted to be down. Dontae and Julian's brother had been handling his pledge process during the week. Julian skated easy. That Friday though Julian's brother and Dontae were going home. At 5:30 that Friday Julian was Len and mines!

I told Julian to meet me at my room with some jeans and a tee shirt on. Dontae and Julian's brother were there. Dontae and Julian's brother told us they was rolling Julian was in our care. Julian's brother must have not loved him because he would not have left that boy with us. As soon as that door closed hell was in session.

The first words out of my mouth were, "Mutha fucka you got some money?" I didn't wait for a response I said, "Get me a damn fifteen pack and two fifths of *Orange Jubilee* and you have one hour to get it!" I asked Len if he wanted anything he wanted two quarts of Colt 45. I gave Julian three dollars and Len gave him two. Julian looked puzzled I said, "Yeah punk make up the rest!"

Before Julian left the room I asked him what his line name was he said the Medic or something. I laughed and said, "Drop that shit, it is going to change! Now go time is running!" Julian left running. Len and I already had some liquor so we started on that. I was scheming on how I was going to make Julian drop line. I asked Len, "You think the fool could come up with the rest of the money?" Len said, "Yeah, his brother know we don't like him so Julian is going to do what he can to impress us." I grunted and sipped the liquor and continued watching *Little House On The Prairie.*

Six-thirty came and Julian wasn't back yet. Len and I had finished our stash. I was getting anxious, Julian had my last three dollars. Plus I wanted to milk Julian the whole weekend so I could stay drunk.

Six forty-five a knock on the door, it was Sherbert. Sherbert wanted to know what I had up for the evening. I told Sherbert about the pledge and his lateness. Sherbert pulled out a splif, joint, and lit it laughing at us. Sherbert felt we were getting shitted on by our pledge. I took the joint from him and hit it hard. I'm thinking thoughts of murder in my head. Here was another fool who was going to have to pay. The weed was gripping my brain like crazy. I said, "Man what the hell is this?" Sherbert snorted through the smoke, "Monkey paw, the weed grips your head like a monkey's paw!" He then busted into gales of laughter.

I didn't know if that was true but my head was reeling. I took another hit on the joint and passed it. Len didn't want any so the twin finished it. Sherbert got up pulling on his crotch and said, "I'm headed to the girl's side to fuck a bitch!" I looked at Sherbert his eyes were bloodshot red. As I looked at his I wondered about mine. I told Sherbert I would holler at him later and he left.

Seven-thirty I'm buzzing out of my damn mind trying to keep violent thoughts in my head. But I kept wanting to fall asleep. Then there was a knock on the door. Len went and opened it. It was Julian. I perked up immediately I snapped, "Get in here!" Julian walked in with bags of stuff. Julian had the brew, the wine and had picked up some burgers from Snap's. I was ecstatic inside because I was hungry as hell. I knew though if I ate I would fall asleep. I wanted to meter out some punishment.

I grabbed the Mad Dog blessed the bottle, said a prayer and broke the seal. I took a long pull out of the bottle. That good cold wine knocked the witch moss off of my brain. I looked at the clock and said, "Where you been?" I guess Julian thought that I would be happy because he had brought all of the items. "What" stumbled out of Julian's mouth. I was happy but I could not let him know it.

I continued, "Boy get your coat off! You got two minutes to take your coat to your room and get your weak ass back up here!" As Julian rushed out the door I hollered, "Tell your girl not to wait up for you!" Julian slammed the door. I looked at Len who was laughing and eating a burger and asked, "How many did he bring?" Len held up four fingers. I said, "Put mine in the fridge." I felt revitalized by having that cold wine in my fist. I hurried up and took another big swig Len said, "Oh shit!" Len had seen the way I was guzzling the wine he knew what time it was.

I said, "Julian is dropping tonight!" I held the bottle out towards Len and asked, "You want some?" Len waved it off and reached for a quart of brew. Julian knocked on the door and entered the room.

I locked the door. It was time for hell to be paid! I shouted, "Line up! What is your name boy?" Julian started to say "Medic." I cut Julian off, "Wrong get into the cut!" The cut is when you bent over getting ready to get paddled. Julian looked at me with a crazy look on his face. I grabbed my weapon, my paddle, and looked at him. Julian tried to ask me what had he done, I cut him off. I shouted, "Shut up pussy and get in the cut!" When you pledged PFA you were considered a pussy until you crossed.

Julian mumbled something as he was bending over Len shouted, "What! What did you say boy?!" Julian didn't say anything. Len continued, "Keep your fucking mouth shut when the brothers are talking!" If Julian was thinking about responding I cut the reply off with the paddle. I swung that paddle like the mighty Thor, whack! Julian shot up and grabbed his ass cheeks! I laughed and so did Len. I then told Julian his new line name. I had come up with: Arab bastard white punk, fruity cause I got three holes in my ear.

Len busted out laughing. I didn't crack a smile. I was feeling vicious. I got in Julian's face and said, "Say your name!" He stuttered, "Arab white boy" I shouted, "Wrong! Bend over!" Julian blurted out, "What is my," I screamed, "Shut the fuck up!" Julian had bent over, whack! Salvation had been brought down! I hollered, "Your name is Arab bastard white punk fruity cause I got three holes in my ear! Now say it!" "Arab white boy fruity" the fool stumbled again. I shouted at Julian, "Bend over!" He began, "What did," Len cut him off, "Bend your punk ass over!" Len's food had digested, he was ready to rock-n-roll. Whack! "Stay bent over!" I shouted, whack! It was hell on that boy I figured Julian would drop after an hour of this. Julian didn't though he had a piece of heart in him.

After the wine was gone I started on the beer. I made the fool, Julian, stand in the corner and jump in place while I drank and watched television. I then came up with the notion I wanted Julian to run around the dorms. I told Julian to go get his coat and be outside our window in two minutes. By now Len was high and screamed, "I'm timing your weak ass!" Julian left. I grabbed a burger I had to get some food on my belly. I didn't want too much because it was still some beer left to drink. By the time I wolfed down the burger the fool, Julian, was by the window. Julian was hollering up to us because we were on the third floor.

I told Len, "Shut that silly mutha fucka up!" Len hollered, "Bitch shut up!" I said, "Make his dumb ass run a lap around the dorms. Let him know we'll be watching him at various check points!" Len relayed the message to Julian and the fool took off. Len left the room to check to see if Julian ran past the front windows of the dorms. I drank a beer and looked out of the window thinking of more devious things I could put Julian through. I glanced at the tennis courts and seen some fresh snow had fallen and there were no footprints in it. I had an idea how to get some in there!

Dumb Julian came running into view with steam coming off of him cause it was cold outside. Len came into the room. I asked him, "Did he do it?" Len said, "Yeah he was running his ass off!" I looked out of the window at this fool and hollered, "Jump in place! Then make some snow angels!" After Julian finished this I told him to do something I thought was impossible. I told Julian to leap the fence to the tennis courts in two bounds.

The fence for the tennis courts was one of those high ass wire fences, designed to keep people out. I told Julian to jump the fence in just two bounds this had Len laughing. I laughed too because I knew Julian couldn't do it. I couldn't do it and I was 6'3" this fool was only 5'6" or 5'7". Dude turned looked at the fence and took off! Julian leaped like Jordan hit the fence at damn near the top of it and pushed himself over and landed on his feet! I looked at Len he was still looking out the window amazed. I couldn't believe it myself!

Oh well it was time to get back to business. I hollered to Julian, "Write PFA big as hell in the snow using your foot prints!" When he finished the letters looked cool as hell. I then told Julian to get his ass back up into the room. Julian came back up into the room. Julian knew he had done well by the look on Len's and my face. That high jump still had us tripping. If I mention it to Len today we still shake our heads over it.

I made Julian go stand in the corner and jump in place. Len and I commenced to drinking again. I had a bright idea to have Julian face the other way while he was jumping. I started running into Julian like a safety hitting a receiver. I was drunk and dude was grimacing in pain but I kept doing it. I was laughing all while I was hitting him. Julian was jumping in place and I was running and hitting him in the back. Mommy this is what they taught me at Willyfarce.

I eventually cabled Len up to hit Julian. Len was about 5'9" 230 pounds and he was lightning quick on his feet. Len was drunk though. Len got a bright idea to open the door so he could get a running start. Why Len did that I don't know but he did. The results were disastrous. Len came rushing into the room full tilt and hit Julian like Jack Tatum hitting Sammy White in the Super Bowl! Julian shot back like a rocket and slammed into the wall and just collapsed! I hurried up and shut the door. I was sober as hell then!

Julian was laid out on the floor not moving! Len was bent over Julian shaking him. Julian finally started moving. I breathed a sigh of relief. I lifted Julian up on his feet and asked him, "Can you move, are you all right?" Julian had turned red as hell. Julian nodded yes though. Then when Julian tried to move his arm he could just barely move it over his head. I thought quickly and said, "You tough as hell, Julian you have earned the rest of the night off." In order to keep him honest though I told Julian to be in the room the next morning at 6:30 with breakfast for Len and I. Julian nodded painfully and left. Len and I just looked at each other and breathed a sigh of relief. Then we laughed until late in the night at Julian.

CHAPTER XII
1990

The winter semester of 1990 was the beginning of my senior year. By then I was known in the circles I ran in as a top-notch drinker. I was also called a fool in some circles, behind my back. This was because of the way I carried myself. As I said before I had no intentions of entering corporate America and holding my ass tight. There seemed to be more to life to me than becoming white. I really didn't want to stay in the suburbs around whites and didn't want to be around phony blacks. I was a man without purpose burning daylight at the first black college in America.

My college routine had become; go to class, come back to the room drink, sleep. That was all to it, I had done everything that I could do at Willyfarce. From stepping at parties to making the Dean's List and even creating my own brotherhood I had done it. There were some fun academic times also. The best one was the time I took biology with Dr. Bean.

Dr. Bean taught biology at Willyfarce. At the time people were thankful to get a C in his class. Dr. Bean was a good instructor. Dr. Bean caught people up because he gave a lot of notes. You had to be there in class every day to get all of the notes. I remember taking the first test and flunking like the rest of the class. The good doctor threw out one test grade. I knew that one throw away grade was gone so I had to ace the rest.

When the next test came I didn't study the way I should have so when it came time to get the test back I was nervous. All bullshit aside I wanted to get an overall GPA of a 3.0 for graduation and this class carried a lot of weight. As Dr. Bean was passing out the results I was looking at peoples faces and their reactions. It was bad. This uppity yellow girl who sat across from me winced at the thirty-eight percent she had received. I was tense Dr. Bean looked at me and handed me my paper. It read an eighty-three or eighty-eight percent, I had a "B"! The yellow girl looked at me and said, "How did you get that?" I was too relieved to rip that nerd up for insulting my intelligence. I knew at that point it was on, I wanted to an "A" in the class.

At that time Dr. Bean had only given one "A" out in his class to my knowledge, that was to his child. I was determined to get an "A." This was the last time I gave a damn about a class at Willyfarce and maybe the only time one made me think. The next test I had a 93, an "A." Then I got on a roll and aced the next two with a 94 and 95. I had a "B" wrapped up, if I had of aced that first test I would have an "A." This would enable me to not have to take the final exam. Well I didn't ace the first one so I had to take the final. There was one more thing I was going for in the class, a 100 on a test.

Dr. Bean had told me that he had only had one person get a 100 on one of his tests, it was his kid. I was going to be the next and I told him so. Most people were sweating and asking for extra-credit just to get a "C." The drunk of the school was battling for perfection.

When test day came I breezed through the test. I finished in ten minutes or so. When I know something tests only take me a minimum amount of time. If you see me taking a long time on a test I don't know what the hell I'm doing. I handed the paper to Dr. Bean he asked, "Are you sure you're done?" I replied, "Yep." I turned and looked at the class before I walked out. The idiots were sitting there sweating and trying to cheat. I left laughing to myself.

I went back to get the results for the test. Boy was I in for a let down! Dr. Bean handed me my paper with a grin on his face. I had gotten one wrong! I had a 98! I know you people out there weren't thinking I was shocked because I had failed, if so shame on you! Dr. Bean said, "You didn't read all of the answers for the question you missed." I looked and sure enough Dr. Bean was right. It was one of those questions that had two answers and I had checked the first one I read cause I was rushing so I was only half right. The real answer was d, both a and c. I argued that I was right, he just shook his head. I was sad because I wanted that hundred so bad. True enough I had gotten an "A", the first he had given out in awhile but it wasn't enough. It is funny though I'm writing this ten years later and I still feel salty about it.

The next semester people were flunking Dr. Bean's class and he told them they should contact me to help them. Dr. Bean later told me that when he mentioned that he had a student on the yard whom had gotten an "A" and he would help people the students tripped. One reason they didn't know who Frank James was. Then when he described me and mentioned PFA they tripped. A few students even said things like, "Dude a drunk!" Remarks like that. I guess Dr. Bean waved that off. Dr. Bean told them to get with me. The only ones who would ask though were freshman. All they wanted was my notes. It didn't bother me, I had my "A" and the real notes were in my head.

I went home for the summer feeling good that year. I knew the next fall semester would be my last one. That in itself was enough to make me jump for joy but I soon got another surprise.

After I got back to Racine my mother or somebody, got in touch with my cousin in Los Angeles. My cousin was working in the movie field and was supposed to have the hook-up. I talked to my cousin and she felt that I would be able to make more connections and get some experience if I came out and stayed with her in Los Angeles. She didn't have to ask twice. I had some money coming sometimes that year from the accident I had gotten into the year before. So I asked Mama and Chuck to loan me some money to go to Los Angeles. They did because I know they didn't want to put up with me.

The night before I was to leave for Los Angeles I went out drinking with my aunt Darla and her fiance Rico. My plane was leaving out of Chicago at five in the morning; I partied until two or three. I barely made it to the airport in time to catch my flight. Mama was glad to put me on the plane and she told me so on the way over there. As I was walking through the airport I was grinning to myself thinking, "I'm going to LA to live the lifestyle of the rich and famous!" Reality would set in as soon as I got on the plane.

As I told you I had been drinking the night before so that turned out to be the worst flight of my life. It was one of those cheap flights that lands two or three times before you get to where your going. I was sweating out liquor and feeling like I was going to throw up and shit on myself all at once. I went into the bathroom and blew it up. I then went back to my seat and told the stewardess to bring 7-up and to keep it coming.

I think they got tired of me and gave me some sleeping pills or something. One of the stewardesses came over and handed me two white pills that she said were for my stomach. I took them and woke up over LAX. Oh well I was in LA and feeling better. Now I have to find my cousin who I haven't seen since I was little.

I found Alice, that was her name, or rather she found me. Alice had seen pictures of me. Alice was very nice and her daughter was too. We went to her place Alice lived in Hollywood. I was ecstatic because Alice lived right around the corner from two movie studios. In my mind it was on!

After I changed and got dressed we went to a talent agency to get me registered. It was wild, as we pulled up there was one of the stars off of a sitcom walking down the street. I laughed because the star looked like he was a drunk. While I was registering the company told us that they were looking for extras to work on Oliver Stoney's film *The Deers*. They asked us were we interested which we were so we had the job.

I had only been in town two hours and had a job as an extra on a major film. Things seemed to be on the way up as they say. Alice also had a hook up that landed me a job as an extra on Rickey Towney's movie *The Six Headaches*. This was the film I wanted to work on. I could care less about Oliver Stoney's flick, everybody I knew would go see Rickey Towney's movie so I had to be seen on film.

I enjoyed working on the *Six Headaches* because I got a chance to see what black stars are like when they aren't acting. Boy was that an eye opener when it came to dispelling the myths Hollywood creates! First off when you get real close to them you realize that a lot of the good looks are make-up. I also learned that a good cameraman and director can make an ugly person look good.

Another thing I learned was many of the actors were fake as hell. Some of them would not speak if you said something to them. I remembered some advice I had gotten years before from a dude who said, "Stars aren't nothing but cats who have gotten a break. They are no different than you." I was armed with this mentality so I was never awe struck when I met the stars. I was mainly trying to see where their heads were and if they were real. In most cases the ones I met were fake as hell.

Don't get me wrong there were some cool ones who gave me good advice. Mich White was the coolest person I met on a movie set. I wrapped to Mich while he was getting ready to do a scene and he kept it real. When I snuck into the wrap party Mich came by the bar and we talked some more he was cool.

I remember meeting Ken Ebony Wills at that same party. What struck me about him was the fact that he was taller than me and built. In my head I was thinking he should have been playing hoop. Ken was cool, I asked him if they were looking for new talent on his show he wasn't. But he was cool about it. There was one thing that closed the book for me on the LA lifestyle, the homosexuality.

When people say, "Everything is not as it seems." They must be talking about Hollywood. I remember being on *The Deers* set and seeing this dude walking around hovering over this chick. From the back it looked as if she was kind of tight with long hair. That was back when I was thinking I was the mack so I'm scheming in my head as soon as the dude stops hovering over this broad I would go check her out. They did a lot of takes for the same scene and I didn't get the chance until lunchtime.

Dude left to go get the chick some food or something it was time to strike. I eased over in range to see the broad from the front. I felt like a line out of an old Blowfly song, "What I thought was bitch was nothing but a man!" This revelation had me tripping what I thought was a damn chick was some fag in a wig! To make matters worse the big dude was catering to it like it was a woman! This was ridiculous to me it was too many fine women out there to be gay.

The real shock hit me when I was on *The Six Headaches* set. That's where I saw that some of the black actors on that set were flaming hot! I mentioned it to Alice and she just laughed it off saying, "Many of the actors are gay, they act manly while the camera is rolling but once it's off they come out." It was sickening. There was some fine black women just hanging around the set of *The Six Headaches*. They were just waiting to be pounced upon and these fools wanted to be gay. What a waste, this is what lead me to want to go straight home.

Now it wasn't all bad in Los Angeles there was my cousins who lived off Crewshaw, they were fun. The first time I met them, when we pulled up, one was chasing the other with a rifle. I thought, "These are my kind of people!" I wanted to hang with them in the hood I didn't want to be bothered with Alice and the gay Hollywood lifestyle. That had gotten old fast, I wanted to be around some real blacks. Alas that was not to be though, I was stuck in phony Hollywood.

Alice must have gotten the wrong impression from my mother when Mama told her I was about to graduate from college. Alice must have figured I was one of those pro-Negroes ready to grasp the American dream, wrong. I was ghetto as they come so I was not impressed with buying five dollar hamburgers at Jimmy Rickets. Or spending twenty to thirty dollars at a store that sold second hand clothes.

I remember asking Alice, "Whose clothes are these? Have they been donated by stars or something?" The answer was no they didn't know who donated the clothes. This was stupid to me cause the prices were just as high as if I would have went to Target or some place to get a new pair of Levis. This was the Hollywood way though no wonder everybody was gay. I was miserable living there. I could not drink. Alice wanted me to do the things she liked, which to me was garbage. It was time for me to go home. I had saved me two hundred dollars for just this type of emergency. The coup de grace came one night.

I had walked to the store and was guzzling a forty when I seen this big booty chick on the bus stop. I hollered, "Where the party at?" It turned around and said, with a voice that sounded like James Earl Jones playing Darth Vader, "What kind of party you want?" I threw the brew down crossed the street and went home. The next day I told Alice it was time for me to go home. The following day I was at LAX waiting on my flight back to reality, thank God!

When I got back to Racine everyone wanted to know what happened in LA. "Why was I back so soon?" Was the question on my parent's lips. When I tried to explain how the situation was nobody wanted to hear it, so I stopped trying. I tried to tell some of my partners I had been in a movie but no one believed me. This was the first time my eyes became clear to the fact that most people can only grasp what their environment gives them. The people I had attempted to tell my experiences to had let their reality be defined by Racine. They could no longer imagine anything but what they saw day to day. I stopped trying to tell people about my adventures in LA. It was some years later when I started telling a few people about me being in *The Six Headaches* and then it was only a whisper.

That summer was a trip. Mama had sold the Ultimate Homeboy Car so I was back to having to borrow her car again. The county didn't want me back because I was going through the process of getting paid from the accident I was in the previous summer. I wound up getting a job working in a foundry that made parts for car batteries. It was a stupid job but it kept me in beer money and I was able to save some scratch for school. I had just about worn my parents out as far as staying with them so I was glad when the end of August rolled around. It was time to go back to Willyfarce one more time.

My last semester at Willyfarce was just a formality. I was tired of school and just wanted to get the hell out of there. I really hadn't been challenged there since junior year so I was burning daylight just to get out. I took twenty-one hours that last semester, all bullshit classes. I had taken all of my major courses my sophomore and junior years so I had a bunch of elective courses. The classes didn't interest me. My hopes of graduating with a 3.0 flew out of the window. I really didn't care. I received my only "D" of my college career that semester.

The class I received my "D" in was music. The teacher was white, the class was a joke. The class was supposed to be about music history, not. The fool came to an all black school and was trying to tell us music started with the Greeks. I knew the man was wrong so did my other two partners, Nick and Carlo. We mentioned the African drum and the fool blew us off like it didn't exist. This to me was an insult to Willyfarce. How the hell could some white man come into a black school and tell these lies and not be fired? You think a Negro could go to Harvard and tell lies? I think you know the answer to that.

All I needed to pass the class was a "D" so that was all I wanted period. I had slacked off so much though I was worried about an "F." I will never forget the day I went to pick up my final grade.

When I walked into the teacher's office he was sitting behind his desk with a smirk on his face. The imbecile thought he was in control of the situation, wrong. I had come with Nick and Carlo, the three bold radicals of the class. We were the ones who laughed at the man in his face. I went in first to get my verdict. The teacher looked at me with mock pity on his face. I already knew what kind of fool he was so I said, "Did I make a C? I need a C." The teacher pulled out his grade book with a sorrowful look on his face and went to my name and said, "You made a 68 average. You missed a "C" by two points."

I looked at the man and asked, "You mean my grade is a "D"? He looked at me like he really cared and replied, "Sorry you were so close." the idiot was going to go on I busted out, "Hell yeah! That's all I needed to get out of this punk ass place!" The bastard looked dumbfounded then it hit him and I nodded, "Yep, I thought I had an F goodbye."

I left his office and told my guys the good news. I had finished college. I sat down and waited for them to come out. Nick and Carlos were back there awhile I thought, "Damn they taking a long time." I got up and went back to where the boy's office was. I seen Carlos standing outside of the office I said, "What's up?" Carlos said, "We both got D's." I looked in the office Nick was attempting to get the dude to re-figure his grade. I looked at the cat he was glowing as Nick asked him to move him up to a "C". I heard the dude say, "You were so close." I pulled Carlos to the side and asked him, "What did he tell you?" Carlos replied, "He told me I just missed a "C". I said, "Carlos the fool told me the same thing! He wants us to beg, the man's trying to run a game on us!" Carlos thought for a second then said, "Skip that I need the grade." I turned and walked out of the room. I don't know if the moron changed it or not for them. I could have used a "C" instead of a "D" also, but I never would have kissed that peasant's ass to get it.

One last thing happened before I left Willyfarce. Right before it was time to leave for the semester I received a letter from the resident director for all of the dorms. It informed me I had to come to the director's office and talk to him before I left. I went down to his office a few days before I left. The director told me that I was a bad influence on the younger students. I was also trouble in the dorms. In short I was kicked off campus.

95

The next semester I would have to stay off campus. I looked at this fool and asked, "You mean next semester I can't live in the dorms?" The director replied, "Yes!" He said the shit with force like Marty Albit does after a score. I sat and looked at the dumb Negro and wondered, "Where do they make negros like him?" I then laughed in his face and said, "Fool I'm graduating! This was my last semester!" I got up and walked out I didn't even bother to turn around to see the look on the Negro's face.

My four-year ordeal was over. I had graduated on time. I did not have to stay an extra year or even an extra semester. Four years for a four-year degree, basic math any first grader can do. I remember when I first thought about college. The thoughts that came to my mind were *Animal House*. That was how I wanted my career to go. Well at the end of *Animal House* the Deltas were suspended from their campus. If I had to go back to Willyfarce I had been thrown off campus. I had succeeded.

PFA had become just me, the other brothers had left and created some other garbage. I was glad they left they were nerdy as hell anyway. I hadn't really learned shit about television from Willyfarce but the black history I had soaked up outside of the classroom carried me a long way.

CHAPTER XIII
1991

The New Year came and I was skeptical about the future. Not many people come out of college with the hook-up I had. I only owed five grand in college loans. I had nine thousand coming to me from the accident I had gotten in two summers ago. So technically I was set, mentally I wasn't.

The only thing I knew for sure was that I did not want to sell out. At Willyfarce I used to hear people talk about the revolution was coming in 1995. Well I thought I have four years to burn until it happens. My original plans were for me to move to LA when I finished college but after my adventure there that wasn't an option. As I stated working in corporate America wasn't my bag of tea either so what should I do? Party like never before, that was the ticket.

I took the money I got and bought a car from my boy Brian. Mama and Chuck were tired of my bullshit so I had to go. I understood. I found an apartment on Jacato drive where all the blacks lived. There wasn't anything but women on that street and I loved it. The apartment reminded me of a college dorm except for all of the kids. Now that the housing situation was taken care of it was time to party big time.

Brian and I hooked up a deejay gig at the New Yorker. This was the bomb! We already went there every weekend any way now we could get paid for it. Around this time I broke one of my own rules I followed the next man's advice and path about a situation.

I had met and boned a lot of women in Racine at this time. Brian and I were damn near doing who we wanted too when we wanted too. I didn't give a damn about anything except filling my glass and busting a nut when I could and on who I could. Enter Halle.

The situation went like this. I was hanging up at Lafayette center just acting a fool tripping when Halle came in. I tripped because I knew Halle when we were younger. Halle was just a skinny chick who looked like Morris Day. Now Halle was a woman thick as hell. Needless to say I had to see if Halle still had the schoolgirl crush for me. I'll never forget thinking, "Damn, Halle tight as hell. I hope she don't remember some of the stuff I pulled." What I had pulled was to play Halle for my ex-girl Tina back in highschool. Halle didn't hold it against me, at least that is what she said so we hooked up.

Halle lived in Milwaukee so I would come up and see her once or twice a week. To me Halle was just another freak, something to relieve tension in. So one day I was rapping to Brian about some freaks we were hooking up with and he mentioned Halle. I told Brian Halle was just a sex thing. Brian then ran some game that everybody needs a main girl, some weak noise like that. Alarm bells were going off in my head because that was never my outlook on life. I lived for the challenge of the birds in the bush, skip the one in the hand. I should have stuck to my guns on that topic. What changed my mind was stupid.

One Friday night I was up at Total tripping with PJ and Fats when Halle got out of a car with her friends and started walking past. PJ said, "Yeah Frank don't you feel sick look at old girl now. Don't you wish you could fuck her?" PJ was grinning at me. Fats was laughing and saying, "Damn Halle tight as hell! Look at dude's face!" I had a funny look on my face because it was dawning on me the chick was fine and Halle wouldn't be a bad main squeeze.

So to save face, PJ and Fats didn't know I was already boning her, I said, "Halle come on let's go!" Without hesitation Halle turned and went to my car. PJ and Fat's mouths were open. I just looked at them and grinned and walked away. I felt like a top "G" at that point. As I got into the car Halle was already inside I glanced at her thighs and thought, "I can live with this." and drove off.

That was one of my worst decisions I ever made. I regretted that decision like Hitler did for invading Russia. Before it was over the girl had ran a game on Keith. Halle started boning him and my buddy Dee and whomever else she could. Poor Keith I think he went crazy over her. Keith didn't realize the broad was crazy. Halle had never forgotten what I had put on her back in school. Halle was trying to get me back by doing all of my friends. The situation hurt for a minute because Keith was my guy. A female should have never come between us. Oh well it happens I still have love for him.

After I got out of that crazy six-week relationship I just basically chilled at my apartment. I worked every blue moon when it suited me. I spent money though like it was water. My grandmother wanted me to sign up for general assistance. I balked at the idea. My father told me to go ahead and do it so Grama wouldn't be mad. I got one months rent but that was basically it. I never would be at home when the care worker came to check on me. The situation was ridiculous to me. The little money they were giving people you could make more working at a $4.25 slave job. The welfare system just wasn't for me.

May of that year I got a letter from Willyfarce asking me was I going to participate in the graduation exercises. I laughed because graduation didn't mean a damn thing to me. Mama was all excited about the graduation. The problem was that Willyfarce's graduation was on the same day Mama was scheduled to graduate from Gateway with her Associates Degree. Mama was willing to forgo her graduation to come to mine. I did not want that to happen at all. I didn't give a damn about my degree. Mama on the other hand had studied hard and was graduating in the top percentile of her class. I had blown my 3.0 GPA my last semester. I finished with a 2.86, some garbage. To me it just made sense for Mama to go to her own graduation.

Also deep down I really did not want to share my graduation with anybody. I did not want all that, "Look at my baby," talk around me. That whole scenario always reeked of phoniness. I felt no one deserved to be proud of what I did but me. Why put on a sham show. I had cut my ass while I was staying with Mama and Chuck, so why go all the way to Ohio to fake it? I told Mama I was not going to the commencement. Mama seemed disappointed about it. I was not. I really did not give a damn about it.

Ronnie, the twins' cousin came by the pad and told me he was going down to Willyfarce to see the twins walk the stage. Ronnie wanted to know if I wanted to ride down there with him. I was intending on going to Mama's graduation so I told Ronnie no.

Somehow I wound up down at Willyfarce chilling at the exercises. Even though I was down there I did not want to walk across the stage. I just came down there to drink with my partners one last time. When I was in the hallway talking with some friends Mrs. Bean saw me. Mrs. Bean was my academic advisor while I attended Willyfarce. Mrs. Bean was also my favorite instructor down there. When Mrs. Bean saw I did not have a cap and gown on she wanted to know why. I told Mrs. Bean I was not walking I was just down there to see my friends walk. I had left the college environment three months ago. The thrill I once had was gone.

Mrs. Bean wasn't buying the story. By this time one of the ladies who worked in the library came up. The woman knew me from being in the library so much. I guess the woman liked me because she pulled her black gown off and handed it to me.

I was shocked and embarrassed to say the least. I tried to wave the two ladies off but they insisted I go into the gym and sit down. The said I had paid my dues and I deserved to walk with every other graduate. They flagged an usher down and had him escort me in.

As I walked in I looked around at all of my fellow graduates. They were all nice and fresh in their cap and gowns. I had on someone else's gown and no cap. The only place the usher could sit me was up front.

So here I am walking in late and being escorted up to the front of the gym. I seen some heads turning looking at me. I heard someone whisper, "He graduating?" I quickly stated "Yeah, what you thought fool." As I sat down it dawned on me. Since no one had seen me around campus that spring they figured I had just dropped out. The students had played me cheap.

The only reason I had to come back in the fall of 1990 was the fact I sat out one semester to roll dope in 1989. I guess some fools thought I was behind or just coming to school to party, wrong. I went eight semesters, two a year, for a four year degree. Nothing more nothing less.

Anyway once the exercises got started I really stood out. These fools had been down there practicing for two or three days. They were turning and doing different things. I was lost. As usual I just didn't seem to fit into this type of scene. I just laughed.

The big moment came. My name was called last because I got there late. As I walked across the stage I felt like laughing at the absurdity of the whole thing. This school was a joke. Here I was about to receive my degree and shake hands with the president of the school. Keep in mind a few months before, the president had seen me drunk and acting a fool at a basketball game and made a comment about I need to be on the cheerleading team I was so hyped. I guess the president felt that way because I had grabbed some cheerleader's pom pons.

I grabbed my degree out of the president's hand and shook his other and walked on. I looked out at the crowd and smiled to myself. I was glad I didn't have my family there cheering me on. I would have felt cheaper than I was already feeling. I was ready to hit the liquor store. It is funny. I have graduated from high school and college but I do not have one single picture of me in a cap and gown. Thank God!

Back in Racine things were getting kind of tight. My scratch was running low and I could sense a change coming upon the horizon. I could see the handwriting on the wall the party was over. Before this happened though I had one last memorable event in Racine.

The neighborhood centers were the place where everybody hung out at in Racine. I had finished school and had been living back in Racine for about two or three months. I rarely went anywhere though I would only go to centers every once and awhile. I didn't want to become "Racinefied."

One day I went up to Lafayette with Brian and we seen PJ and Fats. We went over by them and started talking. Big K pulled up he had just had his car painted and a new system installed. Big K had a Seventy-Eight Oldsmobile clean as hell. So we hopped in to ride around to see how it rode. We made a few blocks when PJ wanted to go back up to Lafayette. So we headed back, by this time it was a crowd up there.

Everybody knew PJ and Fats. Most people knew my face from being with them even if they didn't know me. So Fats came up with this idea to throw some one-dollar bills out to the crowd. I was cool with it. We dropped PJ off and sped around the corner to get our money together. Fats had about twenty one dollar bills, Big K had about twenty or thirty and I had twenty. So we set the tape in the car to the Geto Boys' tune *City Under Siege*. It was agreed that we were going to pull up in front of the doors and look straight ahead looking hard while the song began.

When we got around to the center the crowd was bigger and it was like they could sense we were going to do something. Big K was driving. Fats was sitting in the passenger seat and I was sitting on top of the car out of the sunroof. The song started, "I like to teach the world to be a dope man just like me, I like to front the world some dope and let them sell for me!" While this was playing people had come close to the car to see what was going on.

I had on some black sunglasses and Fats and Big K were sitting looking hard facing the front. I had my arms crossed so after the song said, "For me!" The bass line came in and the lyrics went, "Born in the ghetto as a street thug at age sixteen I started selling cheap drugs!" When that bass line hit Fats, Big K, and I threw the dollars into the crowd! From my position I could see the money I threw just flutter into the crowd. The crowd went crazy!

We had to pull off because they were getting too close to the car in their frenzy to get those dollars! We sped out of the lot tripping cause the scene was hyped! We went around the corner and I got Fats bankroll and Big K's and added it to mine. When we went back into the lot I was still in the sunroof looking hard people started coming to the car screaming like we were stars. I just sat there and fanned myself with this big roll of twenties and tens. Looking down on them like I was a king.

The next day the phone rang Mama was on the other end. She said, "So Frank James you got money to just throw around huh?" At first I didn't know what Mama was talking about then it hit me. Someone must have told my mama about my exploits. The news spread like wildfire. I saw my sister Chasity and she asked me for some of that money I was throwing around. I looked at Chasity and she told me how people were coming up to her at school talking about what had happened. They were saying I had bought them lunch. Chasity had gotten tired of hearing about it. Chasity really got pissed when she went to class and the teacher started talking about some guy throwing money around. I laughed that was a small price to pay to have such a down brother.

That was my last hurrah in Racine, Wisconsin. Little did those people realize that two weeks later I would be damn near broke wishing I had those ones. I took a trip to Detroit to kick it with Len. I met a chick Len was screwing named Diedra. Diedra was also doing a big time dealer and told me if I came over there she could get me on. I didn't have a damn thing to lose and I was damn near broke so I told Diedra I would be back in a week to take her up on her offer.

The main reason I left though was I could feel a change coming. I'm not saying I was all that in Racine but I did have a kind of image to uphold. The way things were heading I knew I was not going to be able to uphold it. I didn't want to lose face in front of people who I grew up with and had respect for me so I left. As they say you can run but you cannot hide, I knew this. At least it would not be in front of people who knew me from the old days. Detroit here I come, it was here that I became, "The Man."

CHAPTER XIV

Detroit

The motor city is the rawest city on any map. Detroit. Since I was little I always wanted to move to Detroit. From Mojo to the status of being the murder capital of the world Detroit always held a kind of fascination over me. It was just natural that I moved there when I finished college.

When I first got in the city we partied very hard on Ward. Our house quickly became known as the party spot. Mary J, Len's mother, drank *Martell*. Ned, her man, drank *Mohawk* vodka. Len and I consumed gin and *Ole English* like fish in water. Diedra was working on getting me hooked up with some dude to get some work. I never once tried to go and get a professional job when I got to Detroit. I guess I came for the fast life and wouldn't settle for anything less. Diedra called about two weeks after I got there to tell me she had put me down with her boy. I was supposed to meet him at Diedra's house the next day. I was a bit nervous but I thought, "This is what you came for so it is no time for second thoughts now." I had to at least see what the game was like in the big city.

The following day I went by Diedra's house to meet the cats she had hooked me up with. When I got there Diedra ran the situation down for me. Diedra had told the dude I was her little brother. Diedra told him to look out for me. I thanked Diedra and then asked, "What will I be doing?" Diedra didn't know that but she did say I would probably be in southwest Detroit. I sat back on the couch and chilled. A few minutes later a horn blew and Diedra went outside. Diedra called me out and I was introduced to these two cats in a big Bronco. They told me to ride with them. I gave my car keys to Diedra and said, "I'll holler." We then pulled off to go to the spot.

I forgot the dudes' names whom I was riding with because they really didn't talk much. When we go to the area they were working out of I remember saying, "Damn, there are a lot of burned out houses." The guy on the passenger side said, "These are the results of us trying to keep a hold on our area. Niggas tried to come in the area and sell we had to burn their ass out." I sat back and thought, "Whoa, this is a long way from Sixth Street." I was upbeat though because I knew there was a lot of money to be made. It was just asking for a down brother like myself to pick it up. They introduced me to an old man who was moving work for these cats. My job was to be his bodyguard, protect him from some cats who wanted to burn his house down. The dudes I was working with were supplying the old guy and I guess he was valuable to them. Before the dudes I rode over there with left one gave me a beeper number. He told me to beep him if any trouble came my way. They drove off.

I started talking to the old man to see what kind of scenario I was in. The old man ran his hustle down for me it went like this. The old man was rolling for two different factions at once without either knowing about the other. In short the old man was playing two sides from the middle. One more thing was my pay was two hundred and fifty dollars a week, plus ten dollars a day for expenses.

I was tripping off of this salary plan. I was used to getting a percentage off of every hundred made. The salary thing really got ridiculous after I seen how this house was booming. After I had sat there about two hours I could tell that this man had a gold mine. The old man had to move around fifteen hundred to two thousand dollars a day in rocks. I felt like I had been shitted on but I chilled because Diedra had my car. Also I really did not know where the hell I was. I decided I would learn as much as I could from this old fool and use it later. The old man's operation was cake I'll have to admit. The old man had some white boy who handled all of the sales so he didn't sell nothing. While the old man was showing me the place he told me about the trouble he was running into with some other cats. The old man was having problems because he was selling dope in their area. The way the old man was talking had me tripping because in Racine you sold where you wanted. This was wild because these fools were over here burning up there own neighborhood for the right to sell illegal drugs. Quite literally fighting for the right to go to prison.

The trouble the old man was having was taking place at night. The place never closed and the old man was having trouble guarding the rear of the joint. The old man had already dodged one bullet when someone had tried to firebomb the place. The firebomb bounced off a wall and hit the ground still intact. This enabled the old man to grab it and dispose of it. This was why the old man needed me to guard the rear entrance of the spot, whoopee!.

We were walking back into the front when a crack-head approached us. The crack head was a burnt out young white girl. She beckoned the old man to the side and they whispered something when the old man turned to me he was grinning. The old man said, "I have to go take care of business with this client. Make yourself at home your job starts at night fall."

I went to the fridge and grabbed a brew and watched as the old man escorted the white girl into his bedroom to take care of business. I had noticed there seemed to be a lot of white trash around this area. I laughed as I thought about the old man. I figured that old fool was in seventh heaven with all of these young white girls who smoke dope. I was betting that the old man tricked off more dope than he sold getting his fill of white meat.

As I was sitting in the front I watched the people come and go, this place was booming. I needed my own spot so I could come up. I was pissed cause here I was the greatest criminal genius on the planet, the black Lex Luthor, guarding an old trick. To me this was a great waste of talent. I was remembering to make sure when I got big that I never blow such talent on trivial pursuits.

The old man came out zipping his pants up and said, "Brother, you want to get you some of that? She fresh and sucks a mean johnson trust me." The old man winked at me knowingly. I looked over his shoulder into the room the white girl was looking at me rubbing her nipples. I looked at the old man and said, "Man, I'm here to make money. I can get laid anytime." I guess the old man seen the look on my face and could tell I was serious he went back into the room and shut the door. A few minutes later the broad came out of the room clutching a little plastic bag she was rushing to get out of the house. She had gotten her pay and was off to smoke it.

There was one major set back that I noticed about the old man's operation, it was hot as a firecracker. I figured if this place was booming like it seemed to be doing then the police had to know what was going on. I also knew enough about America to know that if you were black and was exploiting white folks your days were numbered. This old man's clientele had a big percentage of Caucasians. This was trouble in my book. I was keeping my eyes open for the raid van or whatever the hell they use in Detroit. I didn't need a state sponsored vacation.

Later on in the evening when it was getting close to dark the old man came up to me and said, "It's time to go to work." The old man then turned and walked into a room and I followed him. The old man went to a dresser and opened a drawer. It was full of rifles. The old man grabbed a machine gun and asked which one did I want I chose a riot action pump. The old man led me upstairs to a balcony that was overlooking the back yard. The old man then said, "Watch the back yard and garage, this is where they will most likely try to burn us out from." I agreed and the old man went back down the stairs and cut off the light. I hollered to the old man, "Lock the door and don't come back up unless you holler out cause I'm blasting if I hear anything." The old man agreed and added, "I'm glad to have you watching my back." I grunted and the old man left. I heard him bolting the top lock on the door downstairs. I sat back in the dark and relaxed holding the pump thinking about the situation. I was tripping because this was not the way I envisioned my career to start, watching some spot for another fool. I had chosen my path though and it was too late to turn back. I look back on that picture now and laugh at the situation.

Here I was ready to blow some fool into oblivion, or at least bust some rounds off for some other man. I wasn't even making the big money just a flunkey and I was ready to kill or at least attempt it. Add in the fact that I had only shot a gun twice in my life and the situation really is a laugher.

As I was sitting in the dark looking down into the back yard, I heard a noise in the stairwell. It was showtime. I cocked the pump and faced the stairs ready to cut loose on who ever came up those stairs. I was cool as a cucumber ready to blast when I heard the old man call my name. I asked the old man what he wanted, relaxing my finger off the trigger. The old man called up, "We have to shut down, the police are rolling heavy and it looks like they may raid us!" I glanced out over the back yard then eased down the stairs.

The old man had left the door open and I went outside and then entered the back door to the kitchen. The old man was inside telling the white boy to shut down all operations. The old man then went into a room and started stashing dope. The old man then held his hand out for the pump. I grabbed a towel off of the table and wiped the gun off where my hands had been, the old man seen the play and nodded approvingly.

After the old man had stashed all of the weapons I asked him, "What is the deal?" He replied, "We about to get the hell out of here." The old man then walked out of the room and I followed him outside. We started walking down the block. My luck must have carried over from Wisconsin.

As soon as we were halfway down the block a detective car pulled up in front of the house. The old man glanced back and said, "Damn they see us!" I asked the old man, "Are you clean?" He replied, "Yes." I said, "Keep walking then." While we were walking narcos, narcotic police, rolled up next to us cruising. I kept looking straight ahead walking at an easy pace. I wasn't worried because I hadn't sold nothing. The cops flashed the light on us but we just kept walking and they just drove off.

I relaxed and looked at the old man I asked, "What now?" The old man looked back towards the spot. I could tell that the old man wanted to open back up but I had enough of this. I decided for him I said, "Man they only waiting for you to open up so they can catch your ass dirty." The old man looked at me and I continued, "I'm your bodyguard but I'm not no fool. We both know we just avoided a case or at least harassment by the police by five minutes. Let's close we can make it back up tomorrow." The old man thought a moment and then agreed.

We went up by another spot to grab his van. The old man said, "I'll take you home." I was glad the old man volunteered to give me a ride cause I sure as hell didn't have a way home. Before the old man took me home we rode past the dope house first. As we rode past we saw the white boy trying to sell dope again in front of the house. I said, "Man you better stop that fool." The white boy saw the van and walked over. The old man told him to shut down and lay low. The cat got mad but he went back in front of the house and we seen him waving customers away. After we saw he was shutting down we drove off.

I had the old man drop me off on the corner of Plymouth and Schaeffer. I really didn't want the old man to know where I lived because I was through working with him. Before we parted ways I made sure I got my ten dollar food pay from the old man. The old man gave me instructions on how to get back to his house but I wasn't listening. I knew I wasn't going back. I told him he should go somewhere and lay up tonight and be cool. The old man agreed and drove off. If I seen that man again in Detroit I did not know him. Hell if he walked into my apartment right now, I wouldn't recognize him.

I took the ten spot and went by the store and grabbed me a forty ounce and walked to the pad. I paged Diedra and told her to bring my ride. Diedre asked me how it went I told her okay. Diedra was cool I didn't offer details and she did not ask. I knew I was not going back to work for those cats because they needed flunkeys and minions. Those two characteristics were not in my job description.

The next day I decided I would try the number they gave me to page if I got into trouble. I wanted to let them know the deal. It has been eight years since then and no one still hasn't returned the page. This pissed me off. I was tripping because this let me know that these Negroes were full of shit. I was glad I wasn't in any real trouble because they didn't have my back. That observation just made it easier for me to quit. I told Ned about the job I had and what had happened when I called to check in. Ned said, "Man fuck them niggas. At least you seen how they was cut before you really got into business with them." I agreed with Ned whole-heartedly.

A few days later Diedra came by. I guess the dude Diedre hooked me up with gave her some flack about my performance. Diedre came by questioning me and attempting to charge me up. Diedra was upset because she had looked out for me and I had flaked out. I just sat and listened to Diedra. I remembered an old saying I had read as I listened to Diedra rant on. "Never argue with a fool because people walking by cannot tell the difference between you and them." I just kept on drinking brew. The situation wasn't worth explaining.

Since my hustle had fell through I had to get a job, I needed money. Ned got me hooked up with this janitor job cleaning a dry-cleaning factory. It was only twenty hours a week but it was scratch. This was my first job in Detroit.

It was hot as hell in that factory. I would go in at four or five in the evening and it would be burning up in the place. I was a trooper though I used this to start losing some of the weight I had gained in college. I also started doing push-ups and sit-ups. I was trying to get myself in some type of shape. My plight seems wild now because here I was with a Bachelor of Arts taking out the trash for $4.25 an hour. I never looked at it that away when I was working though. I was doing what I had to do to make it.

After I got my first check Len came home and said, "We going to a bachelor party for Hugh." Hugh was a guy who was marrying a girl Len knew. I was cool with it I was always down to party. We went to a place that was filled with wonder, a place where dreams are lived out. We went to the Black Orchid. This was when Detroit started to get interesting.

I'll never forget the first time I walked into the joint. I had never been to a topless bar before in my life. As I walked in the door after being patted down my mouth dropped. I tripped because there were women up on stage dancing naked! This really tripped me out because the females were fine as hell! Me with my country self couldn't figure out why women this fine would be up there shaking their ass.

I was cool though until this fine sister came in. She walked in with some biker shorts on and a biker top, man my penis got hard! I nudged Len and said, "Look!" He did and I remember saying, "I know she ain't going to take her clothes off and dance!" Len didn't reply because some other female was standing over him putting her butt in his face. I stopped looking at the fine chick with the clothes on and started eyeballing the yellow one dancing over Len and I. I was enjoying this!

Just when I thought it couldn't get any better I looked up and old girl was up on stage in nothing but a g-string. My mouth dropped. My damn hands started sweating, I downed my drink and hollered for a double of *Jack Daniels*. Len must have seen the look on my face because I heard him say, "Damn she is fine as hell." She was on the main stage Len hollered, "Go tip her man!" I was just sitting enjoying the view. A fine black woman always brings a smile to my face no matter what I'm doing or how I'm feeling. I'm surprised my head didn't split in two because I was grinning like a damn jack-o-lantern. I got up enough nerve to go up to the stage and get a closer look.

This chick had it going on! Her stomach was flat as an ironing board and she had to be around 5'8" or 5'9" at least, a stallion! I pulled out my scratch, wishing I had one of my dope dealing bankrolls, and held out some ones. She came up to where I was standing and leaned over smiling and asked, "Are those for me?" I don't think I said anything I just nodded my head. She laughed I guess she got a kick out of this trick who was standing in front of her with a school boy first love look on his face.

She stood up and jiggled her butt in my face then bent over and put her breasts right on my face real quick! Man I almost fainted then she put her leg by my hands so I could place the ones in her garter belt. I mumbled, "Damn, you fine ass hell. What is your name?" As she was looking down at me she noticed my hands were shaking as I put the money in her garter. She laughed and leaned back over and said, "Thanks. My name is Yolonda." and walked away. I gave her every dime I had and every dollar I could get form Len. I got a lap dance from her but what I really was trying to do was get to know her better. She told me she had a man while she was putting her breasts in my face. I was reduced to the stage of just babbling like, "You can use me for whatever needs you have, toilet paper even." All of this was to no avail I couldn't score. This was probably the best thing that could have happened to me. One reason was even as I look back upon the scenario I still know I would have been married. If that female would have given me half of a chance I would have fell hopelessly in love. But she didn't and I'm not so forward I say.

To finish things off I left there broke and smelling like some wonderful breasts and covered in body glitter. Two things became clear to me. One, Len was a square as far as the streets were concerned. Len had been in Detroit all his life and knew nothing of the Black Orchid. Two, only tricks give up their money to dancers. These were the first of many lessons I was to learn in my adventures in the "Dirty D."

Detroit was haven for a party person. Back in the days I was the black male version of Spuds Mackenzie. Len though did not share my views. Len only wanted to drink play cards and stare in his girl's face. This scene wasn't for me! Hell I did not come to Detroit to learn how to play Bid Whist. I came to see the sights. The only reason I was even looking to Len to kick it was the fact that we had kicked it so tough in college. I guess though those were Len's college days, he was so much older now, twenty-two, that he could no longer kick it.

I was cool with that though but it would get funny when I would mention places I had heard about. Len would not know how to get there and Mary J would hint that those were rough areas. I'll be damned if I was going to live in a city and be scared to go outside. Detroit was rough but I figured if you give respect you get respect. The answer to all of this was simple; roll solo and I could live with that.

After about two months reality started setting in. It was four people in the house and it was never anything there to eat. One reason was the fact that no one ever had any money. I look back upon that time and thank my lucky stars that Mary J did not put me out. The deed Mary J did by taking a broke man in is one I'll forever be in her debt for and is greatly appreciated.

For the first time in my life I didn't have a dime to spare. I learned how to roll pennies up. I remember rolling pennies up and going to buy a loaf of cheap bread and salami for two dollars to grub on. I did this more than a couple of times. Don't get me wrong I wasn't looking for Mary J or anybody to feed me, my hard times were my own. Many days Ned would look out for me. Ned would buy food and didn't care if I ate or not.

I needed some fast work and I needed more than twenty hours a week. In came the temporary services. I went to work at these type of places because you could go to work on Monday and get paid Friday. I always needed fast money. I never had the luxury to wait on a position to open. Give me the first place that has an opening I don't give a damn where it is or what the job is as long as it pays. The joint was Switch-Pro, the job packing auto parts. Our job was to switch the auto parts that came in out of Japanese boxes and into American boxes. How ironic the same American companies that scream American made were buying parts from Mazda and other Japanese companies. I met some cool people there. Leroy was my kick it buddy for a while and Cleveland became a good friend too. Cleveland had a big family that included a set of the finest twins I have ever seen in my life. These females make those two flakey ones that were on TV look like what they are, crap. My main guy though was BJ.

BJ was cool. BJ would talk trash with me all night. We were working second shift and didn't get off until one o'clock in the morning, so you needed something to make the time go by. Trash talking came in very handy. When we weren't talking trash on the job, we were drinking at lunchtime. We would go to the store and buy us a beer or half-pint to sip on to make the time go by. BJ was one of the few people who could crack on me back. This made him cool to me. When we got our checks on Friday we would go pick up a fifth and drink and chill, Cleveland him and me after work.

The fall of 1991 I made a decision to get finger waves in the top of my head. I had seen some cats with their hair done and I thought it was tight. What really made me get it done was the fact that I had overslept one Saturday morning and couldn't get my haircut. Mister Del's, the barbershop I went to opened at five o'clock in the morning. If you were not there at five-fifteen waiting, you were going to be there all day. The line would get long fast as hell in there. On this particular morning I overslept until six thirty. I told Jaime, Ned's son, "Man I'm going to get finger waves." Jaime didn't believe I would do it. When Jaime heard me getting information from Mary J about where her hair salon was, he jumped up and wanted to go.

The Ritz was the salon and Wanda was the hairdresser. I remember tripping because it was some fine women in the place getting their hair done. Wanda who was hooking me up was fine as hell also. I was in seventh heaven. I told Wanda I wanted waves in the top and the sides faded. Three hours later I stepped out into the lobby where Jaime was, in the immortal words of Fred Sanford, "Fried dyed and laid to the side!" Jaime said, "Look at the pretty boy." I waved Jaime off laughing. When I got home Len said, "Look out world here come Goldie!" I grinned because my hair was tight. As I look back. I realize that the longer my hair got the more screwed up my situation became.

CHAPTER XV

I worked at Switch-Pro about six months just burning daylight. It was then that I noticed one truth that has been with me on every bullshit job I had since then. The main supervisors were white and the majority of the work force was black. Just like the plantation the whites had their hand-picked Negroes to do their dirty work for them.

One supervisor named Rico had my boy Leroy in his pocket. Leroy thought Rico was cool. I saw Rico as just another greasy piece of beige trash. I say beige because Rico wasn't all the way white he had some Italian or Mexican in him. All Rico wanted to do was try to bone any black chick he could. I had to cut Leroy loose because of his dedication to Rico. Leroy went along with Rico, even when Rico would do foul stuff to the brothers. Leroy and Rico would sit back and watch a cat run the wrong labels on his packages and then tell him the job was wrong. This came after the brother had run two or three thousand of the packages. All kind of crazy stuff that should have lead to Rico and Leroy getting their skulls cracked.

The icing on the cake was one night I had ran the wrong labels on some parts. I told Leroy about it. It wasn't very many so I could fix it myself. I told Leroy and turned to start fixing the problem. The next thing I know Rico is over in my area looking and making comments about I should have caught the error. I looked around and who was standing at his side looking weak as hell, Leroy.

I couldn't believe it, this was the same dude who had went out drinking with me. Had rode in my ride when he needed a ride even been by my house! The Negro had turned me over to the beige man. I just kept fixing the problem ignoring Leroy and Rico. Eventually they walked away talking amongst themselves. BJ walked up and started saying, "That's your boy, that's your boy!" BJ laughed and then started helping me fix the packages.

After that I didn't have anything to do with Leroy. Soon after that incident I was placed in charge of a line that consisted of all females. Anybody who has ever worked with a lot of women know they basically work at their own pace. Add in the fact that some of the females were cute and you really have a problem.

I really didn't give a damn what they did as long as they treated me all right, which they did. Rico would hover over certain lines then pull people up front to reprimand them for working too slow. Rico did that with some of the females on my line. Instead of reprimanding them he told them something about production was off. This meant I was going to get fired. Now you know everyone of the women on that line was cool with me so they listened to this fool then came and told me.

I left the line and found Rico by another line. I pulled Rico to the side and told him, "Man don't never tell nobody else about my job performance. If you have a problem with me tell it to my face." Rico started saying things like there was no problem, it was all hearsay. I walked away Rico was a punk. The trick probably was telling the females that stuff to make himself seem big. I didn't give a damn what type of ploy Rico used to eat cat just don't bring me into it. There were plenty other house Negroes Rico could play with in the joint.

My problem was solved when Cleveland looked out for me and got me assigned to help him run the wrapping machine. I didn't have a boss I just walked around and wrapped packages. That went on until one day a silly fool riding the high-lo ran into a rack and hit Cleveland and I. The first thought in my head after I made sure I was all right was, "I'm suing!" That was my last day at Switch-Pro. I received workman's comp. But other than that I didn't receive a dime. All of this mess carried into 1992 and this is the year things really started getting kind of hectic.

1992

One night was up at Coney Island getting me some food when I spotted a big dude in the line. It was my boy Priest from Willyfarce. Priest was down as hell and we soon hooked up. We were kicking it and coming up with moneymaking schemes. Priest had an idea to move some weed. I was skeptical because I had sold weed before and I knew if you had clientele it went fast but if not it was slow going. We needed a hook up for weed so in stepped Ned.

Ned claimed one of his old buddies was a big time weed dealer. Ned felt he could get a big play if we gave him two hundred dollars. I told Priest about it and he was down so we gave Ned the money on a Friday. That night after I got off work I came in the house and Ned met me upstairs. Ned pulled out a plastic bag full of weed. Ned said, "This is the best play I could get." I nodded and took the weed and called Priest. I told Priest to come by the next day and we could bag the weed up. Priest was relieved to hear I had got the weed because Priest didn't trust Ned with the money.

The next day we bagged up the weed. It was an okay play but it wasn't what we expected. The way Ned had made it seem his boy would damn near give him a pound because they were tight. Ned's guy had given him about two ounces maybe a little more. The one thing was he had hooked Ned up with was some fire weed.

We were in the weed business. Priest was selling his part of the weed to his friends, I sat on mine. I sold some bags to a few people from Switch Pro but the business was just too slow. I gave Len a few bags to sell to his woman's family. Len came back with a crazy story about the weed wasn't any good. The play was getting frustrating. Add in the fact that I was getting tired of chilling around the house all the time and you get the results that happened.

One Friday night I was just sitting in the house chilling and looking at TV. Jaime was over and Len was at his girl's house. I was bored as hell and stuck in the pad because my car wasn't running. This led to me just rolling joint after joint and smoking them. Jaime was there and he snuck a few puffs off of the joints. I was so high and pissed off at my situation I just jumped in my car trying to make it run just to get away. It ran to the store where I grabbed a forty and took it to the head and drove back home where it quit on me.

I got out went in the house and just went to bed. The next day I called Priest and told him to stop by. When Priest came by I told Priest whatever he had left he could keep the profits. I was through with the weed business.

I was out of work, out of weed and hoping for a big settlement from Switch-Pro. I spent the majority of my time loafing around the house listening to Ned. Ned was an enigma, he had a heart of gold but he couldn't put the bottle down. Ned's brain was sharp as a tack when he was sober but when Ned got hold of some Mohawk that was another story.

With Len basically moved out Ned became my hanging buddy. We would drink and Ned would tell me stories about things that went on in Detroit back in the day. In the evenings Carter, Ned's buddy, would come by and drink with us. Carter had a shitload of stories also. I'd just sit and listen to the stuff they had to say about the old days. Their favorite drink was *Mohawk* vodka. The garbage was billed as Detroit's number one vodka. I noticed later on that every one I knew who drank the stuff had a drinking problem. *Mohawk* tasted like turpentine but since I was broke I had no choice but to indulge. When I had some scratch though it was a half-pint of gin and a forty for me.

The drinking used to drive Mary J crazy. Mary J blamed Carter for the fact Ned would drink liquor with him. Mary J damn near hated Carter because in her book he was making Ned drink. This to me was ridiculous. I had seen Ned wake up at ten o'clock and make his way over to the store to get a half-pint to drink. This would be followed by a return trip at twelve for another half-pint. Carter was nowhere to be found when this was happening. I didn't say too much though because at least Mary J was focusing on Ned and not me. My delusions of a big settlement collapsed and I had to get another job. I wound up working at a sheet metal factory in Livonia. It was cool I got paid every week and money was something that I needed severely. I had been in the "D" almost a year and was still living with Mary J. This was going to have to change quick. Len had moved out months ago. The move was ironic Len left our house where it was four of us. To go live with fifty people in one house. Pussy will make a man do crazy things and in his case it had to be that. When Len first left things were really messed up. Len had came and took some things out of his mother's house to take over his girl's mama's house. I remember coming home and Len was moving mattresses out. This hit Len's mom hard. Mary J would ask me questions about why was Len doing the things he was doing. I didn't have any answers for Mary J because I rarely seen Len anymore.

I remember once I hadn't seen Len for a few weeks in the winter. I went by his girl's house to holler at him. I went by to tell Len something about a freak and me. I got the shock of my life. Len stayed clean every since I first met him. The dude kept a fade and Len had brush waves that would make Farrakhan jealous. The man who was sitting up in this little attic where him and his girl slept couldn't have been Len. The cat had just let his beard go and was just wearing some old pants and shirt. This was the same man who turned me on to wearing three-quarter leather coats with fur around the collar and silk shirts. I looked at Len's situation and I vowed to never let a woman bring me down. Maybe Len's woman wasn't bringing him down but Len damn sure was looking down.

Around this time Mary J would get sad about Len's leaving. Mary J was feeling betrayed. It was a real bleak time at on Ward. Len was and still is my guy but I felt like he was making a big mistake. I never really let Len's mother know this. I felt Len had jagged his life away on a rot gut female. That may sound hard but that was how I felt at the time.

This was enhanced to me when Mary J started telling me that she was getting some crazy phone calls from Len's girl. This was real petty. I guess

Gilda, Len's girl now his wife, would call and be charging Mary J up over some he said she said garbage. Mary J isn't the loud arguing type of female so she didn't know how to get the fool off of her.

I knew: a size thirteen in Gilda's butt, but remember I was the outsider my hands were tied. I know I was only getting one side of the story but the way I saw things Len could have stopped that from ever happening. Old girl should have known to never even think about saying anything but hi to Len's mom. I knew this type of interaction would never happen to my mother. For one my mama was raw and would check the fool with a "trickness" if it ever came her way. Two, a female better not mention my mother's name in a loud voice or sleep may suddenly overcome her. I don't think Len ever said anything to old girl so I had to see his mother cry. Maybe Len didn't know what was going on so he couldn't stop it. Whatever the case it was time for me to move on. I couldn't be the replacement son and I had my own issues and didn't need to subscribe to anyone else's. Don't get the wrong idea no one was asking me to be involved but when you are that close to people and you care about them you are bound to be drug into their struggles.

Also Ned was getting worse. All Ned was good for was drinking and sleeping. I knew then that one day I was going to stop drinking. Living with Ned enabled me to see the real side of alcohol. I did not want to wind up unable to get out of bed unless I had a shot of liquor. I had to find a place to stay. It was time for me to fly solo in the land of the freak home of the paid.

CHAPTER XVI

The sheet metal joint was keeping me in scratch I also had qualified for unemployment from Switch-Pro. I was holding onto a little scratch. One day I went to see this broad who was digging me who lived around the corner in some apartments. When I got there she wasn't talking about sex so I nonchalantly I asked her about the rent. She told me the rent was two fifty a month with heat included. I was cool with that so I left. I contacted the landlord and set up an appointment to view an apartment.

I set up an appointment for July fifth to meet with the landlord. I went to Racine and kicked it with Wally. Wally had gotten out of the joint and had a fresh pad. Wally was doing well so I hung with him for a few days then I returned home. Racine was where I was born but my home was Detroit and I liked it like that.

When I got back to the "D" I met with the landlord and her daughter. Len came along with me to see the apartment. When we got there the landlady was there with this fine Hollywood type chick. I let Len do all the talking. Len seemed to know the right questions to ask. Len was talking to the old woman while I was trying my damnest to flirt with the Hollywood type. Who, as it turned out was the landlord's daughter. The Hollywood type's name was Gwen. Gwen was fine as hell.

Len was doing such a good job of setting me up in the apartment that when it came time to sign the papers the landlord was handing the papers to him. I stepped in and said, "Thanks," and started filling out the papers. Gwen asked, "Are you the one staying here?" I said, "Yep, and you can come visit anytime." This brought a grin to Gwen's face but she dropped it when her mother looked at her.

I remember that scene like it was yesterday. Even down to the fact that Gwen had on some white or cream colored pants and her butt was giggling like Jell-O. The reason being she had to have on some g-string draws or a thong. Hey I was a very sick man at the time.

The day I moved I remember I just came home and moved my stuff. My boy Dennis came by to help me because Len was to busy pussy-sitting. I got my stuff moved in and just stood back and thought, "I got my own crib in Detroit," I was overlooking the fact that there wasn't a damn thing in it.

After I moved Mary J remarked, "You moved like a thief in the night." This statement may be true but it was time to go. It was one of those things you cannot explain but you know it is true. I only moved two blocks away so I was still in walking distance to the old house.

One plus was Cleveland was staying down the street in his sister's house. That worked out fine because it gave me someone to kick it with. The female I knew stayed across the hall but I had my rule: no chicks in the same apartment building I live in. Aside from her I didn't say anything to the other people who stayed in the building.

I got two chairs from a white dude on my job. One was a desk chair and the other was an orange piece of crap. Add in my mother's old bean bag and my furniture ensemble was complete. The building itself was in turmoil. Some young girl lived down stairs and she kept young fools hanging around. Also the front doors wouldn't lock so people used the building to cut through to go from Sorrento to Ward. It was a trip. It wasn't unusual for me to come home and step over people hanging in the hallway to get to my apartment. Even though all of this turmoil was happening my apartment never got broken into.

Cleveland introduced me to this cat who lived in the hood named Jazz. We hung out and got lit. It was Jazz who introduced me to Nino my other road dog. Jazz couldn't kick it at the time because he was shacking with this female. Nino on the other hand didn't have any such inhibitions.

The first time I met Nino Jazz told me he was a Vice-lord. This tripped me out because I didn't think Detroit people got caught up in stuff like street gangs. I always had this vision that they were more advanced and was all about the money. So seeing as I knew a lot of Vice-lords and Disciples from staying in Racine I started quizzing Nino to see where he stood. I knew some gang history from a report I had done in college about street gangs. I wanted to see if Nino was real. Or had Nino just adopted something he seen on Nightline.

It turned out Nino had went to Job Corps and met some dudes from Chicago. These cats were Black Gangster Disciples and Nino had gotten down with their clique. Jazz was all wrong about Nino. I laughed when Nino told me the scoop. I also told Nino that everybody I knew was black gangsters or claiming to be down. Nino tripped and started calling me

Folks. I had more nicknames than anybody else I knew. Jazz called me Pharaoh because I had dropped some knowledge on him about Egypt. In the barbershop they called me Goldie. I don't have to explain that one.

Now it was really time to kick it. Before, I felt funny about meeting females and having them call over Mary J's house. If Mary J didn't answer the phone and Ned was drunk when he did, I would never get the message. It was also foul to have to try to schedule females to come by when it was just Ned and I at the pad. I looked at Mary J as a mother to me. So just like my mom I had to be respectful. I was also still getting a feel for the city. I had learned my way around the city and I knew how to get to and from so it was on.

I started hitting all the spots I had heard about before but never made it to them. From Club Inferno to the Shamrock on Seven Mile, if they were partying I was there. I was having a damn ball meeting new people and hollering at some of the finest females on the planet. This was the reason I moved to Detroit to live the good life. Just thinking about those days still brings a smile to my face.

I noticed one thing about Detroit no one had any driver licenses. I had changed my license over to Michigan the previous year and they were still in good standing, until the fall of 1992.

One Friday Nino and I were out partying at this strip club on Woodward. We were in there messing with all the dancers and drinking like fish. We had cornered two females a light skinned one and a dark one. We were attempting to take them with us. The dancers were down with it. But the dancers wanted us to wait until the club closed so they could make some more scratch. Nino came up with this bright idea about us heading over to Club Inferno 2 for a while, then coming back for the women. I was game and the females were also because the manager had started giving them a hard time about just chilling with us. So we vamped.

I was feeling good as hell. For one I was nice and high off of gin. Two, the yellow chick had the kind of body I loved thin and flexible. I was looking forward to doing some exercises on her. As we were leaving the parking lot Nino said, "Make a right and go down Woodward." I did this and hit it. We were rolling down Woodward fast as hell. I was waiting for Nino to tell me where to turn when I looked over at him. The dude was sleep. Little did I know I had crossed Eight Mile road and was now in Ferndale.

I nudged Nino and he mumbled some gibberish and stayed sleep. I said, "Fuck it." I hit a U-turn and headed back towards the club to see if I could talk my girl out of there early. This type of thinking got my pulse racing, which led to more acceleration. Before I could get back across Eight Mile to the safety of Detroit the cops were on me.

I was drunk as hell and Nino was passed out. I was thinking D.U.I., driving under the influence! I grabbed a paper bag and tore a piece off and shoved this into my mouth like gum. As I'm doing this I noticed the bag had the remnants of a pint of gin in it. I shoved this bottle under the seat. I saw the cop coming towards the car in the rearview mirror and I hollered, "Nino the cops is coming!" This fool was still dead to the world.

By this time the cop was at the window so I let it down. Standing there was one of those serious faced cops with one of those state trooper hats on. The first thought I had was, "We are going to jail tonight." This was the time I remembered the plates had expired on the Celica two months ago, oh shit!

The cop said, "You were going fifty-five back there." I replied, "Officer the speedometer doesn't work in this car." Hell it didn't. The cop continued, "The plates are expired." I said, "I know. I just got the car fixed and took it out for a spin." I continued, "I took a wrong turn and that is how we wound up out here." I motioned to Nino and said, "I'm just trying to get him home." The cop looked at Nino and asked for my license he took it and went back to his car.

I tried shaking Nino to wake him up to no avail. I was getting nervous, was the cop calling for back-up or what? I was in deep thought when I looked up and the cop was standing pecking on my window. The cop handed me my license and two or three tickets and walked away. I was still saying thanks when the car shot past. I said, "Nino we are lucky as hell." Nino just grunted and rolled over in the seat sleep.

I pulled off. When we got on Davidson I pulled over and got out and pissed. After I finished I reached into the car and grabbed the pint out and took the last few shots to the head. I laughed and felt my pocket and pulled out the dancer's name and number. She had written the number on a napkin. I thought, "Oh well the night wasn't a total loss. I hopped in my ride and went home, I was tired. Those tickets would come back to haunt me later.

Another time Nino came bamming on my door saying, "Let's roll!" I said, "Nigga what are you talking about?" Nino walked out the door. I grabbed my keys and followed him. When I got outside, Nino was getting into a new Chevy Cavalier or Z-24, it was one or the other. I didn't ask questions I hopped in the passenger side.

When we pulled off Nino said, "A friend asked me to come and relieve her of her car note. She paid me well to do it too." I laughed and said,

"Well where is the gin and how much time do we have until she calls it in?" Nino replied, "We have a few hours." I said, "Let's party then."

We drove the hell out of that car all over Detroit. We hit club after club and got drunk as hell. We had a close call in Highland Park though.

Nino was driving fast as hell drinking a brew. I was taking shots out of a pint of gin we had picked up when we blew by the police. I said, "Nino we just shot past the cops!" Nino said, "I know, the girl's house is right up here at the corner. When I pull over get out and start walking towards her pad." I knew the rest if the cops pull over after us then take off running. I geared myself to get ready to do my John Carlos imitation when I got out. I knew we were busted and our few hours that Nino said we had to play were up hours ago. When we got by the female's house the police were picking up speed trying to catch us. Nino and I both got out fast and started walking towards the girl's house. The police were coming up the block slower now. We kept walking up the sidewalk towards the house. We were walking like we were headed towards the back door.

The police just slowed down and looked at us. They did a U-turn and shot back the other way. Nino and I both breathed a sigh of relief. By this time the girl was on her porch she asked, "What's going on?" We both looked at each other and laughed. We had dodged another bullet.

Working at the sheet metal factory was paying pretty well and the bosses liked my work and were hinting that I could get hired permanently. I was cool with that because they made something like eleven or twelve dollars an hour. This was not to be though because my car broke down. I could not get to and from the job. There was a brother who was willing to give me a ride but I messed that up. One night I hung with Len and one of the females he knew drinking gin and missed my ride. The next day the temp service told me to wait until I got my car back before I called them. Oh well skip them I got another job at Joe Louis arena working in a kitchen. It never crossed my mind to attempt to fire off some resumes to work in my field of study. That was as far from my mind as Uranus is from the earth.

One Sunday Nino came down the block and told me that on Sundays they have female dancers at Henri's palace. I asked were they tight Nino said they were. I told Nino I was down with the program and we agreed to meet later on that evening around eight. The problem with this whole scenario was that it was 11:30 in the morning. Too much time for me to blow off before we went.

I got dressed stopped by the liquor store and got me a half-pint and went visiting. I stopped by BJ's house to talk some trash with him. We went to the liquor store and got a liter of gin. I sat by BJ's house talking and playing dominoes until 4:30 or 5:00. It was still too early to go to Henri's so I went by Len's house.

Len wasn't doing anything and was glad that I had stopped by he wanted to drink. I was one to never turn down an offer went to the liquor store and got a fifth of gin to nibble on. As we were drinking I could see the family life was getting to Len. The wife and kids scenario was wearing Len down. I asked Len if he wanted to kick it. If he wanted to go see some butts shake. Len looked up at me like a man defeated and started telling me about Gilda and responsibility. I hopped up and cut Len off by saying, "Man I'll see you later."

I left I didn't want to hear that death speech. I don't even think Len believed it. Len was just telling himself something to make himself feel better and accept the limitations he had allowed to be placed upon himself.

It was about 7:30 now so I rode back by the crib to see if I could spot Nino. I stopped at the apartment for a minute to make a few calls. I was hyped though I definitely did not want to be there. I could feel the liquor catching up with me. Sleep was on the horizon so I quickly left. It was 8:15 now and no Nino, I left.

I stopped by the store and grabbed me two quarts to keep me awake. I went on to Henri's drinking the brews high as hell. By the time I got there I was drunk as a pig. When I walked through the door I look on stage and they had about fifteen females on stage bent over doggy style shaking their rumps like there was no tomorrow. "Poor Nino", I thought, "He would have loved this!" They were having a contest to see who could pop they butt cheeks the best. I was honored to have the privilege to view the talent and cast my vote. As I got closer to the stage I walked from side to side. I wanted to make sure I got full view of all of the contestants. I got right up close to the stage. To make sure my view was unobstructed. Low and behold there was this fine yellow chick popping her butt like popcorn, and guess what I just happen to know her. Her name was Lena I had met her before at Tony Julian's, another strip club, and boy was she looking good. Lena seen me and winked, hot damn! My penis raced down my leg because I knew I could holler at Lena and tap that cat. I only had one problem I was too damn drunk.

I went and sat at a table and when the waitress came over I ordered more gin. I told her to tell Lena to come holler at me when she got the time. I sat and watched the other broads take money from fools who were tipping and laughed. I had learned my lesson back in the Black Orchid. I had observed the fact that the females really didn't give a damn about the fool who gave all his money away and treated them like a piece of meat. You tended to get further if you played it cool and talked to them like they had a brain and offered to buy a drink for them instead of getting lap dances.

I think when you went the lap dance route they viewed you as a trick. I guess if you had long money that was fine for you. But seeing as I didn't I had to take the other road. Plus I knew everybody wants somebody to make them feel good, someone that they can relax around. I wanted to be that guy to every fine female in Detroit.

Lena came up with a tight dress on barely covering up her snatch looking sexy as hell. I grabbed the drink and damn near downed it, I had to play cool if I was going to get this right. I said, "What's up?" "Me", was the reply I got from her. I had to grin and said, "I know that's right." Lena sat down. I offered to buy Lena a drink she turned the offer down. We chitchatted for a minute when I got down to business. I said, "You know you looking good as hell." Lena said, "Thank you, what you doing in here?" I said, "Looking for you." She replied, "Yeah I'll bet."

I knew from the previous time that I had met Lena that I had a chance to get close to her. I was determined not to blow this opportunity. I said something that went like, "What time are you getting off?" Lena said, "When they close, why?" I knew I couldn't stay awake that long. It was time to go for broke so I said, "Can I take you home with me?" Lena looked at me for a second, scanning the merchandise, and said, "Maybe." That froze me.

Lena beckoned for the waitress and got her pen and a napkin. Lena wrote her number down and said, "Call me tomorrow and we'll definitely get together." I was ecstatic on the inside but cool on the outside as I replied, "Cool."

Lena got up and walked away. The tricks were tipping and she wanted to get her fill. I wasn't mad because I knew I was in as far as I was concerned. As Lena walked away I looked at her and said to myself, "I want that ass tonight!" I was determined to see if I could stay awake long enough to cash in my chips that night.

I got up to go to the bathroom I couldn't see ten feet in front of me I was so high. I pissed and went back out into the bar and looked at the stage Lena was up there dancing seductive as hell. At this point the only thing alert on me was my penis. I went and tried to play Ms Pacman. I knew it was time for me to go when I almost fell asleep playing the game! It was time for the dog to roll.

I walked past the stage where Lena was dancing and motioned that I would call her she nodded and I left. I hopped in my car and threw my Kilo cassette in and peeled out. I remember thinking damn this baby running good, I was flying. The next thing I knew I was a block from home turning the corner in third gear. I was feeling good so I was going to powershift and make the wheels spin midway through the turn. Half of my brain was screaming, "Don't do it!" The other half was already hi-fiving itself because the procedure worked, wrong.

I remember jumping out of my car screaming to George, this dude who stayed on the next block, "Somebody shot my tires out!" To me that's what seemed like what had happened. Don't ask me what really happened because I don't know all I know is my car was messed up. The front wheel was bent in. I was so disgusted and pissed I didn't even want to drive it home, George did.

I ran into the house and called Priest. I was screaming about somebody shooting at me into the phone. The man calmly said, "Nigga you drunk get some sleep." I looked at the phone and mumbled goodbye and promptly blacked out. The Celica and I had taken our last ride together. From there it was all downhill. When this happened in the fall of 1992. It was a prelude of what was coming in 1993. The crazy thing was the next day I caught up with Lena and she came by the pad. I had cooked some chicken and noodles for dinner. I didn't want the grub because I was still thinking about my car. When Lena got over she remarked, "Damn you can cook? You are the total package." I wasn't feeling like anything but a package of shit. I was so pissed about the car I didn't even bone old girl that night. Add in the fact that I had wanted the sex the previous day the situation turned out to be a zero.

I finished out that year catching the bus to and from Joe Louis Arena. Priest had came by and fixed the tire rod on the Celica but the control arm was bent. Priest told me the rod should be fixed and I agreed. Priest took the Celica around the block and that was the last time she drove anywhere. For some crazy reason I just parked the car and said I would fix it in the spring. Don't ask me where I came up with that idea it just made sense at the time.

I also started singing a song that I hadn't heard in years. I started singing *It's All Right* by The Impressions. That song helped me dig deep inside myself when the times got hard. I could have punked out and went back to Racine defeated but the stanza that said, "If you got soul everybody knows it's alright," kept me going. To me this meant as long as your black everything is cool. I damn sure was black physically and more important mentally. A few bars of that song carried me a long way when the outlook was bleak as hell.

This was the first time I had caught the bus regularly since twelfth grade. This was a trip. The cool thing was I could catch the Grand River bus right downtown and walk to Joe Louis. It was a straight shot and the

Grand River bus ran regularly. It was funny I just adapted to this new way of life and kept on rolling. I just felt you have to do what you have to do. Joe Louis wasn't paying much but it was fun to work down there. It wasn't anything but blacks working in our kitchen so all we did was talk trash all day long. It was a whole slew of us down there so I won't even attempt to name all of the brothers. We would do things like bring half pints in to work. Then go up to the fifth floor and get juice to mix the alcohol with. My man Purvis called me Farrakhan down there because I was always talking pro-black. I told them Joe Louis Arena was the plantation and they would laugh.

The situation was plain as day to me for this reason. All of the head chefs at Joe Louis were white all of the servers were black. Add in the fact that all of the dishwashers and prep assistants were black also. What do you get? Sounds like the big house to me.

Joe Louis was getting old fast. The end came on New Year's evening. We smuggled two fifths of gin into the job because we had to work a party that night. I was pissed off because I had to bring in the New Year working. I was determined though to party the same as if I was at home drinking in my living room. The place was packed there were Caucasians everywhere lining up for that slop that we served. I was pissed because I was going to have to help the dishwashers at the end of the day so I started drinking as soon as I got to work.

I had already drunk a half-pint on the bus so I was well on my way to feeling real good. I talked all evening looking at the rich whites walk around and socialize. The crew started really hitting those fifths hard around 10:30. When the head chef brought in the free champagne at twelve o'clock, we were all drunk.

I was walking around trying to see if I could get this waitress to come under the bleachers with me. The waitress had been up on the fifth floor with another dude in the kitchen serving him. I had seen Purvis taking her under the bleachers a little later. I was figuring it was my turn. It was not to be so I just drank all the gin I could and washed it down with champagne. At the end of the night the head chef told me to punch out and rest I was that bent.

The next day I was scheduled to work I called. I had the worse headache I had ever had. It was that bullshit champagne I had mixed with that good Seagram's Gin. When I finally did go back to work they had some type of new regulations that were supposed to limit the number of times we could call in. The regulations were garbage.

I was telling the dudes down there they were only doing us like that because we were black and the head chefs figured they could get away with it. The brothers weren't trying to hear that line. I told them skip this place I was quitting. The job wasn't that serious in the first place. I just wanted to work there because Len worked there and he said the job was cool. The only other dude who seen it like me was Purvis. Purvis quit the same time I did, that day.

There was one thing I have to mention that happened to me while I was at Joe Louis. At the time my favorite food was pork chops. Pork chops and rice was a delicacy in my book. When I discovered pork steaks are big pork chops in a sense I was in seventh heaven. It is important that you understand this to get the gist of what happened to me.

One day the menu had grilled pork chops on it. I'm sure everyone is familiar with the thin pork chops that you get a restaurant. Well on this day I was getting a chance to do some prep work and guess what they had me working on? Grilling the chops, oh baby! I ate at least twenty-three of those babies while I was grilling them. It seemed like every time I put some into the pan finished I put two or three in my mouth. I ate some more later on that evening before I left to go home, I was a happy man.

When I got home I drank a forty and chilled. I went to sleep and woke up screaming! I was having a bad dream. I say having because I swear I was wide-awake with my eyes open and the dream was playing on the wall like I was at a movie theater! I scrambled out of bed and cut on the lights only then did the dream leave my vision. I had to give up pork!

I know what you are thinking, "What the hell does this have to do with pork?" Everything, because in the dream I had eaten pork and was changing into a boar! The dream was wild I had eaten some swine in the dream and been contaminated by the substance. I had to be quarantined and that's when I started changing into this wild boar! I woke up when I seen the horns growing out of my nose. Well I tried to because the dream kept playing on the wall. That did it for me. I have not touched pork since then with the exception of eating some head cheese once in 1993. As far as pork chops go I never ate them again.

CHAPTER XVII

1993

I had quit Joe Louis so I needed another gig. Back to the temporary services. They hooked me up with a job at Harrow Garments. This job was way on the eastside so I would catch the Grand River downtown and transfer to the Vandyke bus and get off on Seven-Mile. Sometimes I would walk the mile to the job sometimes the Seven-Mile bus would be there and I could hop on that instead of walking.

This place was different from any other place I worked at because it was all females there. One thing stayed the same though it was still slavery. We had to work fast as hell for peanuts. The same way a slave worked for old boss. I had figured it out by this time. I knew we never left the plantation we just thought we did. The same white boss was still on our ass only instead of whipping us he fired or reprimanded us. There was one bright spot that was this female named Amanda.

This woman was tight as hell. What made the woman so amazing was the fact that Amanda told me she was thirty-six or thirty-eight years old! I could not believe this! Amanda had many dancers beat. As I write this I have to wonder was Amanda lying or not. Well if Amanda was or wasn't looking up at the front seeing her made a lot of days go by quicker.

I used to get off at ten o'clock and I used to race up to Vandyke to catch the 10:06 bus. I used to walk with this cat who had been in the service and this man could walk. Walking with him I never missed the bus.

All the walking in the world couldn't keep me from losing the gig. They said I was too slow. Oh well no loss I just called up another temporary service, Renaissance this time. Ken-Strip here I come.

I was hired at Ken-Strip to do one thing that was to paint. I literally painted the whole damn factory from floor to ceiling. To get the high spots they put me in a basket and raised me up with the hi-lo. This was wild because if you moved to the front of the basket it rocked forward. This movement would scare the shit out of me because I would be twenty or thirty feet in the air. I was glad as hell when I finished painting the high areas and could just paint where I could either reach or stand on a ladder to reach.

The first week I really didn't have any conversation with too many people. I just painted and left. At break time I would just sit in the break room and listen to the brother's talk trash about females and sports. Both subjects were my forte so one day I decided to join in their conversation.

There was one cat who everybody kind of looked up to his name was Gray. Gray liked the Knicks and was screaming that New York Knick garbage. My team at the time was Charlotte. The reason being my dog was Alonzo Mourning and Larry Johnson was the hardest cat in the league then. Gray was at the table looking at the sports talking trash about Patrick Ewing when I cut in and said, "Charlotte can beat them." Gray replied, "Yeah right." It was on we debated the fact the rest of the break period.

When lunch came around I was talking with Gray and some of the other cats who worked there. They told me when they first seen me painting they thought I was trying to be hard because of the way I was looking.

This is the one thing that we as black people have to work on. Our facial expressions towards one another can easily be misinterpreted. I also have a saying: if you are going to mean mug blacks then keep it real. Keep the same face when you get in white faces. I can respect people who look hard no matter who's in their face. The ones I can't stand is the Negro who is hard as hell with other blacks then when Mr. or Mrs. Charlie comes around they are a grinning jack-o-lantern.

To enforce this point everybody at the job figured I was trying to be hard because of my facial expression. They were reading me wrong. I had to laugh because as I told them I had the crazy look on my face half the time because I was scared. As I stated before the basket was rocking back and forth this kept me on edge. When I told them this they laughed, it broke the rest of the ice between the rest of the brothers and me who was working at Ken-Strip. To seal things Gray blurted out, "I thought he was a damn homosexual type deviant!" Everybody busted out laughing at this insight. I had tears in my eyes from laughter.

Gray became my main man. Gray could talk trash with the best, me. We would go at it sometimes but we mainly cracked on everybody else. Talking with Gray made the day go by quicker. I was actually having a good time working at Ken-Strip.

Once I finished painting the whole damn factory Gray talked to Chad, the guy in charge of the place, and got me placed on the line. This enabled me to keep a job since the painting was through. There was one drawback Chad knew Gray and I talked all day. Chad placed me on another line to separate us. Chad put me on Ed's line, the wash line. Chad put me in hell.

Ed was the type of brother who attempted to have class and separate from the uncouth Negroes. Ed rarely talked to anyone else on the job and walked around like he was better than the other blacks. Ed wanted to show management that he was different from everybody else by working like a slave. Ed had the misguided notion that if he worked hard enough they would reward him with a job or something. This was as far from the truth as saying two plus two is seven. The factory was a stripping plant that stripped paint off of parts and sent them back to manufacturers to be repainted. Kenstrip stripped a lot of things but the main staple of the joint was tire rims. On certain lines you had to wear rubber gloves to keep from getting burned. Ed's line, the wash line, was the only one where you didn't have to worry about the acid.

The first day I was over there Ed ran the line like we were getting paid piecework or something. As we shut down and were walking to the break room Gray asked, "How did it go?" I said, "Man do that fool ever stop?" Gray said, "No, Ed hates for his line to stop. The only people in here who can put up with Ed are Brad and Chad." Then Gray added, "Plus Chad told Ed to work the hell out of you." I thought what kind of black man tries to break another one for the white man? Slavery was still in effect. I told Gray, "My arms are tired but I'll bet I never leave this place tired again." Gray laughed and gave me five and we walked off.

I went home that day and went to sleep at 5:30 that evening and slept until 5:30 that morning. The next day I was ready. Ed was running the line like there was no tomorrow and I was on it. The Negro didn't realize he was messing with a big dog there isn't anything I cannot do when I put my mind to it.

As the time went on I got to the point where I was working so fast I would load the line up and go talk shit with Gray while it was still running and not miss a beat. Ed loved this. We were turning out big numbers and Ed was milking this fact to the max.

We worked side by side Ed would blow the water out of the seam of the rims and I would place them into the rack. This gave me the chance to rap to the brother. It turned out Ed was cool but he didn't know how to be cool. I came to find out Ed had done a bit in the joint when he was younger. Ed was just another dude out here trying to make it in the madness called America.

Nobody in Ken-Strip liked Ed though but he was cool with me. The one thing that pissed me off with Ed was how fast he ran the line. I asked Gray about it one day and he just shook his head and said, "Ed just do that shit nobody knows why." I figured Ed was just trying to show, the man who ran the place, he was a good worker. Ed was hoping the company would hire him. I knew this would never happen because in the whole joint there was only two permanent employees. Brad started missing work and got fired. I had to go to the back of the line and load it.

I was back there all by myself with nothing but a radio to keep me company. Even with Brad gone we still averaged two to three thousand rims a day. I am estimating that because some of those racks had forty or fifty rims in them. We did as many as we could in those ten hours we worked. As I said before Ed never stopped the line.

The line had racks for rims and pin hooks for parts that were sometimes ran called Redar. When we didn't have redar to run Ed would run and jump on the hi-lo when the pin hooks came through to load the line up so it wouldn't stop. This was down right ludicrous. We worked like slaves for four twenty-five an hour. Oh forgive me I think Ed was making five twenty-five an hour. For these mere scraps we worked like fools. The job became a game to me. I had the job so down pat I could load up the line and run up front and talk with Gray and never miss a rack. One day a new dude came on the scene. His name was Stan. This dude was huge. Stan was cool, he and I vibed right off the top. I had bought a Grand Prix from a guy who worked at the joint for two hundred dollars. I was rolling again.

My license was screwed up from the time Nino and I had gotten pulled over. I was just like everybody else in the "Dirty D," no license. The car didn't have an exhaust on it. The exhaust was so bad one day I was driving and kept hearing a scraping sound. I pulled over and pulled the catalytic converter off. I threw it in the back seat. This was going to be my excuse to the cops if they pulled me over. I was just going to say my exhaust just got messed up, or something to that effect.

I never even got the car registered in my name because the dude couldn't find the title. No problem, I just got the hook up from my girl Rena. Rena had these fake licenses applied for papers for your back window. I invested in some and it was on.

Gray, Stan and I hung tough together. I drove us home after work and we usually stopped by the liquor store and got something to drink. All we would do is talk trash. I would pick their heads for schemes to run on females. Both Gray and Stan had done a bit in Jackson penitentiary so they knew the streets well.

Gray had done his bit for narcotics so I always liked the stories he told about Detroit in his heyday. Stan, I think he went up for robbery or it may have been drugs. Stan had done some time. I remember Stan told this cat who was trying to talk slick in the lunchroom, "Man I'll knock your punk ass out, lay you on the table and fuck you in the ass." Stan said it real calm the dudes who heard it were tripping.

Stan then turned to me when the guy walked off and said, "See Frank, mutha fuckas don't think. He may come back and kill me after I've finished but he will never be able to take back what I've taken from him." Stan then walked into the plant. These dudes may have been criminals but they were deep as any college person I had ever met.

One day while we were drinking I told Gray and Stan I had a degree. They both just turned and looked at me and asked, "What the fuck are you doing here?" I told them, "Man, the professional world wasn't for me. I wanted to pimp ho's or sell dope anything but work for whitey." Little did I realize that by doing one of those professions I was being a bigger tool for whitey. Gray just looked at me and shook his head and said, "The pimp days are over. You can sell some dope and make some money but pimping is dead." I tended to disagree because I had a plan.

I outlined my plan for Gray and Stan it went like this. I intended to get me a house with three or four bedrooms. The plan was for me to fix the house up real nice. The next phase was to catch one of those hot ass eighteen or nineteen-year-old females who was sucking and fucking like a champ already and turn her out. Once this was accomplished put the young girl in the house and tell her rent was a specified amount per week.

The way the girl could come up with the rent was to satisfy some of my friends who would come around on the weekends. The girl would never know how much money was coming in from her work just the fact that she had satisfied the rent for a week. Once I had her up and running, it would be time to fill the other bedrooms in the house.

To do this I would invest in her some fresh gear and a old car that looked good. Then I would have her go around her old friends who didn't have anything. They would see how the girl was coming up and want to know what she was doing. In I would come with the house and rent proposal.

By me setting the girl up in some gear and clothes she would become the best recruiter I could ever get. Her girls nine out of ten would be freaks already anyway so they would just need a little nudging in the right direction. By showing them the house and explaining the rules I figured I could swing that. Plus I would have my girl telling them the setup was gravy and look what they got. They only had to serve my friends on the weekends what they did during the week was on them.

Some of the cats I knew would serve as security for the joint so there wouldn't be anything jumping off. It would be a safe place for people to come and relieve tensions. The girls were actually getting a deal. For one they were probably living at home so now they would have their own pad. The crib would be fresh and they could have their own phone lines. The only responsibility they had to me was to be there and serve my friends on the weekends. If they made more during the week that was fine also as long as they gave me a cut of about twenty percent to cover costs.

Once this house started jumping I planned on buying more. I intended to have one house on each side of town. I also intended to rotate the females every few months. This was to ensure that there was always fresh meat in the houses. This also kept people from getting too attached to customers and clients. I knew I would never run out of employees once the scheme got started because the school system was turning them out the same way Chrysler turned out cars.

My ultimate goal was to have a place where the rich people could come and feel comfortable to trick. This would be my palace for the ballers and businessmen to come get their hands on some fresh meat. After I finished telling Gray and Stan my plan they looked at me. They both agreed it was tight but they just looked at me with pitiful looks on their faces. I think they pitied me for wasting my mind on such garbage.

CHAPTER VIII

Ken-Strip was getting old but it was cool because I could go trip out with Gray when I got bored. I had my job down to a tee. The owner Al would walk through the plant and everybody would jump and try to look busy. When Al would walk back to my area if there weren't any rims to load I would be sitting down listening to the radio.

One time Al came up to me while I was chilling and asked me. "Shouldn't you be doing something?" I just kept looking straight ahead ignoring the fool. The dummy stood there for a second like he was expecting a response so I just turned and looked at Al with a vicious look on my face. Then I just turned and looked forward again. That fool speed walked getting from out of my area. Al raced up front and talked to Ed and Gary the man who took over for Chad. I guess they told Al I worked like hell so let it go, and he did.

The job had become easy to me. Even the biggest rims they ran had become light. Since I had the job down it was time for Ed to pay for his sins. I still remembered the slave act Ed had pulled on me the first day on the line. Ed had worked me for the white man so now it was time for a field niggas revenge.

Ed's demise came on a day when we had to run rims and redar at the same time. When we ran the two together we usually only put four or five pieces of redar on the pin hooks, that way we could keep the line running and you know Ed loved that. When I first started I could only get two or three pieces on the hooks and Ed let me know his frustration. Now I was the man and hell had to be paid.

I pulled all of the excess pin hook racks that were lying around and loaded them up with redar pieces. Instead of trying to add pieces I would just replace the whole rack with a full one. So instead of four or five pieces coming through the line there was twelve coming at Ed on each rack. Ed wanted to work well dammit let's work!

When I first started replacing the racks it caught him by surprise. Gray worked across from Ed and said, "When we heard all those pieces coming through the line we turned and looked." Gray then went on, "Man Ed's face dropped! The fool started scrambling trying to keep up, sweating like hell!" The old fool had to stop the line. Now keep in mind Ed never wanted to stop the line for anyone else to catch up or give them a rest, so I wasn't having it.

I started the line back up from my end. Ed stopped it again so I walked up front with my hands on my hips pretending to give a damn. Gray and his line had turned around because it was funny to see Ed busting his ass. I said, "What is the hold up? We got to get this shit out!" I turned and walked away. Man that dude didn't know what to do. As I walked past the start button I hit it to fire the line back up.

I kept the pace up on him, every rack was full. It got so bad that Ed started missing pieces and they were being washed twice. Usually I would go to break and that was when Ed could go on break because the rack would be empty, not today. Gray called for me to come on and I waved him off. Gray later told me Ed looked back there and seen me working through break and his head dropped.

At lunch I went into the break room Gray was laughing his ass off. Ed was still out there trying to get caught up. Gray said, "Man you working the shit out of Ed!" Everybody agreed and said that's what he gets. I nodded my head but inside I didn't give a damn about what they thought. I was doing this for me. The dude had to get out of that steppin fetch-it act and learn how to be cool. After lunch Gray and I were walking back to the line to go back to work when I seen Ed still working. I looked at the end of the line and noticed the pin hooks were coming back around to my area. I knew that Ed was counting on me missing those hooks so he could go to lunch. I took off running and started replacing those racks fast as hell!

I only missed one rack and the rest was full after that one. I laughed because the old bastard had to stop the line. I promptly hit the start button and Ed stopped it again. This time Ed came back where I was at, yelling. I cut him off by saying, "Break is over, I thought you wanted to run this shit out?" The man wilted before my eyes. Ed just walked back up front and grabbed his water cup and went to the break room. I went up front and Gray gave me five. Even though Ed was up front I was the king of the line. Everybody in the joint knew it. The rest of the time I worked there Ed got cool and even took a drink with me from time to time.

By the time the end came for me at Ken-Strip Stan and I were drinking Cisco Red every day at lunch. We would be high as hell in Ken-Strip talking big about we run the plant. I still had another dude who drank Mad Dog bringing wine to work in the morning. I would be drinking this stuff at 6:30 in the morning on an empty belly. Then at lunch it was time for Stan and I to get our daily fifth of Cisco that was the routine. After work we always stopped at the store for brew and more wine. I was just having a good old time drinking myself to an early grave.

My last day on the job started as usual me bitching to Gray about how we were being played by the whites, the usual sermon. Later on in the day we heard that they had given certain people raises for their performance. I was not one of the ones who garnered a raise. That was fine by me because the few people who got them were cats I was cool with like Stan and Gray so it didn't faze me. Then I heard this lazy Negro got a raise. I snapped.

The company had pulled me up to $4.75 but I heard they had given the lazy Uncle Tom Negro five dollars an hour. I wasn't buying this. I was arguably the hardest worker in the joint. I fed a whole line by myself. Ed and I ran just as many rims as the other rim line that had four people on it. If anyone deserved top dollar it was me! It really wasn't so much as the quarter it was the fact that the dude who got the raise was a grinning buffoon. Also add in the fact that it was time for me to move on and you get the results of what happened.

I went looking for Gary who supervised the shop. I found Gary in his office. I told Gary about himself and the job. I told Gary something and closed with the fact that he was a red-neck. I stood hovering over dude looking down on his fat ass thinking about committing a felony. Then going and finding that fag Al and running him through the wash line. If Gary thought about trying something he forgot it because Stan had come in the office to tell me to chill out and Gary knew how we ran. I grabbed my things out of the locker and went back into the plant. Gray was standing off to the side he had heard everything. Gray gave me five with a sad look on his face. I knew I was going to miss him and the atmosphere with the brothers. I stopped by and hollered at Ed, he even looked sad. Ed gave me his number and told me to holler at him. I slapped him five and waved to all my other friends and walked out the door. I hopped in the Grand Prix and peeled rocks getting out of the parking lot. I would miss the brothers but it was time for me to roll, skip Ken-Strip. I went to the pad and called Renaissance and told Valerie what had happened. Valerie told me she would look into the situation and get back with me. I also let her know I wanted to be working as soon as possible.

Two days later I called and Valerie told me to come in and take a test for a job. The pay was six dollars an hour if I passed the test. I went out there and aced the test. The job was at this place called Halm. My job was to count and re-stack old manuals.

My hair was getting long as hell. I wanted to cut it but you know how that goes so instead I decided to let the sides grow in. This would give me a full head of waves like the old school players I heard so much about from Gray. I still kept in touch with Gray and Stan. We still hung tough drinking and talking trash. One day I was telling Gray and Stan about how I had ran this cute little chick named Skeet away. I was running it past them because I couldn't see why Skeet wouldn't trust me. I had gotten Skeet over the crib playing Mr. Nice then went gangsta pimp on her. I was running the scenario down to Gray and Stan. Gray was laughing so hard he had tears running down his cheeks. Stan on the other hand was silent. Stan took a drink and said, "What young chick going to trust you?" I looked at Stan he continued, "What young girl going to trust you when you have a Goldie fixation, a seventies mentality and a *Superfly* move up your sleeve?"

Stan went on, "Shit she would be a fool. If the girl got any sense and she listened to you she would have to be thinking you would have her up on the corner selling ass at the least."

Gray stopped laughing for a second and added, "Frank man you too hard. Female's are attracted to you because you are tall and well built and handsome. But the minute they talk to you, you freeze them. You come off so raw like, 'Bitch I'm the shit what use are you to me?' Find one or get gone."

Gray was serious now and said, "That was the impression you gave Rita." Gray was referring to a friend of his wife who I had scoped once but never followed through with.

Stan added, "Man if you were born in the fifties you would have had it made but these dames ain't trying to hear the shit you talking these days." Gray added, "You too hard man. Women these days like these weak ass niggas who cater to them." I blurted out, "I ain't buying a bitch shit not even a condom to fuck them with!" Gray and Stan just shook their heads and Gray said, "Frank you too hard." This statement lead to us busting out laughing and toasting the old days when pimps ran wild.

In my sick mind I was straight. If it came down to me soft shoeing females I just would not have any. Plus I wasn't worried there was always some broad who was willing to cheat on her man or husband who liked tall brown skinned dudes. When it came to these type of females eight out of ten they had a soft sucker at home. This type loved a raw dog to fuck over them every once and awhile. I was just that man.

While we are on the subject let's clear one thing up, getting laid was never a real problem. This shouldn't be a problem for any man who has a little sense. This is the reason I haven't gone into detail about the sexual exploits I have partaken. It would be petty to a true one because every man has sex. The key is to have sex on your terms, not out of weakness but strength.

There have been times I would have been out on Front Street blowing my horn to get in a female's pants. When these occasions arisen I would play it cool and walk away. This was to get the girl to doubt herself. Then the next time the roles would be reversed she would be all on me. Now it's on because I'm playing cool as hell. You want to mess with a real fine woman's head play her off.

Don't get me wrong if you just want to bone her then you can sweat her. You may get the ass physically that's it. On the other hand if you play her like she ain't shit, especially if she is flirting with you, you are starting to fuck her mind. This is what leads to control over somebody.

Keep in mind you are taking a chance. If the cutie is real down then you may blow her. But be realistic if she is down and you jump on the pussy first chance you become a bitch to her. You may be fucking her but really she is fucking you. Why because the cutie is doing it on her terms not yours. When the cutie says no more, you will be the one all hung up on emotions. The cutie will be gone on to the next hard penis.

On the other hand if you play it right and get the cutie to doubt herself and make her please you, then you screw on your terms. This leads to a better ride because she is trying her damnest to please you. Remember; no matter what she does you have to act nonchalant, emotionless.

There is one adverse side effect to this method, once you start this route you have to finish it. What this means is if one day you decide you love the broad you cannot go to acting soft. You started hard so you have to finish hard.

Why? You ask. Because remember the dude the cutie fell in love with was a dog not Richie Cunningham. When he leaves nine out of ten she leaves. Does the game work? I have to say yes because I ran it for years. Brothers beware though because this same game can be ran on you by a down female. Trust me because I had it done to me. Three females flipped the script on me and even though I knew what was happening, I was still hurt. I figured it out the hard way emotions mess you up. So to keep emotions down I had a personal freak and one good married woman when I was running wild in the "D."

Around the end of the summer I was driving down Grand River when wham! I was rear ended by a brother in a Ford Escort. I jumped out and the dude started apologizing. I was moving quick cause I didn't want the damn car to blow up. My gas tank leaked and you could see inside it from the outside. Add in the fact that there was no rear bumper and you can imagine why I was moving so fast.

I told the dude not to worry and to give the next brother the same break I gave him. The guy gave me some scratch to buy a beer and drove off. I took the Grand Prix home and parked him, he never moved again. It was back to the bus for FJ.

When the Grand Prix got totaled my life fell into a rut. My assignment was over at Halm. I knew I wasn't going to get called back. It was not because of my job performance it was because of my attitude. To the few people I worked with I was crazy. Gene, this one dude I worked with, told me I missed my time I needed to be back in the sixties with H. Rap Brown because of how I talked.

To me it was simple we had to get rid of the white folks in order to get back on top. I still believe this but it is a mental thing now we have to get the white mind out of our head. But in 1993 I had no qualms with talking about the only good white man is the dead ones on money.

I remember once on the job they were talking about how this pro athlete's father had been killed. The white guy said something to the effect that even if the man was dead when those boys found him they had no right to take his belongings.

I butted into his conversation and said, "Look a dead man ain't worried about no damn watch or ring. He has other issues on his damn mind. Plus a dead person can't claim shit so it ain't robbery." I added, "Hell if you drop dead right now I'm going to check your pockets." The man turned red and said, "That's wrong. You mean to tell me if I dropped dead you would help yourself to my belongings?" To give him his answer I asked, "Do you carry Mastercard or Visa? I need to know what stores I can shop at." Needless to say the guy was one of the permanent people who had a say in who kept their jobs and who was not called back.

As I stated I fell into a rut of just going to work and coming home drinking brews. After the Halm assignment was over I just chilled for a while and put in to get my unemployment. I needed to do something until the money started coming in so I worked a few weeks at a seat plant for GM. I was basically burning daylight.

I was getting fat from just sitting in the house drinking brews and frying chicken wings. I became good friends with Mr. Pyle. Mr. Pyle was an old man who lived in the building. I rarely saw Len or Mary J anymore. Even though Mary J lived right around the corner. I knew their thing was card parties and that had gotten old to me two years before.

I looked out for Mr. Pyle because he was a kind old man who had retired from Chrysler and stayed in the building. Mr. Pyle had lived there so long he remembered when white folks lived in the building. My phone had been cut off for a year so I would use his.

I sat up there almost everyday drinking brew and listening to Mr. Pyle tell stories of the past about Detroit in its heyday. The only social activity I had was going to get my hair done. I got my hair waved once a week even though I wasn't going anywhere. It was my one release in life. I was tired of my hair and the waves but I had gotten so fat I knew I would look crazy without it. My face had grown fat from inactivity.

One good thing that happened was I met this cat named Vince. Vince caught my attention because one day we were sitting in the break room at the seat job and he farted. The cats around Vince moved away and he said, "Don't worry it doesn't stink. I don't eat beef or pork." I laughed because Vince was eating what looked like a hamburger Vince seen me looking and stated, "Turkey my boy, I don't play with the beef." I asked why Vince started dropping science about beef hormones and how beef was bad for your health. That was only the beginning Vince was a genius.

The reason I say this is because Vince knew history back and forth. Vince talked about meditations Atlantis and Lemuria, things I had only read about in comic books. The thing that made the Vince so amazing was the fact that he tooted heroin.

Vince would take him a bump on the bus on our way to work and nod off. When Vince woke up he would be dropping science about the dynasties of Kemit, the workings of the black body stuff only a damn scholar would know. To me it was amazing.

Vince talked about things that put me on the path to higher learning because I wanted to see if he was correct. A lot of Vince's information was on point I can't say all because to this day I cannot remember all the books he told me to go find. I kept in touch with Vince up until I left Detroit.

Around the end of the year Mel, my barber, mentioned to me he had a friend who would give him plays on some cocaine. I had become cool with Mel because he had been doing my hair for a while so I told Mel I was down let me know when he wanted to get started. It was two months before we attempted to get going. But the groundwork had been laid so I was cool with it. I figured I had one more go around left in me before it was time to retire.

New Year's Eve came and I was sitting in the house looking back on the year analyzing my situation. It was pretty bleak in the forecast. I had been out of school for more that two years and had not worked any type of permanent job. I was over weight and had a damn seventies doo on my head. I was broke and had bad habits up the ass, the main one was drinking. I had to make some changes.

As I sat there listening to the gunfire sound off I toasted myself. I had a fifth of gin and a few forties of St. Ides. I looked forward to a New Year. I drank and grinned to myself and popped *The Mack* in the VCR. 1994 was here.

CHAPTER XIX

1994

January of that year was hell in the Motor City. It had to be one the coldest one I had in Detroit. I was straight though my money was coming every two weeks via mail, unemployment. I did not have to leave the crib except to get food beer and liquor.

I spent a lot of time rapping with Mr. Pyle drinking brew and talking trash. Another cat had moved into the building with his woman, his name was Dennis. Dennis was cool and came down to kick it with Mr. Pyle and me sometimes. One thing that was a constant though was getting my hair done. My hair had gotten long as hell. This is what I was hoping for why I don't know. Nino would come by and shoot the shit with me every once and awhile.

Around February Mel let me know he was ready to get started moving some rocks. I went in half with him on an eight ball to get started. We bagged up about four hundred in work from the play Mel had gotten. I had let it be known I would roll the dope out of my apartment. I went to work.

There was one dope fiend living in the building at the time so she became my best customer. The fiend had a good job so she was reliable to buy most of the product. Other than her though it was real slow. I moved enough though so we could re-up. I felt I would mess with it awhile longer.

I was getting tired of the action but I felt I would give it a chance that way when I stopped this time I would know that the dope game wasn't for me. This would enable me to walk away with a clear conscious about the dope game.

Mel and I were supposed to take turns selling the dope. Mel never did come by the pad to sell anything which was fine by me. I wasn't doing a damn thing anyway. We re-upped and this time Mel's source gave him a big play and we bagged five hundred up off of an eight ball. I knew if it was going to happen, start booming, it was going to be off of this play.

One reason was the word had leaked out about rocks being for sale on Sorrento in the building. This is what I wanted in order to get big. But I was being realistic moving eight balls was sucker plays. I could work four twenty fives and make more money with less hassle. This was my last fling.

The night we bagged up the dope, Dennis sat with Mel and I while we bagged it up. Nino stopped in and hollered, then he left. When we finished I suggested we go to the strip club and watch some females shake their ass. Mel agreed, I put the dope in the safest place in my apartment, under my bed. After I did this we left.

When we got to the club wasn't nothing happening so I told Mel, "Let's roll." Before we got to my house I told Mel to stop by the store so I could grab me a brew. When Mel dropped me off I told him I would catch up with him tomorrow and let him know how it was going. When I first walked in the apartment I knew something was wrong. The apartment wasn't torn up but it felt funny. My closet door was open and I knew I had closed it. I went into my bedroom, my bed was moved. My bed where I kept all my drugs and money had been moved. Yes my dope was gone along with my scratch. Nothing else in the apartment was touched. I glanced at my bedroom window and seen the plastic on the window had been torn off. The sons of bitches had come through the window so it seemed. After I looked at the situation more closely the robbery looked more and more like an inside job.

I ran upstairs and knocked on Dennis's door. He came to the door half sleep I told him someone had broken in and stole my dope. Dennis grabbed his clothes and came downstairs to check the scene. Dennis looked at the window and shook his head. I went up to his pad and paged Mel. When Mel called back I told him the deal I also told him he should come right now. Oh yeah bring heat.

As I sat and waited for Mel I realized that I was in a dilemma. The only people who knew I had stones were Nino and Dennis. This lead to a problem because these were the two people I was counting on to help when I got rolling tough. I was just using Mel as a springboard to get started. These were the two people I trusted the most if one of them turned out to be untrustworthy then I was screwed from the start. If I couldn't trust them with the little money then what would happen when the big money started coming in? As I was sitting there pondering this situation I cracked the brew. Dennis was sitting there with me and I offered him some. After about an hour of waiting on Mel I told Dennis I was hitting the sack I'd catch up with him later. As I lay there in the bed I thought that maybe this was for the better. I knew I was thinking about quitting anyway so this made the decision easy. The next day I tracked Nino down and told him what had happened. Nino helped me fix the window and we drank a brew. Dennis came down and kicked it with us then Nino rolled out. We sat and watched television until around two thirty, that is when Mel showed up.

By the time Mel came over I had already realized that whoever took the stones did me a favor. One, they showed me that my clique was weak. As far as Mel went he should have been there fifteen minutes after I called him with his pistol in his hand if he was down. This dude didn't show until the next day in the afternoon! If we were going to find some answers that night they were gone the next day. Also if Dennis or Nino took me off it was good that it happened early in the game and not later.

When Mel came by I showed him the window. Dennis was there and he was watching the proceedings. I was explaining to Mel what happened when he pulled out this 380 automatic. I'm looking at this fool tripping on the inside cause to me we needed the heat last night not now.

I told Mel, "Man someone stole from us last night. You came a day late, the trail is cold." I continued, "We have to chalk it up as a loss. You can put the piece up we needed that last night." All while I was talking I was looking Mel straight in the eyes to see his reaction. Mel put the gun up and didn't say too much, why I don't know. Mel walked out onto the porch and hopped down and headed to his car. I hollered to him, "Schedule me an appointment for Friday!" I still had to look good.

This made Dennis bust out laughing but it was true. My hustling days were officially over. I would no longer have the dreams of big money that had clouded my vision every since I had a taste of fast money back in 1989. I have to say I felt quite relieved.

I never did find out who took my stones, dope, for sure. To tell you the truth I really don't want to know. All I do know is that they did me a big favor in helping me give up one of my fantasies. So this thank you is to them, thanks from the top of my heart.

Now that my dope dreams were over I was basically on pause mode. I had came to Detroit three years before with illusions of Mercedes Benzes in my head. Reality had set in I didn't even own a Yugo. I had actually gone backwards because I came with a fresh Celica and had donated it to the junkyard. I was broke.

One thing I had going for me was the fact my hair was getting longer, whoopee! I just sat around the pad and drew unemployment and drank brews with Mr. Pyle. The days of Willyfarce were long past. I had forgot that I even had a degree. I had almost hit rock bottom. Before I did that I had to do one more thing, go to jail.

One day I was sitting around the pad and Stan came through. Stan was drinking on some cheap gin saying we could go to work in a packing house in Westland today. I was registered with the temp company that was sending people there so I called and the company cleared me to go out there to work. We went and hopped in Stan's ride a big Mark IV and rolled.

We were going to Westland where the place was located when Stan realized he didn't know where the hell we were going. We stopped at a gas station and got some shaky directions. I noticed the police were out on this stretch of highway tough. I told Stan, "Man let's go back to Detroit. You know these fools don't want us out here." Stan replied, "Man we out here now we may as well work one day and get the check to make the trip worthwhile." I agreed and we kept driving.

The place where we were going to work at was on the left-hand side I said, "Stan you just missed the turn." Stan stopped and signaled too turn left to go up into the driveway, flashing blue lights. The police, damn! I knew we had broken the one law of Detroit, we had gone past Middlebelt Road into the suburbs. The rule was blacks had free reign in Detroit but wander into the suburbs and that was your ass. Well it was mine because I had warrants out for my arrest in Detroit and Ferndale.

The warrants were all garbage. The Detroit warrants I wasn't worried about they would never put a hold on me for the petty stuff. Ferndale though this was another story, these people ate blacks for breakfast, lunch and dinner. I was beginning to feel like a T-bone steak.

The cop came to the door and Stan started explaining because he didn't have license the first. The cop kindly escorted Stan to the squad car. At this point I was thinking I have two licenses, Wisconsin and Michigan. The Detroit one was suspended and had the warrants on it, the Wisconsin one didn't. I should have had the Wisconsin one in my hand waiting for the cop to come back because I knew he was. I didn't though. Bad move on my part.

When the cop came to my side I started pulling my wallet out. By this time the cop was standing by my door. I grabbed the Wisconsin license out and tried to hand him that. The cop had seen the Michigan one and asked for that one too. I was kicking myself, hard. To this day I don't know why I didn't have that Wisconsin license out waiting for dude. This still grinds a nerve with me.

I just settled back because I knew barring a miracle I was going to jail. I glanced at the sky and no the clouds were not parting, jail was on the horizon. The madness was just starting though.

The cop came back to the car and told me to step out of the car. The fool read me my rights and handcuffed and led me to the car. This is where the scene got bizarre. The cop walked to the other side of the car and opened the door and took Stan out and uncuffed him. The cop then proceeded to inform Stan he was free to go! I sat spellbound as I watched Stan drive away. I was glad Stan got away because he was still on paper from his bit in the joint. My arrest was stupid to me. I was just the passenger in the car. Logically if anyone should have gotten a break it should have been me. I waited until Stan was out of sight and asked the cop why he was holding me. The cop went to saying something about fairness in society. Maybe it was be kind to a Jig day or something, the whole thing was retarded to me. My only comment to the cop was, "Only in America." That got him to shut up.

My main problem once we got to the station house was how long they would hold me for one of the other counties to come get me. I knew Detroit wouldn't waste their time coming to pick me up. Ferndale though had made it known they wanted me to get to know their jailhouse. The precinct had called Ferndale and they told them they would come and get me. I sat there cussing myself out. "That's what I get for trying to work in this garbage." Is what I kept thinking.

After they booked me they asked me if I had two hundred and fifty dollars to bail out. I just laughed I didn't have two hundred and fifty lint balls in my pocket, much less money. The other cops asked the moron who arrested me what was I doing to be picked up. The cop told them the story and mentioned Stan. The other cops looked at him and asked, "You let the driver go and brought in the passenger? How stupid!" I laughed out loud.

I was also hoping that Stan had gone back to Detroit because that cop was red as a beet. That cop would drive all the way to Jackson, Michigan now to pick up Stan just to save face.

I had the right to a phone call. Maybe Mary J or Len could come spring me. That was the proverbial wish in hell. I called anyway Ned answered the phone drunk. Here I come Ferndale County Jail.

My only hope was that Ferndale would not come and pick me up. This would lead them to release me because I didn't have any warrants in Westland. That was some weak wishing because deep down I knew those imbeciles were coming for me, my luck had ran out for a moment.

I stood in the cell pacing hoping for a miracle damn where was Jesus? The cell door opened was it Jesus? Hell no the Ferndale police was here to escort me to Ferndale's public college for disruptive niggers. I just shook my head these fools had nothing better to do than to track down a man for traffic tickets.

The two officers who came to pick me up looked at the arrest warrant and asked, "You are wanted for a speeding ticket?" My only reply was,

"Yep." They shook their heads I guess the situation was ridiculous even to them.

As they transported me to Ferndale they pulled my coat to the fact that Ferndale was overcrowded and I would be shipped somewhere else if I didn't make bail. That was it for me. Up until that point I was thinking I'll do the five days or whatever and get the hell out. When the cops started talking that shipping out garbage, alarm bells went off in my head. I didn't want to get lost in Michigan's messed up penal system. They processed me and placed me in a cell with a pay phone. It was about four o'clock in the evening. I had to bail out before seven or I would have to wait until the morning. I pulled out my ace in the hole I called Mama.

I remembered Mama had said a long time ago that anyone can mess up once and deserved to be bailed out of jail. I had one time for Mama to come bail me out she wouldn't do it twice. The sun was still shining on me because I had never had to use my get out of jail free card before. There was no better time than now.

I called Mama and told her what had happened. Mama listened and told me to call her back. I called Mama back and she told me Elsa was coming to bail my ass out of jail. Elsa was Mama's friend who lived in Detroit. I told Mama I had to get out fast she let me know I should have thought of that fact when I messed up. Before Mama got off of the phone she reminded me that this was my one time to get bailed out and hung up the phone. Whoo, what a relief I was getting out.

The cops brought dinner a Coney Island hamburger deluxe. I could eat it because I knew I was getting out. I looked around the cell and shook my head. It was cold in there. I thought about my partners who were doing time and felt sorry for them. It didn't take me long to realize that the joint was not the place for me. Ice Cube had a lyric that said something about the county was cool because you know everybody. Oh no! I wouldn't give a damn if my whole family was in there it still wasn't the place to be.

Finally the cops came and told me I was free to go. As I walked out I looked at the row of cells with brothers in them and said to myself, "Never again." Elsa's stepson had come and bailed me out. I had never been so glad to leave a place. I had been locked up maybe four hours and I had learned that jail was not the place to be. Before I left they reminded me I had to go to court. I was not going to forget and you can believe that.

Court day came I caught the bus and walked about two miles to the courthouse. I got there early hoping they would use my bail to pay my fines, yeah right. The judge kept the fine and told me I owed another C-note for retrieval service. I had to pay for them to come get me and place me in jail. I was pissed and needless to say I didn't have a C-note on me either.

146

My only hope was if the mailman had brought my check. I had to go home and check the mailbox.

Luck was on my side my check was there. I borrowed Mr. Pyle's car and raced back out there to pay the fee. Len had stopped by so he rode with me. I willingly paid the fine and made sure they hadn't ordered any other bench warrants out for me. I was sick of Ferndale justice so Len and I went and got a fifth and chilled.

After that I just chilled and got fat. I just drew unemployment and bullshitted around with Nino and Rickey. I needed a change of pace it was time to go back to Racine. It was May and my sister was graduating from school. Also Mama and Charlie had stated they would help me get a car. I was on the first train smoking headed to Racine.

CHAPTER XX

When I got back to Racine I figured I would kick it around Racine and chill for two weeks. I had to be back in Detroit in two weeks to turn my unemployment paper in. When I hit town it was cool because I hadn't been there in a year, I hadn't worn my welcome out. It took about four days to do that.

My lifestyle was totally different from when I left. I was serious about kicking it. Me coming in late night and waking up Chuck wasn't wearing to well with the home team. I was basically used to just exploiting and doing what the hell I wanted to people. So when I came back to Mama's house I wasn't used to walking softly. Mama was also getting tired of me using her car and bringing it back smelling of beer.

To solve this dilemma I checked the paper for a used vehicle. I spotted a 77 Coupe Deville for sale. Mama and Chuck said they would help me get it. We went to check it out to see if it was worth buying. When we got there it was rusty on one side but it was clean as hell on the inside. Plus the car ran like a champ. I had my first caddy. My car wasn't a Cadillac it was the Mackalac.

The problem was I was so broke I couldn't afford to buy the plates to make it legit. I wanted Wisconsin plates because I had burned my tail in Detroit. I figured this would keep the police from noticing me and pulling me over with no license. Either Mama or Charlie sprung for the plates on the car. This was probably to ensure that I left. I had worn out my welcome in ten short days maybe less. Before I left though I had to attend Chasity's graduation and holler at Brian. The graduation was on a Sunday I checked out Brian that Saturday. What a blast that was.

That Saturday night I hatted up and went to Milwaukee, the mission find Brian. I hadn't seen my boy in four years I had to kick it with him. When we got by his house the first thing Brian did was trip when he seen the Mackalac. Brian couldn't laugh too hard he was rolling a raggedy red Escort. I was glad to see the dude because it had been a long time as they say.

My cousin Barry had rode up to Milwaukee with me. Barry claimed he could hang with the big dogs. I don't know if he could but we were damn sure going to find out. It was gin time so we grabbed a liter to start off with. I convinced everybody to try mixing it with Rose's lime-juice, this was my latest drink.

Barry hollered, "Man I haven't ate yet!" My reply was, "So! If you want to eat go to a buffet but if you want to drink, hang with me." I had not eaten either. I had learned a long time ago food interferes with the liquor brain process and I definitely could not have that. While we were drinking Brian's boy Elton came by. I knew the guy from Racine. I wouldn't have kicked it with Elton but he was Brian's friend. Elton came in trying to drink up all of the liquor. I watched this negro try to guzzle all of the gin and try to act cool. What a trick Elton was. We decided to cruise town in Elton's car. All while we were riding dude was looking at the liquor like it was going to run away or something. We stopped by some girl's house I knew and kicked it with them for a while. The party was supposed to be downtown so you know that was where I had to be. We headed downtown to scope some females.

On the way downtown Elton started saying he was sick. Elton claimed he was feeling too drunk to drive. I was starting to get pissed because nobody told Elton to try to drink up gin. The situation reached a head when this fool pulled over on the highway to throw up! I threw my hands up and looked at Brian. Brian just laughed and shook his head with his hands in the air. When dude got back in the car I said, "Take us back to my car!"

When we got to my car Brian, Barry and I jumped in. Where Elton went I don't know and don't give a damn as long as it wasn't with me. I asked Brian, "Why you hang with that weak pussy?" Brian just shook his head and laughed. I turned to Barry and asked him, "You rolling?" Barry said, "Yeah!" The liter was gone so I asked Brian where is the nearest liquor store, it was time to re-up. Brian's reply pissed me off, "Man they stop selling liquor around here at nine o'clock." Brian saw the disgust on my face and suggested we hit a sports bar.

When we got there I ordered a round of gin and juice. There was one problem with the scene, no music. I couldn't feel the atmosphere in there because of the lack of music and dance floor. To me the scene was stupid to just get drunk and look at TV and buy women drinks. Give me the juke joint with the dance floor in the corner. So Brian mentioned Vandomes another club in Milwaukee that was supposed to be hyped. Plus Timothy worked there, a dude we went to school with, so it would be free.

We sped to the joint. I was damn near full tilt rolling that big caddy. I was hyped up because I was glad to see my boy Brian and feeling good as hell. By the time we got to the club Barry had passed out in the backseat. When we got there I slapped Barry awake. I asked Barry, "Man you going in? He replied, "No" and started pulling off his shoes laying on the backseat.

Brian and I went up to the door. Sure enough Timothy was standing there grinning like a fool. Timothy waved us in after we rapped for a piece. On the inside they were playing Luke. I thought, "This is more like it!" I snatched me a freak up and headed to the floor.

While I was out there trying to rub the freak's butt I heard the dee-jay announce, "Gin and juice for a dollar for the next ten minutes!" I left the girl on the floor. There was liquor to drink. I went up to the bar I motioned for the bartender to come by me. When the bartender did I told him, "Give me ten gin and juices! I want Rose's lime juice to be the mix you use. By the way don't give me the weak gin use Seagram's the real thing!" When the drinks came I gave Brian four but he gave two back. I had eight drinks around me all of them good ones as far as gin content went. I heard the deejay holler, "Last call!" So I saw a dude I knew from high school and gave him two and chugged the rest. I was messed up royally.

They put us out. Since I hadn't squoze a female I was ready to roll. Barry was still sleep in the back seat. I hopped in the Mackalac and punched it. I had that four-twenty-five howling rolling down 76th street. Brian wanted to go get something to eat at some joint.

When we got there I drove up in the exit driveway and forced the cars that were trying to exit to back up and let me in the parking lot. After I done this we realized the place was too crowded so we left. Brian suggested Hardee's. I didn't argue because I was hungry as hell by then. I hadn't ate all day and the gin was starting to wear on me.

I sped down Capital Drive to get to Hardee's. When we got there the line was out of the lot. I just snapped. I pulled in the lot and shot past every other car that was waiting. I pulled next to the car that was ordering. I hollered, "If I can't eat ain't nobody eating!" I then started blowing my horn and squealing the tires.

I was making as much noise as I could so they wouldn't be able to place their order. Brian was rolling, Barry was looking around drunkenly I was dead serious.

I did this for a minute or two then pulled off. When I got to the exit the police were pulling into the lot. I played it off and pointed the other way like I was talking to Brian. I pulled into the street as I watched the cops go around the building where I had been. As soon as they went around that corner I punched the accelerator.

We got back to Brian's house in no time. Brian was laughing all the way back to his pad. I made a U-turn at his block and my hubcap popped off I was going so fast. I threw the Mackalac in park and ran my hubcap down. This event really sent Brian into gales of laughter. When we got back to Brian's house I went in and passed out on the couch.

When I came to the next day Brian's girl was cooking breakfast. I wolfed down my eggs and told Barry, "Let's roll." I hugged Brian and hit the highway. Chasity's graduation was that day and I didn't want to miss her walking across that stage.

When we got back to Racine I was feeling like crap. I dropped Barry off and went home and showered. I had worn all my good clothes. I had to throw on my Mickey Mouse shirt and some shorts and roll. My hair was shot so I just slicked it back and rolled.

I got there about three names before Chasity was about to be called. When I looked into the gym sure enough the biggest lips in the world was walking across the stage. I had made it just in time. I lingered in the back for a while kicking it with my cousin Miles until the ceremony was over. As Mama was leaving she spotted me I guess I looked like hell because disgust came over her face. Oh well I thought it was time for me to leave anyway. By the time I got back to the house everybody was over there. I kissed Chasity, she swore I missed her walking I tried to tell her different but she wouldn't listen. I think my appearance was disturbing Mama. Oh well it was time to hit the highway. Elsa Mama's friend was riding with me back to Detroit I told her I was ready to leave. I waved goodbye to everyone and hit it.

I drove about fifteen or twenty minutes until we got to the first tollbooth. I was worn totally out from the previous night's festivities and I needed slumber. I told Elsa I couldn't drive any more could she take over. Elsa obliged and I got in the back seat. When I woke up we were in Jackson, Michigan an hour from home. I dropped Elsa off and went to the pad but before I went to sleep I had to drop my unemployment form off. I had to get paid.

I needed a job my unemployment was running out and it was time for me to re-up. I had been through the temp thing too many times I needed a real job. My partner Harry had told me about this place called Ken's automotive. I told him I had a car now and could make it to work, could he hook me up? Harry told me to come early and put an application in and drop his name. I got there early one morning and filled out an application.

While I was filling it out Harry walked past and waved. Harry told me he would holler at the foreman. The next week I was working at Ken's.

At the beginning of the summer tragedy struck my small world. My main man Gray was found dead. I remember earlier in the year Gray's wife paging me asking me had I seen him. I remember thinking Gray had left his wife because he got tired of her sorry son living off of them. The wife's son was a joke Gray and I laughed about when we were working at Ken-Strip. The son was grown and still lived at home. This burned Gray up because the dude was always laid up when he got home.

Gray's wife's daughter and husband lived with Gray and his wife. This situation lead to Gray coming to work a lot of days pissed off. So when Gray's wife started calling me saying Gray had not come home I figured he had left her. I remember Gray saying he loved his wife but the kids had to go. I felt Gray all the way. Because I think I would have went crazy looking at all those grown imbeciles when I came home from work.

With these thoughts in mind I really didn't pay any attention to her when Gray's wife would call me complaining. The wife told me Gray had started smoking dope. I really didn't pay it any mind cause in my book she was going through spurned lover syndrome.

One day Gray's wife paged and when I called back she told me they found Gray dead. I was numb she went on saying he had hung himself. Alarm bells went off in my head because Gray and I used to laugh at people who contemplated suicide. By the time they found Gray's body it had deteriorated severely and they could barely identify him.

This is when the police started saying Gray had hung himself. I wasn't buying any of it all I knew for sure was my main man was dead. When it came time for the funeral I was numb going in the parlor. By them not having a body all they had was a picture of Gray. I remember looking at his stepson and blaming him for Gray being dead. If Gray had started smoking it was because of the pressure of taking care of a family full of lazy punks. The whole thing disgusted me.

I remember his stepson asking me was I going to come by and have a drink with them. I just looked at dude and left after telling him yeah. I had no intention of ever seeing them again. I went by Len's house and bought a half-pint of Canadian Club, Gray's favorite drink and poured it out in his honor. That was my main man and I still wish he were here for the black times I have now.

The Last Gin And Juice Fest

I had been working at Ken's about one month when one Saturday Priest called. Priest told me the crew from Willyfarce was in town for a wedding. I asked Priest was Archie in town he said, "Yeah." I told Priest I was on my way.

When I got over on the east side sure enough Dizzy and Dionte was over Priest's house. After I got over there Kay came over and we went to the liquor store. They got *Hennessy* and I got a forty of St. *Ides*. As we sat there we started talking about old days at Willyfarce. I listened as Dionte and Dizzy told all the stories about people who back then thought they were all that who were know burnt up. For example one dude who was cool was now strung out and was sucking cocks for hits. I was laughing my head off when they mentioned the queers.

They just co-signed what I already knew from when I went to that raggedy school. These dudes were giving up the evidence about the fruits. By now Priest was crying laughing at some of the stories they were telling when he made the comment, "Frank had been saying that shit for years!"

The biggest scenario was one Greek who was about to get married but broke down and admitted he was in love with another man. I don't know if they were lying or not but the story had me splitting my sides with laughter. Is this what the American dream was about?

It was time to go to the reception. Dionte, Dizzy and Priest piled into my car. I was buzzing a little from the forty. When we got there it was more people from Willyfarce in the house. One of the twins was there. Herbert. Sherbert was in Maine. I guess I stood out from everybody else because I had on short pants and they were dressed up. I didn't give a damn they had free gin.

I remember going to the bar and telling the bartender to give me gin and cranberry juice and to not skimp the gin. Priest looked at me and said, "Man you a fool the shit is free." I waved Priest off and eyeballed the bartender as he made the drink.

Archie was in the house and I was glad to see him. We laughed about the things we had done at Willyfarce. I remember being the only one who was really drinking like a fish. This kept on until it was time to go. While I was saying goodbye to the people I knew this guard kept trying to rush us out. The guy was starting to piss me off.

The conversation fell into the usual banter. Herbert and everybody else were leaving. But by this time I was pissed and high. In the lot I was walking and loud talking when the guard just came outside and stood looking at us.

I told Herbert to just leave. He was chicken anyway. Herbert pulled out as I hopped in the caddy. Priest, Dizzy and Dionte were riding with me. I rolled up in front of the joint and started blowing the horn. The guard came out I was squealing my tires. The guy started hollering something and I hollered, "Fuck you fag!" This was the time the dude whipped out his badge. I knew then it was time to roll.

I shot out of that parking lot like a rocket! I did a serious G-turn to the left, little did I know my hubcap popped off, and punched it! Dionte and Dizzy were terrified Priest was cool. I came down Vandyke flying weaving in and out of traffic. When it came time to get on highway ninety-four it got worse.

I was talking and looking over my shoulder into the back seat. All while I was doing this I was rolling in the fast lane tailgating cars. Everybody in the car had the nerve to try to put on seatbelts! I was in rare form, cussing and telling them to take them off. Priest tried to calm me down but I thought he was betraying me so I cussed him too. By the time we got to the house we were going to I was drunk.

Priest tried to get me to go in and chill but that wasn't happening. I told them I would holler at them later. Dionte and Dizzy jumped out of the car running. Priest lingered I waved him off I was mad because I felt they thought I was weak. I pulled off. By the time I got to the first stop sign I felt myself going to sleep. I had to let the car take me home.

I knew time was running out so I made an executive decision, blow all stoplights. I remember blowing two or three because I was blacking out as I drove. To this day I could not tell you where I dropped Priest and the crew off. That was how drunk I was. I forced myself to stay awake until I got to Meyers. It was Coney Island time. I was too hungry and the Arabs in there knew my order: cheeseburger deluxe with loose meat on the fries. I grabbed the food hopped in the ride and sped the three blocks to the pad.

Inside the house I undressed ate two spoonfuls of food then, blacked out. I remember my food order because the next day when I came to it was sitting in the middle of the floor. I must have been standing in the middle of the floor and just sat the food down and stumbled into the bedroom. Oh well another day another drink.

I cleaned up and Priest came by Dizzy, Dionte and Archie came with him. Someone had left a camera in the Mackalac and needed to get it. They all came in and sat for awhile. I saw Archie checking out my pad. When we went outside for them to leave Archie said, "Man take care of yourself." Archie was looking at me with pity in his eyes, me the big dog! Archie was looking at me like he felt sorry for me. This had a wild effect on me because I remember I had written a paper for dude back in school for a brick of Mad Dog. We had kicked it together a many of nights at Willyfarce.

I remember thinking, "I have become a disgrace to myself and to what I am." That did it, no more drinking. I owe Archie big time! If Archie had of never looked at me with that pity in his eyes I may have never looked at myself and kicked the liquor. I love you man.

I stayed clean a week then I remember going by Len's house to watch football on a Sunday. I drank two bottles of St. Ides with him. I remember going home and feeling the brain deadness that comes with drinking. I said to myself, "I don't want to feel like this anymore." That was it, I haven't drunk a brew or a shot of gin since that weekend.

CHAPTER XXI

Life After Gin

One of the first things I did was join Powerhouse gym to work off some of the pounds malt liquor had added to my once svelte frame. I was around two-fifteen or two-twenty at the time. This was entirely too heavy for my liking. I had also gotten tired of the finger waves. I wanted to cut them off but I was so fat I know I would not look right if I cut them off before I lost weight.

I gave up beef and cut back on the chicken and I started to slim down. I think the biggest reason I was slimming down was the fact I had given up the malt liquor beer. I really didn't kick it too much with anyone because I was what was termed a square, I didn't drink any more. I basically worked at Ken's and went to Powerhouse gym when I got the time.

After about two months of being sober I started enjoying my life again for the first time in awhile. I had time to stop and smell the roses as they say. My daughter was starting school that fall so I sent money over for her to get some school clothes. This is something that would have never crossed my mind if I was still drinking. I was at peace with myself for the first time since 1987.

When I went to some of my old stomping grounds sober I realized that the scene wasn't fun at all. I still loved going to check out fine females at strip clubs but now I looked at the dancers as wasting their talent. I remember going to The Outcast one night watching the freak show and tripping. I was saying to myself, "Why are these sisters degrading themselves?" The sisters were not ugly at all. The party was wild. One girl was getting eaten out by one cat, while his boys held her up in the air. It was a lot more going on in there trust me. I won't lie and say I didn't enjoy some of the freak show but I didn't have the same mindset I had before. I remember telling people, "If the things you are doing drunk is so fun then try doing the same thing sober. If it is just as much fun sober as when you were drunk then you are really having fun." That was how I started looking at things.

Later on in the year I cut the sides off of my hair. I guess in my own mind I was still holding on to my hair, my ignorance. I remember coming over to Racine for my birthday that year.

I had told Mama that I was coming back to Racine to celebrate my birthday. Mama was glad to hear I was coming over to Racine. Somehow Mama got into contact with Del and arranged for him to pick me up.

I think this was the time Del brought his buddy from the job with him to the train station to pick me up. This was a trip because this Del's buddy knew all about me and I had never seen his face before. Why did Del's buddy know me? Because the dude had went to Willyfarce.

When I got off of the train I seen Del and started walking towards him. I noticed a dude looking at me with a funny look on his face. I didn't know him so I kept walking up to Del. I hugged Del. I noticed the dude was right there lingering by us. Del then spoke up and said, "This is my guy from the job." I forgot the boy's name but as soon as the dude was introduced he rushed up and shook my hand and introduced himself. I stepped back because I had never seen dude before in my life and he was acting like he knew me. When we got into the car he let it be known that he attended Willyfarce. This didn't mean much to me because the boy was at least five years younger than me. The man couldn't have been at Willyfarce when I was there. The dude then went on to say he pledged a brotherhood on the yard, SOB.

When the man said that it all clicked in my head. Del then broke into the conversation. Del told me how when he had heard that this guy went to Willyfarce he mentioned my name. Del said that when he said Frank James to this dude he tripped. The cat started saying, "You don't know Frank, you don't know the creator." Del said he just looked at dude like he was crazy. So Del told him, "Yeah I know him as a matter of fact I'm going to pick him up from the train station this evening." Needless to say the dude insisted that he come with him.

As I listened to all of this I still couldn't figure why a SOB would give a damn about me. I had severed ties with SOB back at Willyfarce. When we got to Mama's house everything was explained.

When we got inside I asked the guy, "How do you know me?" He replied, "Every SOB know you. You are the founder of PFA." "Yeah" I replied "What does this have to do with SOB?" The guy looked at me as if I was stupid and said, "In our history you are still number one. We learned about the split but you are still the founder and the creator." I grinned and looked at Mama and Del.

I told Mama and Del, "See everybody thought I was lying about me having my own brotherhood." The dude cut in, "He was not lying. Frank is a legend in our clique." The dude then went on saying things about how proud he was to be kicking it with PFA number one.

Del and Mama were shocked. They never believed me when I would tell them of PFA's exploits. I went and got my paddle from downstairs and showed it to the guy. The guy went crazy, for a minute I thought he was going to try to keep my paddle. Then he told me how strong the brotherhood had gotten. They were like fifty strong or so. I asked him about Beep. The dude said SOB run the yard now skip Beep. I laughed at that because Priest was a Beep and I couldn't wait to tell him. It felt good to be a legend.

Anyway on my birthday I went to a strip club in Milwaukee with Brian. Brian and Del took me to the place. I was disgusted. The joint had crack heads up there shaking the last vestiges of their asses. I asked them were they joking or not because I was used to fine women shaking tail. It was sad because the brothers in there really were thinking they were doing something.

This experience also pulled my coat to the fact that Milwaukee and Racine were light years behind Detroit. I knew I could never have any type of night-life in Wisconsin ever again because the people were so far behind. This was good in a way because life in the "D" had severely changed the way I looked at things.

I knew it was time for the perm to go. I vowed to cut it before the year was out. This didn't happen because I had a friend coming from St. Louis to bring in the new year with me. I got one last set of waves. Five days into 1995 I cut the last of my hair off. Things really started to change for me.

1995

I went into the barbershop after my friend had gone back to St. Louis looking for Mel. It was time for the hair to go. Mel wasn't there so I got Micheal to cut me instead. I wanted to go back to my little rounded box look. I still had a lot of hair on my head because I still had my top and that was where my hair was the longest. I figured I had enough to go back to the style I first wore four years ago before I got waves, wrong.

When I told Micheal what I wanted he agreed. As Micheal started getting closer and closer to my scalp I noticed I didn't have any new growth.

Micheal stopped at the level I told him to. The cut looked wild because the hair was still straight. I told Micheal to cut down until the perm was gone. The other barbers in there who knew me were looking at the situation because I guess they knew what was coming.

When Micheal finished he put the mirror in my hand and spun me around to look at myself in the mirror. I was bald. I had a total bald head. Micheal had given me a bald fade totally. I had some peach fuzz on the top that was it. The scary part was it didn't look like it was going to grow back either. This was the result of me getting "blasted," this is what I called perms, every three or four weeks for four years.

My scalp was discolored from the perms. I immediately went to the store and got me some green grease to build it back up. My hair started coming back but it stayed sick for three years after that.

The Transformation

This may sound flaky to some but the following statements are true. I was always radical in my thinking about white-black relations. When I cut my hair off it seemed like a whole new world was opened to me. I started receiving information on why I thought like I did and why I wasn't too far from wrong.

I always read even though it was only Stephen King books. All while I was drinking and at my lowest in Detroit I always had a book around. My inner mind told me to keep reading and my brain would not get foggy. The day after I cut my hair I went out to Northland. As I was looking for some gear I found this bookstore. It was called The Truth Bookstore.

When I went in the store just to browse and see the art. I wound up looking at these books that seemed to make all kinds of sense to me even though I had never heard of them. It was like I had a veil lifted off of my head and could think clear again. To solidify what I'm saying the first book I bought was *The Egyptian Book of the Dead* translated by Gerald Massey. I remember talking to the woman behind the counter and leaving feeling elated.

I took a whole bunch of flyers with me to put up in Coney Island and the barbershop. I wanted everybody to get hold of some of the knowledge I was beginning to feel. I had already been exposed to some history at Willyfarce. I also got history from brothers I had met like Priest and Vince. This was different, I was finding this info out on my own. The crazy part was that it felt like I was just re-learning what I already knew but had forgotten.

When I went to the barbershop to put the flyer up Mel was in there. As I was putting it up on the wall I said, "Man they got the word out there." Mel just looked and said, "Oh yeah?" I replied, "Yeah!" Grinning as I walked out.

After reading *The Egyptian Book of the Dead* I was hungry for more. I could not afford all of the books I needed to read. It was time to go to the library. This time I hit the downtown library. This was really like I had entered a whole new realm.

I always knew that Blacks were much more than they had allowed themselves to become. Now I had the proof. I researched the Egyptians and this lead me to other venues of knowledge. I read books like, *Serpent in the sky, Ancient Egypt the Light of the World*. All types of information that just showed how great the Black man was and should be at this time. The information was also exposing the Caucasian for what he was a liar and a thief.

I was reading books at the time that I didn't understand until years later. I was quizzing Priest to death about stuff. Priest finally said, "I could tell you everything but you won't appreciate it unless you find it out on your own." At the time I figured it was a weak excuse to say I don't know. A few weeks later I realized what Priest said was so true.

I also was looking at myself in a new light. I pulled outside of myself and looked at my existence. I had slipped off of my pedestal. I had fallen so far until I had not even been to a nice sit down restaurant in years. To solve this dilemma I watched Priest.

I do not mean I jocked Priest or anything like that. I mean I watched how Priest carried himself, his demeanor and basically his etiquette. I had a hard core ghetto demeanor because that was where my head was. In order to vibe on a higher level I had to take what I learned at that state and apply it on another level. I used Priest as a springboard in order to revive my true persona. Also hanging with Priest was more stimulating mentally than kicking it with Len or Nino. Nino and Len are cool people but they don't vibe on anything but petty topics like the majority of the masses. I was hungry for the real knowledge, skip football. Priest and I would vibe for hours on black topics. We would rap for hours talking about history and how the Caucasians knew who we were and we didn't. This is about the time my materialistic urges left me.

I used to be very materialistic in my thinking. I wanted mink coats and diamond rings and Cadillacs. After reading and realizing what we once had one thing became obvious to me. The crème of this civilization wasn't worth the dirt between my toes. I realized that if the Caucasian had of never bothered black people we would have a civilization greater than the average person could even imagine. To prove this go back to Kemit and you will see that we already had it. We were truly much more than what we had allowed ourselves to become.

I was reading all the time. I read at work at home on the toilet, everywhere. I became a vegetarian. I kicked the chicken to the curb along with the turkey. People at the gig started to notice.

They already didn't mess with me because after working there for one month I threatened to kick the supervisor's ass over my check being wrong. After this scenario they cut me a wide berth at the job. This is also how I know that you don't have to suck up in order to keep your job. I never did and I have never been fired. I always spoke my mind and let my work speak for me. I did a good job so the boss just figured leave him alone and he'll do the work.

As I was becoming more enlightened I was also looking at the brothers around me on the gig. I tell you this was not a pretty sight. The Negroes on the job let the Caucasians get away with anything they pleased. Take for instance the relationship between this old caucasoid Pete and a negro named Calloway. Pete talked to Calloway any way he wanted too. Pete never worried about Calloway saying anything back. Pete laughed at Calloway's wife and his religion. Calloway claimed he was a minister.

One day while Pete was ripping dude a new asshole Pete looked up and seen me looking at them. After Pete finished giving Calloway hell he came over and talked to me. Pete said that he had to talk to Calloway and the other brothers who worked for him like that. Pete went on and said I was different from the others. I looked at the fool and he walked away. I knew that if I let Pete talk to me like that he would be yelling at me.

One time the three brothers who worked under Pete were in the back arguing about something. Pete went back and stood in the doorway of their area and hollered, "Shut up!" Pete continued on, "I better not hear any grumbling from any of you!" You can bet your last dollar on the fact that it got quiet back there.

The brothers who worked up front making motors always said the brothers in the back were stupid. They were not any better. They just made a little more scratch. The white foreman made them jump through hoops also when he wanted to.

Around the beginning of February or March I started drinking *Hennessy* with Priest and Jessie. Priest wouldn't drink any bullshit liquor so we broke ourselves drinking *Hennessy* instead.

This lasted until one weekend Priest bought some champagne. I remember looking at Priest shocked he said, "The wine was cool and delicate on the body." That sounded right to me. All I needed was an excuse to drink. I was slipping back into the drinking mode. I bought a bottle of J Roget a few days later and tried that. I fell in love with the stuff. I was back drinking but only J Roget champagne and *Hennessy* when I went out.

I had everybody around me drinking J Roget. I told them the wine had slow high, that it only took one bottle. Me of course being the wine connoisseur I needed two. Even though I was drinking again it was nothing like before. I would drink a bottle of wine, that's what I called it, once maybe twice a week. I only drank *Hennessy* when I was out clubbing, or at a card party. I had come to the conclusion that I needed my mind sharp in order to break down some of the info I was reading.

The one person I worked with who even attempted to read was a Mexican named Hosea. Hosea was real cool and quiet. Hosea studied history too. One day he seen me reading *The Metu Neter*, when I told Hosea it was Egyptian he nodded like he was with it.

The next day Hosea came in with a book on Osirus that I had never seen before. Hosea also gave me some real old national geographic magazines with pictures of Kemit in them. I put one picture of a Pharaoh up in my work area to let everybody know who was holding the area down.

Around April of that year I was getting bored at Ken's. I had been there almost a year and this was the longest I had ever been at one job. I was also tired of getting dirty and working long hours. My sister came to town and sparked an idea in my head.

Chasity came to town for two weeks in April or May of 1995. Chasity was getting ready to enlist in the Airforce. Chasity must have seen I had changed from the way I was when she visited before and let me know I was wasting my time in Detroit. Chasity suggested that I move back to Racine and put my degree to use. I had been trying to get another gig in Detroit but it was hard because all I had was factory experience. After Chasity went back home I thought about it. I talked to Mama and she let it be known that my Aunt Beth could set me up with some interviews for caseworker positions. This would be working with welfare women. I figured I was just the man for that job because I had the answer, get a job.

I went over and interviewed with some people. I thought I did well but I was still speaking my broken English. I figured the people I needed to reach would understand me. The people who were doing the hiring did not see it that away. From the encounter though I got the impression that I would be able to get out of the factory quicker in Racine than in Detroit. I started making plans to move. I didn't tell anyone my plans I just intended to fade to black.

162

I knew you had to work on year to get a week vacation from Ken's. I was almost there and I wanted to get my vacation check I had worked so hard for. To ensure I got my vacation I put the union rep on the case. I didn't tell him why but I let him know that the week I made a year, that Friday I wanted my vacation added onto that check. The week I was slated to make one year on the job I worked Monday through Wednesday. Thursday I called in sick. When Friday came I walked into Ken's grinning. I told the foreman I was retiring and to give me my check. The idiot had a puzzled look on his face and I nodded yeah. I then asked the foreman, "Where do I go to give them the address to send my last check?" He told me upstairs.

When I came back down the word had spread around the plant that I was quitting. I had also let it out that I had a college education and was going to work in my field. Pete had a look on his face that said, "I knew he was different."

I went and hollered at all of my buddies and told them to stay strong. I gave Hosea the plates off of the Mackalac, he collected plates from different states. I looked at the shop and the brothers and walked out. That phase of my life was through.

I'll never forget the feeling I had walking out and letting everybody know I was quitting. It has to be the same feeling that a convict gets when he is leaving prison after he has been paroled. I felt elated to be leaving that greasy factory. I vowed I would never work and get dirty again.

The next stop was for me to go and get my security deposit for the apartment. This was going to be my last stop for me in Detroit, after this was secured I was going to hit the highway and go to Racine. This turned out to be my biggest pain.

Gwen had told me if I ever moved I could get my security deposit back. I was secure in the fact that I had two hundred and fifty dollars coming. I knew Gwen had let me be late numerous times with the rent during my stay at the building, but she had said that had nothing to do with my money.

I had served as caretaker for the building when Gwen could not get anyone else to do it. I had also played security when some young cats wanted to burn the building down. So Gwen had gotten her money's worth out of me while I stayed there.

I had talked to Gwen earlier in the week and told her I was moving Friday. Gwen had told me to call her at her office and she would cut me a check no problem. The fool tried to play on me.

I called Gwen Friday morning and she told me to call back around one. Fine, I called at one and there was no answer. I paged her and still no response from the here. I tried calling Gwen back, no such luck. The situation was getting hectic because I wanted to hit the road around three o'clock.

This went on until I called Gwen's mother's house and her sister answered the phone. Gwen's sister knew me from being the caretaker at the apartment so I told her the situation. Gwen's sister came right out and wrote me a check for my money it was getting close to five o'clock so I sped to their bank to cash it. Hey you never can tell with African Americans.

By the time I got the check cashed and the oil changed in the caddy it was late evening. I just chilled and spent the night on Mr. Pyle's couch. We sat and talked until late into the night. Mr. Pyle was sad that I was leaving Detroit. I knew I would miss Mr. Pyle and his cigar. I owed that old man a lot.

Mr. Pyle had got my phone turned on in my apartment in his name so I would have one. Before I left I made sure that it was paid up I might add. When I was broke and wanted a beer Mr. Pyle always had one. Mr. Pyle's kindness to me is what enabled me to be kind to people later on in life.

Later on in the evening I called Mary J and Len and told them I was rolling. Mary J remarked that I came into Detroit with a roar, now I was leaving quiet like I stole something. I had stole something while living in Detroit, my mind back.

That next morning I told Mr. Pyle I would see him later and left. I stopped and gassed up the caddy. Before I left the gas station I called Dennis and told him I left him something in my apartment, my weights. I hopped in the car and hit highway 96 until I got to Southfield. Then I took the Southfield freeway to highway 94 west and headed for Chicago. The dog was going home.

I was rolling like Nolan on my way to the pad. I got to the other side of Chicago when I hit traffic. I had my Parliament music blasting just chilling. The oil light came on right before I got to the first toll booth coming towards Milwaukee. This had never happened before but it went right back off. I finally got past the tolls and opened her back up. I got to highway twenty just outside of Racine when I noticed the oil light was back on. I cut the radio off and I heard tapping. "Oh shit!" I thought, "Don't die on me now Mackalac!" These were the thoughts that were rushing through my head.

The tapping started getting louder and louder as I got close to Mama's house. I ran a red light so I could get home faster. As I pulled up at Mama's house the noise was loud as hell now so I hurried up and cut the car off. I went inside hugged my family and went to sleep.

The next day I went outside to check the oil in the Mackalac with Chuck. The car was damn near empty! I was sweating because I was thinking the motor was gone. Chuck took me to get three quarts of oil.

I dumped them into the caddy and got inside to start her if she would. As soon as I turned the key the Mackalac fired right up. The knocking was loud for a second then I guess that oil started circulating and the noise just quieted down. The caddy was sounding like a ninety-five! I was elated I kissed the steering wheel grinning. Chuck just looked at me and shook his head. I went up to the tire place and they told me when I got the oil changed an old washer was used. This caused my oil to drip out and almost cost me my engine. I was pissed to say the least. I then thought about how far I had come driving the car with damn near no oil and I had to grin. It was a Cadillac to its heart baby!

As I look back on the Detroit years I came to this conclusion. Most people go to grad school to get their masters degree I went to Detroit. My graduate training was a hard core dose of the real world and I loved it. I had graduated from the University of Detroit and made it with honors.

CHAPTER XXII

I was back in square Racine. It only took me one week to start thinking I had made a mistake. One reason was the fact I wasn't used to staying with anyone. This was a hindrance but the main problem was there wasn't anything to do. I just read and slept.

The situation was so screwed up in Racine I couldn't even get an apartment. I had scratch but I guess my reference in Detroit was too big of a risk. My once promising job leads had evaporated like water in the sun. My bankroll had gone on a diet also, so I needed some scratch. Guess who I wound up working for, you guessed it a temp company. I was placed at K-wax filling orders.

It worked out in a way because I worked second shift and Mama and Chuck worked first. This kept me out of their hair. I just made the scratch and put it in the bank. I paid Mama and Chuck every week because I was thankful for them letting me stay there. This was getting old though.

I went to see my aunt's ex husband about getting me a job. The funny thing about that was this was the same Negro who had attempted to get me a job five years before. Needless to say he said he couldn't help me and of course he brought up the previous time he had attempted to help me. Skip him I think the real reason he didn't help me was the fact he had something against my mother. Add in the fact that he was screwing white women and you get the picture. As I look back though I realize that everything worked out perfectly. It was never meant for me to stay in that weak city. One Sunday I was up in Milwaukee kicking it with my man Brian. We went by my aunt's house and she told me about this white woman who had cleaned up some apartments. I guess when the white woman bought them they were like the Carter Arms in *New Jack City*, now though they were top notch. I had nothing to lose so I called. We went by the lady's office to check out the apartments.

It was an older white woman who was this miracle worker. The apartment she showed me made my apartment in Detroit look like crap. I was hesitant about getting the place because of all the hassle I went through attempting to rent other places. I had the feeling she was going to bullshit me.

I told the lady the one I liked and she said, "Cool, let's go back to the office and I can run a check on you." The woman knew I was from Detroit because I mentioned my previous landlord talking to her. The test was a credit check. I slumped I knew I was through because even though I had gotten my student loans cleared up I still was all over the credit bureau. I told the woman straight up, "If you are checking that then don't waste your time, I'm in there." She looked and said, "I'll check anyway."

When the woman finished she told me I was not in real bad shape. I knew I had the phone bill from Detroit and the heating from when I stayed on Linden. There were some other items in there but I only owed around a thousand dollars to the bureau. The lady then let me know I could move in immediately if I wanted too. I told her I needed time to get my affairs in order but the fifteenth of November would do me. She said fine and I had a pad.

Brian had been telling me for years that they had a television station that anybody could get on. Well now that I was moving to Milwaukee I could do just that. I started my training on my birthday 1995 three days later I was a certified producer on MATA, Milwaukee Access Telecommunications Authority. Look out world Frank James was hitting public access!

When the fifteenth rolled around I couldn't get in touch with Del or Brian. I had to get Mama to help me to move. It was then that I realized that Mama was aging. I always looked at her as being a super-woman but helping me move took a lot out of her. I felt bad because I didn't realize it until Mama mentioned it later. It was this that made me notice that my superwoman was human up to a point.

After I got all my stuff inside the pad I took Chuck his truck. I then went back to my apartment. I had an apartment but no job and rent was due in fifteen days oh, well welcome to America.

I needed a job quick. I was walking through the mall with Brian and saw a help wanted sign. I went and applied for the job as a joke. I talked to the lady and she told me to come back for an interview. I did and I was working at a T-shirt store. This was the first job I had ever had that was outside of a factory or warehouse setting. It was a million miles from Ken-Strip. I knew though I needed a real job.

I went to Quickie services and took all the tests to get into the office side of the job market. I aced all of the tests but my work experience was all factory and warehouse work. This need I say was not the type of experience Mr. Charlie wanted to work in the house. I told the girl who worked at Quickie, Terri, that I wanted to get a job outside of the factory. Terri told me she understood and would work on it.

I kept working at the store being bored as hell. Around a week later I got a call from Terri. I went to her office which was located in the mall I worked in. Terri had set me up with an interview with channel nine as an assistant producer. I was ecstatic! The interview was set up for the next day. I went to the interview in my best suit, I may not have known anything but I was looking good. The interview was at 9:30 I got there at 9:00. I was nervous but I was cool because I knew if they gave me half a chance, I would get the job.

A tall white woman came out to interview me her name was Peggy. Peggy talked to me for a few minutes in the atrium then we went into the station. I think Peggy was impressed with my appearance. Peggy and the reporter, Tom Flannery interviewed me. To tell the truth I think Peggy wanted to hire me right then and there. But Tom had his doubts about me. After it was over I went home and called Terri and told her what happened. Terri told me she would check it out for me. The next day I went to work at the T-shirt joint.

When I got off I stopped by Quickie services to check on jobs. While I was in the lobby Terri came out and said, "We have been trying to call you all day. Peggy and Tom want to talk to you again." Terri then instructed me to wait while she went into the back to call channel nine. When Terri came back up front she told me to go right over and wished me luck.

This time when I got there Tom was asking all of the questions. Tom grilled me left and right about why would I want the job. Tom kept stressing the fact that it was only a temporary position for a few weeks. Tom didn't know I had done worse temporary assignments before.

Finally I just told Tom. "Man, I'm just looking for a way to get back into the field I went to school for. I know I can do the job all I need is the chance." Tom looked like that prosecutor in the old Perry Mason shows who could never win. Tom finally said, "Okay." He then looked at Peggy. To this day I don't think Tom wanted to hire me. I think Peggy pushed the issue to get me in there, why I don't know. I got the job.

I called Terri at Quickie and thanked her. I went and quit the T-shirt gig, why I don't know and called Mama. Mama was happy for me. As I stated why I quit the T-shirt gig is beyond me because I was only working twenty hours a week. This decision lead to some very hard times. I was past broke. The job though was a different story. I was happy as hell working at channel nine. This was a million miles from all the dirt grime and fuck up of all those factories I had been in. There was one problem though I was too raw, still ghetto in my speech. I spoke Black English to the hilt which was fine in my world. However, answering phones and calling white folks was another story entirely. Example: "Hello, the nine-line, what you need?" This is a little too hard for that grandma who wants to call up and complain about the Maytag man. What I did to get around it was not to change my voice but to put some of those good old Willyfarce words I had forgotten to use. I still sounded harsh but I could pass.

After a week I had even remembered my white voice I used to use. Sometimes I would use that and then bust out laughing after I finished because I sounded so stupid. Peggy told me I was doing fine. I was so glad to be out of the factory I would remark, "I have the best job in the world." This always made Peggy laugh when she heard it.

One day I had to go with Tom on a shoot with a photog. On the way back to the station I noticed the photog. had a federation badge like the one Picard wore in *Star Trek, the Next Generation*. I asked who was the trekkie and the photog. said he was.

We talked about the series and some episodes. We compared the old one with the new one. Tom was shocked that I kept up with such things. It tripped him out enough until he went and mentioned it to Peggy. Peggy later remarked, "Hardcore Frank watches Star Trek."

After two weeks I was holding it down at channel nine. Tom and Peggy even left town for a week and I ran the office. I was the man. I did some good while I was in there. I helped a lot of people get better service by simply just calling the companies.

The pinnacle was I got an elderly couple a new furnace put into their house in winter. These people wrote a letter to channel nine thanking me for my assistance. I was having fun but Christmas break was almost up and the interns would be coming back. My time was running out.

Before I left channel nine though the ice broke between Tom and I. One day Peggy was acting like a real bitch. Peggy was in a horrible mood as far as helping with problems. This didn't surprise me because I never lose track of the fact that white folks are white folks.

Later on Peggy apologized for the way she had acted earlier. It all lead to Peggy saying something to the effect about how she looked compared to other days. Peggy said something that lead to her appearance. I said, "I don't look at you anyway." Tom looked and laughed Peggy looked at me and I just kept doing my job. I could give less than a damn how she looked.

I was here to do a job not oogle white women which as we all know wasn't my flavor.

After that Tom opened up. Tom started talking sports and everything else. My only guess is that Tom was relieved to know that I didn't want to screw Peggy. Tom was probably relieved to know there was one Black Man who didn't covet white women.

One day before my assignment was up I was doing my duties when Tom and Peggy told me to give a resume to Pompei Patterson. This caught me by surprise so I asked, "What?" They went on and said, "Give Pompei a resume so you can get a job working in staging." Hell I didn't know what staging was but I needed the job.

I went over my Aunt Hannah's house and whipped up a resume and submitted it to Pompei. Pompei was a brother and he told me the position was only for sixteen to twenty hours per week. I told him that was all right with me it was my foot in the door as they say. I got the job so I went and told Tom and Peggy. They just nodded their heads. I thanked them for the lead. I later found out they damn near made Pompei hire me for the position. I had a job in TV after all those years it seemed as if I finally was shaking the dirt off of my hands.

I want to clear one thing up before we go on. Peggy gave me a chance and I produced. I filled a position when it needed to be filled. Now most black people feel when this happens, my scenario, they owe white folks. Myself I've never felt I owed Peggy or Tom a damn thing.

The reason being they recognized talent and capitalized off of it. It was an even trade off, they needed help I gave it. I hope black people out there read this and take heed of what I'm saying. These people know talent when they see it and you best believe by you working for them or with them that it is benefiting them.

Heading into 1996 it seemed like things were going to finally go right for FJ.

CHAPTER XXIII
1996

By the time the New Year came around I was broke totally. I had paid my rent with all I had left and I knew working sixteen hours in staging wasn't going to keep the rent paid. My Aunt Hannah told me about a place that was hiring for okay money. Money was one thing I needed badly so I went to work for Tel-Sel, a telemarketing company.

I took a test and I was in. The coolest thing about the place was you could work as long as you wanted. I could only repeat those sales lines only so long so I limited myself to ten hours a day. Working at this place helped me get my diction back in working condition. The job also helped me keep the rent lady off of my back.

I told Pompei to just schedule me for Saturday and Sunday. This enabled me to work full-time at Tel-Sel and still keep my job at channel nine. The only downside was I would be working seven days a week. This really was no problem because Milwaukee was lame as a three-legged dog so partying was not an option.

While I was working I was also putting together spots for the show Brian and I were going to do on MATA. It wound up being my show because Brian didn't want to go on the air. The name of it was going to be "Being Frank with Frank."

I got the name from this guy named Philo from K-Wax when I worked there. I told Philo on the show I was going to be bringing the truth as raw as it could be. Philo said, "You should call it Being Frank with Frank." I looked at Philo and he went on, "You going to be raw right?" I nodded yeah. Philo then said, "You being Frank and you're Frank hence Being Frank with Frank." I liked it but before I ran with it I checked with Brian.

Brian still wanted to be behind the scenes producing. It was my show. A legend was born.

We went out and did a few five minute promos for the show. The promos had me voicing over a black screen with just a white dot in the middle where I was announcing I was coming. Before we could do a big show we had to take classes on editing and shooting. The classes were intense they were wild it was like a four year program jammed into three days.

I remember the first promo we did with me on camera. It had me sitting in a chair with a picture of Milwaukee in the back of me. I was asking people if they were tired of looking at fat unattractive female hosts. At the time I was going to focus on male-female relationships and break them down from a real one's perspective. The funny thing was I had my suit on but I had forgot my dress shoes. So the whole promo had to be shot on a tight shot. I remember Brian setting up shoots at bars. We would shoot pack up and drink then leave. Hell I was still drinking *Hennessy* when I was out and about.

It was finally showtime April 14th 1996 at eight p.m. Brian had the studio all set up by the time I got there. While we were going over the finishing touches a tall cat walked in offering to help with our production. His name was Carver.

For that first show we had all the superstars of public access working on the floor. I had a little studio audience consisting of Mama, Chuck, Beth, Hannah and Cheryl my aunts. The first show went cool I got a lot of feedback from the callers so we went from there. I hosted Hardcore Reports a few times and we set up the format to do more Being Frank with Franks.

At the same time the telemarketing job was getting old. The place was a trip. They paid people on Mondays to ensure you came to work on Saturday mornings. I was constantly complaining about that. To me it was an insult to the people who worked there it was treating them like kids.

We all know that the place was all black except for the front office. To me it was the same old thing white folks regulating black people. Some of the blacks felt me but they were too scared to say, much less do something about it. I wrote a letter complaining so the white overseer knew me but I was a soldier with no army. I started job hunting again.

Once again I had an appointment with one of my aunt's pro Negro friends. This was another Negro who if he could do something for me wouldn't. I knew right off the bat that the Negro wasn't true because he was looking at my suit straightening his shirt out. The Negro then proceeded to look at my resume making statements to the fact that I didn't have a lot of experience. Well hand that man a prize! No duh! This is why I needed some help. The Negro finished with the usual spiel he would do what he could to help me.

While I was walking out the Negro told me F-Star was interviewing and hiring people today. The Negro hinted that I should try to get in there. I knew then that this man would never help me. I didn't know anything about banking. If I said no, he could say he tried to set me up with that job but I refused it. Then if I interviewed and failed the Negro could say he did all he could I just blew my chance. I said okay knowing damn well I didn't want to work in no damn bank.

I interviewed first with a gay white man who informed me that there were some positions open for people without banking experience. My next interview was with Jeanette Kelly. I quickly impressed her with my demeanor and willingness to learn. Jeanette told me the job was balancing accounts and it was simple. Jeanette then asked me did I have a checkbook. I almost busted out laughing checkbook yeah right. I told Jeanette no but I was a quick learner. Jeanette made me an offer and I was in corporate America.

I went to Tel-Sel and gave them my weeks notice. I called Mama she was glad for me. I was glad too, I had a new challenge. I would now wear shirts and ties to work, look out world a field hand has snuck into the big house!

The first day I met my partner Francis. I was assigned the hardest account in the bank, balancing ADP. Francis was from Hungary or something but she knew her job. That account was the hardest job I had ever done before. I knew that after the second day I was going to quit. I couldn't let the job beat me though, I was going to master the job then quit. I got to the point where I could do it by then though it was time for me to get my accounts that I would do daily by myself.

After two weeks the bank wanted to send us to Illinois to train for a week. I was skeptical at first because I didn't want to be jammed up without any wheels. Then the supervisor asked me to drive a van over to Illinois this meant I would have wheels. Okay I played Morgan Freeman and drove four white women over to Illinois to train.

I picked up my job quick, man was it a relief from ADP. I could come to the hotel and relax in the evenings with no worries from the job. I had quickly let the women know that there were restaurants within walking distance, don't bother me. Even though they looked like Ms. Daisy I wasn't playing it.

This was quite routine until one day the two black women and me who went over there to train went to lunch. We were all new to the gig so we were feeling each other out. They started talking relationships. I told them a story about a brother who I thought was down with black power until I seen him with a white woman and three mixed kids. The one sister Shanice just said, "Huhn." The other sister was a different story.

The other sister cut in saying, "Hold on mother fucker! Freeze that mixed kid shit!" I looked she went on, "Yeah nigga my Mama white and look at me I'm fine as hell! So now I'm mixed!" Shanice was looking at her then looking at me.

I did the only thing I could do I busted out laughing. Shanice looked at her nervously and said, "Dude just laughed at you." I thought the outburst was a joke because the broad was only one shade lighter than myself. I stopped laughing and asked, "For real?" The sister said, "Yep." I just sat and looked at her.

I remember riding back in the car wondering what kind of place had I come to where I couldn't tell the black people from the whites. After we got back I quickly got used to working nine to five and working with a bunch of females in dresses. It was kind of funny because it was the same as the factory in one sense, blacks on the bottom whites on the top.

When I finally got my cube it was on. I would just sit and trip all day with my co-workers. I really never did any work the whole year and a half I worked there. I just talked game with females and had fun. I had a lot of good friends in the bank on seventeen.

There was one female though who really brought a smile to my face and the thought of her still does, Candi. Candi was a young intern in the bank when I met her. Man was Candi fine. I had to meet her so I just walked up to Candi and started talking to her. She turned out to be cool as hell.

One thing about me had changed in Detroit I had gained control of my lower nature. So instead of scheming on how to get some I just played the friend role. Plus on the other hand I remembered Clint Eastwood's line in *Magnum Force*, "A man has got to know his limitations." Keeping it real I think deep down I knew I would have been in love with Candi. Candi made the rough days smooth as glass.

For example one day the bank had me thinking hard about a problem in one of the accounts. The situation was hectic because I could not figure it out. I dropped my pencil and bent over to pick it up. As I bent over I felt someone over me. I turned my head and was looking at some feet then legs leading up into some booming thighs. As I scanned higher my eyes passed over a tight skirt flat stomach and some thirty fours topped off with a cute face grinning at me. It was Candi. The view made my heart start sending excess blood to my genitals, but I got myself under control. I couldn't help but to grin, hell I'm grinning now three years later. We talked a minute and I walked her off of the floor. Man that girl was stacked.

After that I raced back to my cube and solved that problem and two or three more that day. It was funny because some of my female friends who sat in the row I did would make remarks like, "He done seen his candy girl now he happy." Yeah I'd grin and think to myself, "Why don't you get your act together?" The sorry bank transferred Candi to a branch. I felt like singing Bill Withers, "Ain't no sunshine when she's gone."

Now before we get off course the bank was cool but the main focus of my life was the show, Being Frank with Frank. As stated before when I first started off my focus was going to be male female relationships from a black man's perspective. That shit changed in a hurry.

I received info on w-2. A racist welfare reform program created in Wisconsin. I put that information out on the air. The show was tight because I was telling people that welfare was over they are going to cut you off. No one listened though they kept saying welfare couldn't be over. Yeah okay later that year wham the party was over. I got some info from some black officers about black on black crime. I showed how we were being manipulated into killing one another. How we were doing Mr. Charlie's job for him. No one wanted to listen though.

I was really getting fed up because no one was listening. The people who I kicked it with daily didn't even pay attention. Around July I was going to talk about how we spend money with people and they don't respect us.

What had lead to this was a sister had gotten beat down in a damn beauty supply place. This happened while the sister was pregnant and because the owners thought she stole something. Other factions had staged a boycott of the business. While they would be out there boycotting other blacks would be walking around them going in. It was ridiculous.

By this time I was seeing Milwaukee as being country as pork sausage. I was feeling pissed so this was going to be my last show. No one knew this but me. Around the end of the show I got a call from a little boy who said he watched all the time and he listened to the information. I finished up and that made me want to keep on going. Maybe someone would wake up and catch the vibe. I started going to the library tougher and all types of doors opened for me at the magic place. I also started receiving info from people about black scholars I had never heard of. I got turned on to Amos Wilson, Chancellor Williams, Anthony Browder, John Henrik Clarke & Frances Cress Welsing to name a few. Now we were getting down!

I met a brother named Kendall who had more info than a little bit. Look out, now I had even more information to back up my beliefs about us being much more than the present picture.

I realized that everything we had been taught was a lie to keep us from finding our true selves. I started doing shows that were really hitting home with the mentality of the Negro. This is also when I realized I had to keep it pure. I wasn't on any side except the Black side.

That August the story broke about the drugs being placed into the community by the government. I was on it like a cheap suit. Realistically any fool knew that the drugs had to be placed in the black community because we don't own any jets to bring it in. I went on the air telling it like it was, and still is. After the show Brian came up to me and told me he was quitting. Brian attempted to tell me why but I told him he didn't owe me any explanation.

One of the reasons was money but I told Brian there wasn't any money in what I was doing, speaking out. If you are doing it right there shouldn't be any money involved and I was determined to do it right. I had gone past the point of trying to get rich off of this. I was at the point where I was doing it because it was the right thing to do period. I knew the black race was much more than what it had became and I wanted everyone to know it.

The only hindrance that came with Brian leaving was I had to go off the air. I had to take the studio class in order to reserve the studio. I had to go off for a few months but when we came back in December we were back and Blacker. I had total control of the physical side of the show and the spirit was handling the other side of the show.

Around September I started getting sick of the bank. The shit was getting old and I needed a change of pace. When I left they threw a party for me, I would miss my friends but not the bank.

I let Pompei know I was able to work during the week at channel nine. One Wednesday I had to floor a show called *Teen Perspective*. I saw this black dude standing there calling the shots. I asked my other partner Dennis who the guy was and he told me Mickey Renfro. Dennis also pulled my coat to the fact that he owned *Teen Perspective* and was cool.

After the show I introduced myself to the brother. Mickey was down to listen to my ideas so he gave me a card. I called Mickey to set up a meeting to discuss some show ideas I had. I threw on a shirt and tie to go meet the brother, if I could get dressed up for a Caucasian I could do it for a brother.

We talked about show topics and we both had the same concept for a teen sports show. Mickey then said something to me that is still with me today.

When Mickey heard the show concept asked, "Why didn't you do it?" I was puzzled Mickey went on and said, "You had the show concept, why didn't you do it?" I sat back and thought. I had fifty million excuses why I didn't do it which lead me to never trying. Mickey took me off the hook by saying he liked my concept write up a proposal and we'll make it happen.

Once again I was over my Aunt Hannah's house typing up some quick last minute work. I wrote up a horrible one-page proposal and it was on. Step-up, Mickey's company, couldn't pay me so I had to get another job. Oh well it was back to the big house.

I went by the bank one morning to draw some money out. I hopped on the house phone and called up to seventeen to see what my partners were doing. I talked to Edna about my plight. She mentioned it to Darlene who told me to call Samantha and get my old job back. To make a long story quite short Samantha convinced Jake to hire me back in my old position.

As far as Being Frank with Frank was concerned I was in limbo. I had to wait until I could get into those classes so I could reserve the studio. I was still reading and analyzing info every day getting more ammo. When I did come back I wanted to be ready and Blacker than ever.

CHAPTER XXIV

By the time November came I was chomping at the bit to take the classes I needed. This time on my birthday I went with Mickey and sold Milwaukee public school's athletic department on funding *Sports Jam*. *Sports Jam* was the title of the show we were producing.

I hope you have kept in mind that all the while I was on TV talking about being positive I was still drinking. I wasn't drinking like back in 1994 but I still would get good and high off of J Roget. Now don't get me wrong I would get high and still be pro-black. But three things happened to me in the last two months of 1996 that lead me to believe it was time to hang up my shot glass.

One I have never dug obese women in my life. I used to brag, "I don't like nothing fat but a money roll and nothing chunky but soup." So around the end of November I got put into a trick bag. I was out partying with an ex co-worker who was cool as hell but we were just friends. I was out drinking and partying having a good time. The party was over we headed back to my house. I knew I had some more wine in the fridge so I was content in that knowledge. We are sitting on my couch and the broad started talking about sex. I'm nodding my head listening to this spiel thinking, when the hell is she going home when she led the question right to me. Now I'm woke. Deep down I don't want to bone her so I told her, "Look I ain't with that relationship con and all I would want to do is bone and that would be that." I figured she wouldn't go for that type of scene anyway, wrong. Before I could get the glass to my mouth to take another drink old girl said, "Cool we can. Do you want to?" I drained the glass and said sure. She got up and I looked and thought, "Damn she got a gut." I almost told her hell no then I remembered I had an unopened bottle of J Roget in the fridge. I went into the kitchen and popped the cork and took it to the head.

I was lit but even then part of my head was saying, "Don't do this she too big!" Another part was thinking, "Bone her and you will never bone her friend, Debrea." I shrugged those thoughts off. Hell I could get what I wanted. I looked down on old girl laying in the bed. She didn't have a gut after all. That was the first sign. When I went to work Monday her girl Debrea was acting funny. I finally got a chance to talk to her. Debrea looked at me with disgust on her face, I knew the deal. I said, "What?" The look on Debrea's face then changed to pity. Debrea then told me that most dudes don't understand women and sex.

To make a long story short Debrea told me that old girl had told her she was going to freak me when I first started at the bank. I was on the girl's "to do" list. I looked down into Debrea's face and seen that she thought I would be able to discern this type of con. I think Debrea held me in high esteem and I had let her down. I could hear the zip lock on that trick bag sealing up. I just walked away cussing the female who I boned and myself, mainly myself.

Instance number two, one weekend Brian and I hooked up with some freaks. These were some freaks Brian knew from back in the day. I picked Brian up along with some wine and we went to grab the women. Brian's girl was thick while her sister was nerdy as hell so I was pissed.

We went to some raggedy hole in the wall type of joint. I was already high from the wine but when I got to the place I started drinking *Hennessy*. The deejay started mixing Luke. I hollered, "Oh shit!" The flaky female was claiming her head hurt. So I asked Brian's female to dance. This woman was nasty.

The first song I guess you can say we were feeling each other out. It was casual. After a few more drinks things got interesting. The deejay threw on more booty music and we hit the floor. Brian's girl was trying to freak me and I was trying to freak her. The girl was rubbing my penis with her hands trying to give it muscle spasms. I was rubbing the female's butt, breasts and cat like Aladdin trying to get the genie out of the lamp. We danced until Brian said he had to go home to get ready for work. I'm good and drunk now and my penis is ready to spit some game. We packed into my car and the first thing I did was take the girl's sister home. I knew Brian didn't give a damn about the freak so I took him back to his car.

I asked Brian's freak in front of him, "What are you going to do?" She wanted to go with me but her loyalties were with Brian. Brian being the player he was said, "Y'all go on out and have a good time." I looked at Brian and he grinned and got into his car. Old girl and I went back to the club.

When we got back there the deejay was playing NWA. This brought back old memories of my partners Wally and Keith. I was obliged to take a few shots of *Jack Daniels*. By this time my hands are damn near in the freak's panties. The bartender told us it was closing time, it was time to go home.

I was ready to take the girl home but one problem her baby daddy was in the club. The dude waved her off so she wound up with me. We got by her house she invited me in. She handed me a can of *Old English* to sip on while she got ready for bed. As drunk as I was I put that *Old English* down I didn't want to mess with that. She was putting her kids to bed in her room because they were sleeping on a pallet on the floor. The next thing I know the freak is standing in the doorway in a red satin negligee.

There was one problem the girl's belly was poking through the slit. It was time for me to go home now. That's when she did it. The nasty slut pulled out her breasts and started rubbing them and sucking on the nipples.

Home was gone from my mind. The freak went and layed on the pallet on the floor rubbing her nipples. I pulled my clothes off hurriedly and stood over her watching the show. I remember bending down to get onto the pallet and thinking, "Man look at yourself check your surroundings." I did a quick scan and seen some roaches on the ceiling but then my eyes fell on those breasts and the rest is history. Now I know many of you out there are thinking what is the big deal. Well first of all I was always finicky when it came down to my women. To have back to back thick women was definitely out of character. Plus the *Hennessy* and the champagne were starting to do me just like gin and malt liquor used to do me. It was time for a change but it took the third scenario to wake me up.

Christmas Day 1996 I went to Racine to holler at my family. They were celebrating Christmas. I was celebrating the next day we were shooting the first footage for *Sports Jam*. I hooked up with Del and we went by my father's house to check him out. I sat over there and drank two bottles of J Roget talking trash. I was high as hell so we left there and went by Mr. Kim's tavern. I'm in there chilling when an old friend of mine walked in Richard Kenney. We started toasting *Hennessy*. Then another friend comes in Victor. It was turning into a south side reunion. This means its time for more *Hennessy*. Then a real blast from the past walked in, Keith came in.

I hadn't seen my man in years. As soon as Keith seen me he hollered, "Bartender give us *Jack Daniels*!" I couldn't pass up my boy's toast. So now I was drinking *Jack Daniels* again. We got drunk and started singing *Gansta, Gansta*. Eventually Keith had to make a run. It was late so I told Del I'll catch him later.

Del asked, "Man where do you think your going?" I said, "Home." He said, "Man please it's blizzarding outside." Del continued, "You're also drunk so come sleep it off over my pad." Like hell I was I had called up to Milwaukee earlier and my ex co-worker had told me to come over. Fat or no fat I was horny.

Outside it was snowing like hell. It was bad out there. I wasn't worried about it I had front wheel drive. I hopped in the Black Mobile and as was about to drive off Del flagged me down. He said, "Man you too drunk pull over and park you are coming with me!" I looked at dude I wasn't mad it was touching. I said, "You're right let me pull over and park." When Del stepped back I pulled off. As I drove away I blew the horn to let Del know I was gone. What the hell did Del think this was, *Cheers*?

It was snowing like hell when I got to the freeway. The freeway was damn near shut down, skip that I'm rolling. I popped in *X-Clan* blessed myself and hit it. I drove fifty-five all the way.

I was passing fools who were only going twenty-five like they were standing still. It's funny I remember looking into the rear view mirror and thinking, "Oh there is somebody who wants to keep up with the dog." I was rolling vibing with Brother J when lightning struck the shit house.

The car started going into a spin. I remembered the car that was right on my tail and I thought calmly, "Well FJ your time is up." Now that I think about it my car had to spin around one and a half or two times. The right front clip was bent along with the left rear quarter panel. The car following me must have missed me because I remember hitting the dividing wall that's it. The engine had stopped but *X-Clan* was still blasting. I tried the motor she fired up. I turned around and kept heading towards Milwaukee. I don't even think I slowed down because when I was getting off of the freeway I spun out again.

I finally got by my ex co-worker's house. I thanked the spirits and went in. When I got there the chick was sitting on the couch. This broad wanted to hold a conversation! The conversation was starting to sound like that moralistic talk that church folk sing. I got up and looked out the window at my car and thought back. I had crashed my car up racing to get to a fat woman. I laughed out loud and told the woman I would catch her later.

As I drove home I started thinking about how screwed up I had become. I had raced to get to a fat girl who sober I would just say hi to. Then I thought about the other porker and boning on the floor. Then it hit me I had whited out another big breasted chick I had ran up in high a few weeks before. I was slipping.

In the shower I thought about all the messed up decisions I had made in the last ten years. Many of them had one similar factor, alcohol. Alcohol had blinded me to what I really had to do. I dried off and went into the basement to look at my car. I said aloud, "Enough! No wine, no *Hennessy*, no nothing. Every time I think about a drink I'll look at my car!" I damn sure did not have the money to get it fixed. The next day I was starting a new show it was time to start a new chapter of my life without alcohol.

I went on the shoot and enjoyed it. It was a learning experience because it was my first time out as a producer but I could do it. When New Year's Eve rolled around I had already made my mind up about drinking. So New Year's Eve I just chilled by myself thinking about what I wanted to do.

The next day was 1997. Time to start fresh. I ate my black-eyed peas and kicked back. I was determined to rule with a clear head. To celebrate my decision I pulled out my dad's blue fur pimp suit. I always loved this suit when I was a kid, that suit and his stacks. I could wear the suit and shoes now so I threw them on. I pulled my Dobbs hat out of the box and stepped out into the world. Once again it was on!

ABOUT THE AUTHOR

Frank James IV is currently working in the Milwaukee public school system as a teacher. Mr. James has also produced several television shows and commercials. Mr. James is an avid reader and considers himself to be a part-time historian. Mr. James has a Bachelor of Arts in Communications from Wilberforce University. He has worked extensively in the television industry and also been in a few motion pictures. Mr. James is currently finishing up a second novel to be named.